THEN SINGS MY SOUL
The Memoirs of a Good-For-Nothing

**An Account of God's Wonderful Providence
That Turned a Booze Maker
Into a Bible Minister**

Dr. David W. Winget

*David W. Winget
The old Seminary professor*

XULON
PRESS

Thanksgiving & Dedication

I must offer a few words of thanksgiving at the outset. First and foremost I wish to express my gratitude to my sovereign heavenly Father and his Son, the Lord Jesus Christ, and the Holy Spirit for the innumerable manifestations of grace throughout my life.

Also to the following persons I say, "Thanks a million!" because without your encouragement and practical contributions to this project it would not have been completed: Michael Winget-Hernandez, Jonathan Wonnel, Steve Winget, and John Hain.

Finally, this monologue is given in loving memory of Norma, my dear wife and queen, who went to heaven on May 13, 2008. Her faithfulness, love, and devotion were a constant encouragement to me for 56 years.

A Preface Intended to Be Read

$\mathcal{E}$veryone who knows me is aware of the fact that my singing is best left to private moments. My vocal dexterity is limited to the non-melodic categories. I can whistle quite loudly, I have occasionally been known to give a loud cheer at a particularly exciting point in a sporting match, and I have invested a lifetime in developing some bit of dexterity in preaching and lecturing. However, I do have a song in my soul that I'd like to share with you on these pages. Its lyrics speak of the amazing grace of God that He has showered upon me and the sure hope that I've been given through His Word of the coming opportunity to join with the choirs of heaven in singing His praises in eternity.

The opening of a story rarely determines the outcome, and the first few lines of a song sometimes hide the thrust of the closing bars. Narratives of shepherd boys overcoming giants, persistent tortoises outlasting sporadic hares, and bands of 300 defeating enemy hordes are the stuff that give moral fiber and spiritual resolve to every slow starter, underdog, or person without promise who ever lived. Nursery tales of the "little train that could" and real-life stories like that of Susan Boyle naturally inspire and encourage us to strive to reach beyond what others might think we can accomplish.

What you have in your hands is a ballad much in that same genre. It's the story of someone who had very little promise going into the game, of someone that most odds makers would bet against, of someone who would not impress the coach during try outs, but who, solely by the intervening grace of God, became more than a winner. He became a trophy – a trophy to that magnificent intervening grace!

Please note: my "soul music" is not about a human hero. It is about a divine Hero Who caused the main character in the song to grow beyond the narrow confines of his childhood. It is about a Savior Who heroically sacrificed Himself so that the primary personality of the drama could live out the purpose for which he had been designed before time began. It is about Jesus Christ and His matchless grace and the changes He wrought in a sinner He saved from his sins.

Ultimately, this story is about a Baby Who was born in a stable to peasant parents in a backwater hamlet on the edge of the empire, a Baby Who was born to die the most ignoble of deaths. It is about a Baby Who grew to Manhood and achieved His purpose of dying, so that the subject of this book could live forever. This song seems to be about me, but it is not.

This song is about Jesus Christ and what He accomplished in my life.

Please note also: my "soul song" is not primarily intended for a merely human audience. Ultimately it is intended as an act of worship and adoration for an Audience of One. It is my prayer that the music that Jesus Christ has authored in my soul will be a pleasing sacrifice of praise to His ears.

> Then sings my soul, my Savior God, to Thee,
> How great Thou art, how great Thou art!

Introduction

*M*y paternal grandfather died many years before I was born. My father's mother passed away when I was an infant. Therefore, I do not remember ever meeting her or, as a child, even learning either of their names. I do not recall ever having seen a photograph of them.

My maternal grandparents were a different story altogether – they both survived until I was a grown man, and I have fond memories of them. Their integrity and morality influenced my life for good, but my lack of contact with my dad's parents bothered me. I wished that I could have had a similar relationship with them as with mom's folks.

It is my desire to keep my grandchildren from experiencing the same lack concerning their grandparents – I want them to "hear" their grandfather's song of the grace of God in his life. Therefore, this autobiographical sketch of my life is intended in large part for the benefit of my grandchildren – Nathanael, Karis, Andrew, Joel, Zac, Josh, Brianna, Mia, and Wilson – and future great-grandchildren.

I want them to understand a little about the many places I lived during my childhood and why we moved so many times. I think that it will profit them to have some idea of my dad's occupation and our family's income at that difficult period of time.

The methods of discipline used by my parents and how it affected me are also discussed because I believe it will be a valuable resource of illustrations of "how to" and "how not to."

Details about the effects of the Great Depression of the 1930s on my generation in general and on my family in particular are set forth because I'm convinced that in coming days those earlier episodes will prove helpful.

The question of how I was affected by, and my possible participation in, the Second World War, the Korean War, and the Viet Nam War will probably arise in the minds of some of my offspring, and they may be benefitted by knowing some of those details.

My memoirs include facts about my schooling so as to serve as a repository of stories that might help them in their educational pursuits and in those of their children.

I want my offspring to know about my life goals, interests, accomplishments, as well as my disappointments, failures, and shortcomings. They will learn how I was deeply concerned with my children's spiritual, mental, emotional, and physical maturation and development.

If they read patiently my children will most certainly see from these pages the radical change in my attitudes, desires, and ambitions when the Lord Jesus became my Savior.

My prayer is that they will seek to imitate any good and avoid any ill that they observe in these pages, and that these musings will be a small means by which the Divine Musician will plant within them their own notes of praise.

The Man Who Was Never Paid For

*T*he first time I saw the light of day was in a farm house in southeastern Alabama about five miles from the Georgia state line and about 25 miles from the Florida border near the town of Columbia. I was born very early in the morning on September 22, 1930 – perhaps that's why I have always liked to get up and get out early ahead of the crowds. The only witnesses on that occasion were Mom, Dad, and an old country doctor whose name is no longer remembered. At the time of my birth my mother was 16 and my dad was 20.

No name had been chosen for me at that early hour. When the doctor later filled out my birth certificate he could not call to ask whether a name had been selected – there was no phone at our simple dwelling, nor electricity, or running water either. The doctor supplied the name "Childrent Winget." Later, Mom unwisely tried to erase "Childrent" and put in "David Ward Winget" on my certificate, my middle name taken from my father, Robert Ward Winget. This, of course, was illegal for a private citizen to alter a birth document, and years later it caused a great deal of trouble to acquire a legal certificate from the capital at Montgomery.

Dad had agreed to pay the doctor $15 for his services on that momentous occasion, but the doctor died before Dad was able to pay him. On more than one occasion someone has quipped that I wasn't worth $15. Others have commented that, in that the money was never paid, I am worth nothing or that I am a "good-for-nothing."

For decades I have used this to illustrate that apart from the Gospel of Christ and the grace of God I am indeed worthy of none of God's great goodness that He has extended toward me. Though I had been created in His image and therefore am of tremendous worth, my sin has rendered me worthy of His righteous judgment. Romans 3:10-11 emphasizes that there is "none righteous, no, not one: there is none that understandeth, there is none that seeketh after God." Only by God's mercy and grace can any good result from me or my efforts (Eph. 2:4-9).

Truly, I am unworthy and do owe a debt because I, and all, have sinned (Rom. 3:23). I owe the debt of death. "The wages of sin is death," according to Romans 6:23. Jesus paid that debt of death in my place. Although all are guilty (Rom. 3:19) – "guilty" means "obligated to pay a penalty" – He took our guilt upon Himself on the cross and died for us (Rom. 5:8). That He died "for us" means that He died "in our place" as our Substitute. He suffered for us, that is, in our stead, in order that He might bring us to God (1 Pet. 3:18). "He made Him who knew no sin to be sin for us, that we might become the righteousness of God in Him" (2 Cor. 5:21, NKJV).

I was 16 when the Holy Spirit caused me to understand the glorious truth of the substitutionary cross-work of Christ. The Spirit enabled me to accept this truth by faith (Eph. 2:8-9) as the full payment for my sins. At that time I experienced peace with God and the assurance of heaven for eternity. I have since learned from God's Word that I was also instantaneously justified, sanctified, reconciled, redeemed, baptized, indwelt and sealed by the Holy Spirit. By "justified" I mean that I have been declared forgiven and righteous before God (Rom. 5:1). By "sanctified" I mean that I have been set apart by God for His use (1 Cor. 6:11). That I have been "reconciled" means that God had brought me from a state of warfare against Him into a state of fellowship (Rom. 5:10). That God had "redeemed" me speaks of His having metaphorically bought me out of my slavery to sin at the cost of His Son's death and made me part of His family (1 Pet. 1:18-20). I was "baptized" into the Body of Christ by the Spirit of God, that is, I was made to be identified with Christ's Body (1 Cor. 12:13). That I am "indwelt" refers to the fact that the Holy Spirit now lives within my body, and that I have immediate interaction with the God of the universe (1 Cor. 6:19-20). The term "sealed" has to do with the fact that God had made numerous remarkable promises to me for eternity and that the Holy Spirit's indwelling guaranteed the trustworthy fulfillment of those pledges (Eph. 4:30).

Years after my salvation the truth of 1 Corinthians 6:19-20 overwhelms me. God says to his children, "Your body is the temple of the Holy Ghost which is in you, which ye have of God, and ye are not your own? For ye are bought with a price: therefore glorify God in your body, and in your spirit, which are God's." We have been bought with the price of the blood-red agony of God's Son. It strikes me with awe that He would pay such a price for a world of "good-for-nothings."

These verses teach me that I was bought with a price by God the Son, I belong to God the Father, and I am indwelt by God the Holy Spirit. Therefore, my relationship to the heavenly Trinity should influence the way I live my earthly life.

While my earthly birth was certainly not a noble or fêted event, my second birth was remarkable and celebrated. Few have been physically born in more humble surroundings, yet God's grace birthed me a second time and even His angels rejoiced at the event (Lk. 15:10).

Hoover Days in the Deep South

Those early years of the 1930s were called "Hoover Days." Many blamed Herbert Hoover, President from 1929 to 1933, for the economic depression and the high unemployment of those days. Many times my dad worked for 25 cents per day, and this necessitated my mother having to earn extra income for the family even though pregnant with my baby sister. But what to do with me? She came up with an ingenious solution.

When I was still in diapers I wore long-tailed shirts – both the diapers and shirts were homemade from flour sacks. Mom often set the post of the bedstead on the tail of my shirt to prevent me from crawling away and getting into mischief. She knew that I was safe, and this allowed her to work for a while.

13

Not only was Mom a hard worker, but she also was a very courageous woman. An incident that illustrates this occurred during the Depression before I was old enough to remember. One particular neighbor, a local "redneck" and lowlife kind of guy, stopped by our house when Dad was away. He said he wanted to visit with Mom. She demanded that he leave, but he kept hanging around until Mom finally threatened him with a shotgun. The rascal then began to run away, but mom shot at him anyway. A few bird shot pellets wounded him slightly. That scoundrel never bothered her again. Everyone applauded my mother for teaching that bum a lesson.

Another incident that happened many years later attested to Mom's strong physical constitution. Once while fishing she accidentally stuck a fair-sized fish hook into her thumb. The barb was embedded deep in the tender flesh and refused to be "backed out" of the wound. Her youngest child, Darrel, had to use a pair of pliers to force the hook the rest of the way through her thumb. Throughout the ordeal, Vera didn't even flinch.

The Tribe Increases

On September 3, 1932, my mother gave birth to her only daughter and my only sister. This time Mom named her at the beginning. The name she chose was "Bobbie Mae," because mom's name was "Vera Mae." Mom's third child was born on July 16, 1935, in a tobacco barn that had been adapted for our simple living quarters. The name given to him by Dad was "Robert Earl" because Dad's name was "Robert Ward."

Late in '35, my family moved about six miles east of the Chattahoochee River across the state line into Early County of southwestern Georgia near the small town of Cedar Springs. The hamlet was composed of two or three stores, a post office, an elementary school, and about a dozen dwelling houses. There were no paved streets nor traffic lights, but this period affords some of my earliest recollections, a few of which I'd like to relate.

Uncle Dick

Dad was the 13th and last child in his family, having been born when his mother was 53. I well remember one of Dad's older brothers, Uncle Dick. He had quite a notorious reputation in the area.

Once a robbery of the grocery store was reported. That night Uncle Dick visited us. While we were talking we heard a car stop in front of our house. Dad said, "Dick, that may be Sid Howell." Sid Howell was the local county sheriff. Quick as a flash Dick bolted from his chair and out the back door. Mr. Howell came through the front door as his deputy went around to the back of the house, but before the deputy could circle behind the house Dick had crawled under the house. (In those days most houses around there rested on blocks above the ground. The result was that there was usually a crawl space of some two or more feet between the ground underneath and the flooring above.)

The sheriff said to Dad, "Robert, we're lookin' for your brother, Dick. Do you know where he is?" Dad replied, "I don't know where he is now, but just a minute ago he was in that chair." With flashlights in hand the officers searched carefully, but Dick could not be found that night. Later he was taken to court, but he defended himself and won his case.

Years later Uncle Dick told some of us about another event that happened at Cedar Springs. A well-known, relatively wealthy man – there were very few really affluent neighbors in those days – lived alone and became the victim of a robbery. Dick admitted that he one day went with a saw to the man's house while the man was away and cut out a part of the floor under the man's bed. That night Dick waited under the house. When Uncle Dick heard the man snoring he went up through the hole he had made and stole a billfold from pants hanging on the foot of the bed. Uncle Dick, obviously knew how to take advantage of the architecture of houses in those days.

The surprised man discovered early in the morning that he had been robbed and notified the authorities. By that afternoon the sheriff arrived in Cedar Springs on his way to inspect the situation. Dick saw him and waved to him. "Hey, Sid, what brings you to our town today." The sheriff responded, "Old Man Horn was robbed last night, and my deputies and I are on our way to investigate." Dick asked if he could go with them to the crime scene, and Sheriff Howell let him go along. If Dick was ever asked why his fingerprints were at the scene, he could say that he had gone with the sheriff to help look for evidence. It would seem that architecture wasn't the only thing Uncle Dick was adept at co-opting to his benefit.

I'll share more memories about Uncle Dick later.

New Clothes, Homemade Biscuits, & a Dying Man's Cornbread

During the summer of 1936, before I turned 6 years of age, I picked cotton right along with Mom and Dad, and I earned enough to buy my own school clothes: one shirt and one pair of overalls. I was careful not to soil my only shirt and overalls because I had to wear them to school all week. Every Saturday Mom would hand wash my school clothes and press them with our smoothing iron. This was the type of iron that had to be heated on the wood cooking stove or before the fire in the fireplace.

That fall just before my birthday I began school in Cedar Springs Grammar School. (There was no kindergarten in the area in those days.) The thing I liked most about school was having my own personal desk with its writing top that had a pencil groove to hold my pencil. Sometimes I would return to my desk before the recess was concluded just to enjoy my desk. I guess I've always been a man of simple pleasures.

My school lunch each day consisted of two homemade biscuits with part of the centers pulled out and refilled with thick gravy or molasses and wrapped with newspaper or put into a brown paper bag. While this may sound poor by today's dietary standards, we never felt especially underprivileged. Such a school regimen in those days was fairly typical and I, for one, liked the lunches Mom had prepared.

Upon arriving home I would sometimes be allowed an after-school snack of a stale piece of cornbread. I would take my prized morsel out to the porch swing and sit there munching and singing a song my Uncle Johnny (an uncle on my mother's side) had written, "Sandy Bottom Blues." The gist of the ballad was about a man who'd been in a brawl and was stabbed. As he lay mortally wounded his advice was: "Take warning from a dying man, and listen to what I say..." Those were the only words I knew, but I misunderstood them and so I sang: "Take cornbread from a dying man, and listen to what I say." They seemed appropriate words to croon while I enjoyed my afternoon treat.

Cranking by Hand & Backing Uphill

During those days Dad owned a black "Model T" Ford that had been altered into what we called a "cut down truck." It was, I think, a 1925 model, and had been "cut down" about 1933 before Dad bought it. It was a car that had its top and a part of the rear removed and a flat bed had been attached for hauling things. This type of vehicle was quite common in those days.

The truck had no accelerator to regulate speed. On the steering column just below the steering wheel were two levers similar to the turn signal mechanism on modern cars. One was called the "spark" and the other was called the "gas." To increase the speed one must pull down on the gas lever and pull down on the spark lever, too. To decrease speed the gas lever and the spark lever had to be pushed up. The truck had three foot pedals: one was the brake, one was the clutch, and one was reverse gear. This vehicle had only two gears, low and high, which were controlled by a long lever that came up from the floor on the right side of the steering wheel. For more pulling power or to go slow one needed merely to pull back on the gear lever. To go faster one would push forward on the lever. I think I also remember some sort of lever that came up from the floor on the left side of the steering wheel. It served as a parking brake or emergency brake.

The gas tank was above the engine, just lower than, and in front of, the windshield, and the gas for the engine was gravity fed; there was no fuel pump. When going uphill, especially if the gas tank was nearly empty, the gas would not drain properly into the engine because the line from the tank to the engine was connected in the front portion of the tank. The driver was forced to take measures to place the front of the tank in a lower position than the back of the tank, or in other words, the front of the tank needed to be downhill from the back of the tank. Thus, if we were low on fuel, Dad had to climb hills in reverse so that the gasoline would drain into the engine.

Another oddity to 21st century motorists was the "Model T's" hand crank. To start cars of that era a "Z-shaped" rod had to be inserted into the front of the engine. The exposed end of the rod had a floating handle that was grasped while standing in front of the truck. It was forcefully cranked clockwise several times to create a spark to ignite the gasoline in the engine.

It goes without saying that our car had neither heater nor air conditioner, radio, nor seatbelts. Indeed, it had no windshield wipers because there wasn't any windshield! Believe it or not, there weren't even any doors on this limousine of ours. Dad's vehicle had only one seat, a 12 inch board that was worn smooth from years of use. Don't imagine that this "seat" had any springs under it either.

Bama Jones & Miss Priss

About every two or three weeks we would take a long trip (or so it seemed to us) – about 14 miles – to visit my mother's parents, George and Bama Jones, over in Alabama west of Columbia. On one trip Mom was riding on the passenger side of that smooth board seat holding my baby brother, Earl. When Dad turned left at a crossroads Mom slid off the board and out of the vehicle into the roadside ditch still carefully cradling Earl in her arms. Neither were hurt, but you can imagine they were both frightened, as were the rest of us. (This was another testament to my mother's courage and tenacity that at that point of danger she protected her baby.) Except for a few major highways all thoroughfares were rough dirt roads, and therefore Dad was driving less than ten miles an hour as he made that left turn. Even so, by God's grace, grubby clothes were the only damage from that accident.

When Bobbie and I were between four and seven years of age we occasionally spent a few weeks in the summer with grandma. Once Bobbie "smarted off" at grandma and called her grandmother "Miss Priss," a term which she had heard somewhere that implied vanity. Grandma spanked her for disrespect, a discipline that some in the 21st century would call criminal, but which certainly served to increase the virtue of respect for our elders, not only for Bobbie but for all the rest of us as well. As a result Bobbie's nickname became "Priss" even to this day.

One summer when I was staying with Grandma and Granddaddy Jones I had a very serious ear infection that caused puss to flow from both of my ears. It was so severe that I even lost my hearing for a few weeks. People had to yell right close to my ear for me to hear. Several times a day for several days I had to have peroxide poured into each ear to try to cleanse the infection. Again God's grace was evident in that there was no permanent damage from this ailment.

In 1937, we moved again, this time from just south of Cedar Springs to a farm about two miles north of town. Dad worked for Mr. Plymail for $7 per month plus the income he could get from the sale of crops he could grow on a very small plot of land. The house we lived in had no glass windows, only wooden shutters that had to be opened to let light in.

We used kerosene lamps for light at night and during the day when it was too cold to open the windows. Actually we used kerosene lamps in all the dwellings where we lived in Georgia. In none of the houses we inhabited in Georgia did we have electricity. Our heat was also from flame, in this case a wood fire in the fireplace or cook stove. In the winter the outside temperature seldom dipped below 20 degrees Fahrenheit, but in the middle of the winter the inside temperature was still quite uncomfortably cold. Sometimes water in the hand washing pan and in the drinking water bucket would freeze. It was so cold in our house that we would stand so close with our backs to the fireplace that we'd almost singe our clothes. Of course the summers' heat outside would sometimes soar as high as 100 degrees, and the inside temperature would rise to 80 degrees or more. Those were aromatic days, you can be sure.

Petty Crimes and Paltry Theology

In early 1938, Uncle Dick, a cousin, John D. Lock, and some neighbors were visiting us on a Sunday afternoon. They were enjoying their favorite recreational drink, illegal moonshine whiskey or "bootleg whiskey." Sheriff Howell and his son, Deputy "Buddy" Howell, appeared rather suddenly at the front of our house. John D. grabbed a gallon jug that still had some whiskey in it and ran out through the back door through the corn field. Uncle Dick was sitting in a chair by the wood cook stove with a pint bottle of the booze in his lap. He calmly put the bottle into the wood compartment of the stove before the sheriff entered the house.

The officers searched the house thoroughly. They did find a half pint of the stuff under the mattress of my parents' bed. But Mom had been told that it was legal to have a small amount for medicinal purposes. She told them that that bottle was her medicine, and they let her keep it. They looked everywhere, including inside the oven of the stove, but did not think of looking inside the wood compartment where wood was burned to heat the stove. Therefore Uncle Dick kept his bottle of whiskey. However, it was whiskey that ultimately proved his undoing.

It was somewhat ironic that one of the more notorious members of our family was at times one of the more religious. Whether Uncle Dick ever actually came to saving faith in Christ's finished work rather than focusing on his own occasional periods of good deeds is difficult for me to say, but my uncle was for a time quite regular in his attendance at church and outspoken in his religious views. Once, when one of our family was seriously ill, Uncle Dick knelt and prayed fervently for healing. The sickness soon abated, and my mother was convinced that her brother-in-law's prayer had been the key.

Both my dad and my uncle had the somewhat picturesque habit of creating humorous malapropisms. I'll talk later about some of Dad's curious sayings, but some of Uncle Dick's aphorisms or quaint adages included the following. When he wanted to discuss a story about Jesus he would usually say something to the effect that "Jesus told 'comparables.'" In a more theological vein he contended that there was a significant difference between the Holy Spirit and the Holy Ghost. "The difference," he used to say, "is that the Holy Spirit is like a little Farm-All tractor and the Holy Ghost is like a big Fordsom tractor. If you chained the Farm-All back to back to the big 'ole Fordsom, both pulling against the other, the Fordsom would just drag that other tractor all across the field!" Looking back on it, I don't think I recall that he cited any Scripture to support his hypothesis.

Uncle Dick had been "down front" to the "mourners' bench" on numerous occasions where he had "prayed through to God" for salvation. Uncle Dick was of the persuasion that he could gain God's forgiveness for sins and become a child of God and later, because of unfaithfulness, forfeit those benefits or "lose his salvation," a cycle he was convinced that he had repeated numerous times. As is the case with many who fail to see the simple truth of eternal salvation by grace alone apart from any human effort or works of merit, his opinion sadly kept him from apprehending any assurance of gaining a clear and right standing before God. Uncle Dick was constantly in fear that his many indiscretions severed the fragile relationship he had ostensibly established with God, and he was continually having to try to re-establish the relationship through another round of mournful repentance. I recall him saying once that a believer was "like a barefooted man walking on a board with nails in it." That was Dick's appraisal of the constant vigilance necessary to maintain one's salvation. One false step would result in a painful "fall from grace." He was often heard to say, "The Bible says that you gotta 'work out your own salvation.'"

Uncle Dick didn't realize that this passage in Philippians speaks not about meriting salvation or demonstrating salvation. Paul had previously mentioned his belief that the Philippian church's prayers would result in his "salvation." But surely Paul, though he used the exact same word in both passages, was not talking about his salvation from sin. The Apostle was in both cases talking about a "solution to a present problem": his release from imprisonment in the first case, their settlement of a church dispute in the second. Paul's meaning there had to do with his encouraging the quarrelling church members to "work out a solution" to the problem they were facing.

On one occasion we had been planning to travel to an annual "revival meeting" over in southern Alabama. On the morning that we were to set off on the trip Uncle Dick approached my dad and asked for a drink of whiskey. Daddy was shocked that his brother who had recently rebuked him for alcohol consumption would ask this. "What?" Dad exclaimed. Nonetheless, Dad consented to give Dick a drink. In Dick's mind, he had already "lost his salvation," so a short time later Dick wanted another drink, and then another. Needless to say, he became quite inebriated. At the church he sat on the back row and, in a near stupor, repeatedly "amen-ed" and slurred out "Bless 'im, Laaard!" to various statements the preacher made.

Last, But Not Least

*B*efore midnight on the 21st of May, 1938, Mom started having labor pains – the birth of her fourth and last child was imminent. Dad went to get the midwife to assist Mom, and later Dad took Bobbie, Earl, and me a little ways down the road to Hoyle Daniel's house where we awaited the culmination of the great event. Hoyle was a black neighbor with a wife and three children ages three to seven. He had promised to help out in any way "when the time came." He put a mattress on the floor, and soon, six kids – three white and three black – were asleep side by side on the mattress.

We knew that mom was expecting a baby but could only guess whether he would be a brother or a sister. Early on the morning of May 22, 1938, our guessing came to an end when George Darrel was born. Mom chose the name because her dad was named "George."

For years during the 1930s and early 1940s, Mom helped to support the family with money she earned from the sale of "home brew." From time to time she would make a gallon or two and put it into soft drink bottles. The drink had an alcoholic content about the same as commercial beer but had a much better taste. Every batch was easy to sell. (The midwife who assisted Mom when Darrel was born was paid with a few bottles of Mom's home brew.)

After the birth of our baby brother Dad got a job with the WPA (Works Project Administration). This was program started by Franklin D. Roosevelt who had become president in 1933 – it involved working for the government on various civil projects like road construction. Dad's job on his WPA crew was to keep the drinking barrels full of fresh water for all of the other men on the crew, and for this he was paid the very good wage of 30 cents an hour. My dad was about to become "wealthy" according to our standards, but he needed a more dependable truck to use for hauling barrels of water.

He found a newer, more powerful, Model T "cut down" truck that could be bought for only $7. He borrowed the money from Grandma Bama Jones and repaid her at the rate of $1 per month. This truck, too, had to be hand cranked like the previous vehicles we had, as well as being backed up steep hills when the fuel in the tank was low. That Model T was the instigation for an event that was etched very vividly into my memory.

An Early Lesson in Substitution

Though I loved my dad, I have to admit that, before he became a Christian, he had a problem with his temper. For instance, as we were on our way to our grandparents in Alabama to make a payment on the truck the engine stopped and dad tried several times to start it. He became so angry that he kicked out the headlights.

I want to quickly add that he never abused us kids, but he did discipline us sternly with a switch or a paddle when we disobeyed. (Mom occasionally spanked us, too, when we needed to be disciplined.)

The more significant memory regarding that old truck, however, had to do with just such a lapse on my part. My regular assignment was to crawl under the Model T when Dad came home from work and turn off a valve on the gasoline line to prevent gas from leaking out. On one occasion I forgot this important chore because I was playing with my cousin. Within a few minutes Dad noticed a spot on the ground where costly gasoline had leaked. He yelled to me saying "Come here. I'm gonna learn you a lesson." That was his term meaning "teach you to do what you are supposed to do." He picked up a short piece of old siphoning hose – maybe two or three feet long – with which to whip me.

Mom's courage came to my rescue. She stepped in between Dad and me and said, "No, Robert. David was s'posed to turn off the gas, but he forgot. And it ain't deservin' that kind of whippin'!"

Dad warned, "If you don't move out of the way I'll let you have it!"

Bravely, Mom did not move. Dad struck her once with that piece of siphoning hose against her backside. That was one time that Dad came close to abusing me, but Mom took my place, and he struck her instead of me.

Mom's substitution for me that day was a vivid illustration of a truth I had not yet fully grasped. Jesus had suffered the wrath of my God for me. The difference was that my Dad's anger was unrighteous while God the Father's anger against me and my sin was pure and totally just. God's righteous standard had been violated by willful disobedience time after time, and I fully deserved His wrath. (To be sure, no child deserves such a cruel beating as my father's raging temper intended to inflict, yet the fact remains that I had disobeyed his instruction and did deserve stern discipline. I do not relate this incident to indict my father, but rather to praise my mother, and her brave intervention will always be one of the best illustrations of Christ's substitutionary act that I have ever experienced. I want to quickly add that years later Dad came to faith and his temper, while not eradicated, was moderated and brought under control by the work of the Spirit in his heart.)

If Mom had not endured Dad's rage that day, I would have had to. If Jesus had not endured God's rage at the cross, I would have been obliged to take the full force of His righteous anger against my sin. According to John 3:36 God's wrath "abides on" unbelievers and Ephesians 2:3 speaks of the unconverted as "children of wrath," that is, "people who are worthy of wrath." The fact that my mother took my whipping in my place that day is a good illustration of Jesus bearing the wrath of God in my stead. Mom had not disobeyed Dad, but she bore the punishment of one who had. Jesus never was guilty of any sin. But He took my guilt – that is, my obligation to pay the penalty. He took my guilt upon Himself and paid my penalty in full on the cross in my place. This doctrine of penal substitution has come under intense fire of late, but it is clearly central to the Biblical understanding of what the Gospel is all about.

Yes, Romans 6:23 says, "The wages of sin is death, but the gift of God is eternal life through Jesus Christ our Lord." Romans 5:8 tells us that Christ died for us in our place in spite of the fact that we were wicked sinners standing under the impending and crushing weight of righteous judgment. On the cross Christ substituted for me as surely as my mom had substituted for me, yet there is another very important difference between those two substitutionary acts.

My mother's acceptance of that painful stroke by my father's hand was definitely not proportional to the offense I had committed. On the other hand, the immeasurable agony which was exacted upon the Son of God at Calvary and which He bore for me – not merely the physical torture and emotional distress, but more significantly the spiritual torment of complete separation from the Father – was exactly just and proportional to the inestimable trespass which I had committed against an infinite God's perfect standard. Had the immaculate Godman, Jesus Christ, not stood in my place on that day, and had I not accepted the Father's gracious offer to apply Christ's vicarious payment to my account, justice would have obliged to spend eternity in hell as payment for my unfathomably immense crime. For one to understand the saving Gospel of Christ, he must take into account the incomprehensible gravity of his sin and the inscrutable grace exemplified by Christ's substitutionary death.

Jesus died because of our sins, and God raised Christ from death to prove that He fully accepted His Son's death as a comprehensive payment for our sins. Romans 4:25 asserts, "He was delivered up on account of our offenses; He was raised again on account of our justification." This passage is often misunderstood to mean that Jesus' resurrection was intended for the purpose of His overseeing our salvation. Rather, Paul's construction requires that we understand the second clause to mean that He was raised from the dead on account of the fact that an adequate basis of our justification had been secured. Jesus' went to Calvary because of our sins. He walked away from the Garden Tomb because those sins had been completely paid in full, and the Father was totally satisfied with the payment His Son had made.

A Chevrolet Truck

In 1940, we moved about a mile further north and Dad got a job with the Georgia Highway Department. He purchased a 1931 four-cylinder Chevrolet truck in which he had room to take other men to work with him. Those men shared the expense of transportation to and from work. In some ways the Chevrolet truck was better than the Model T Ford trucks had been. Unlike the old Fords, the newer Chevy had a foot accelerator and a floor gearshift.

As with the Model T, the Chevrolet truck had neither a heater nor an air conditioner, and we still had to start her up with a hand crank. In fact, in the coldest part of the winter when the oil in the engine was cold and stiff, it was helpful to jack up a rear wheel to make it easier to start the engine. When the rear wheel was off the ground the engine could be made to turn fast enough With the hand crank to create a spark to ignite gasoline in the engine.

I don't remember if liquid antifreeze was available in our area or if it was just too expensive for Dad to afford. What I do remember is seeing Dad drain the water from the radiator at night when the weather was apt to freeze to prevent the radiator from being damaged. He would then heat water on the wood cook stove or in the fireplace to refill the radiator the next morning because warm water caused the engine to start more easily.

My 11th Christmas came in 1940; it was the first Christmas that I remember that the Winget kids received any toys. Until that Christmas our family was too poor to celebrate with gift-giving. We were surprised when the four of us kids were given a red wagon. I also received a silver-colored, single-shot cap pistol and even some caps to shoot in it. I can't remember what individual presents the other kids received, but the wagon was enjoyed by all of us. I can recall putting Earl and Darrel in it, and Bobbie and I took turns pulling them around. We enjoyed lots of apples, oranges, raisins and nuts of various kinds, too. After all, we were nearly rich because our dad now worked for the Georgia Highway Department.

I remember some of the adults talking with great amazement about the strange things on some of the new cars. No cranking tool was needed to start the engine. They had automatic starters – a button on the dash was provided that one could press to start the engine. No longer did one need to stand outside the car in the cold or in the rain and work so hard with a hand crank to start the car. What would they think of next? When this was first discussed at our house, someone exclaimed, "Are you joking? Is that true or have you been dreaming?"

Some of the new cars no longer had a gearshift lever that came up from the floor, but the gear lever was attached to the steering column on the right side just below the steering wheel. The driver still needed to manually shift gears as he formerly did when the lever was up from the floor. There was low gear to start off and then the driver had to shift to second gear to gain speed, and finally shift into high gear for top speed. Oh, yes: there was a reverse gear, too.

Nicknames – People & Places

I remember that my young brothers gave interesting names to me. I think it was Darrel who, at about age two and a half, called me "Gaygah" because he could not pronounce "David." Earl called me "Bubba" for "Brother," and our neighbors, Mr. and Mrs. Davis, he dubbed "Mister 'n Miz Bubba," because "Davis" sounded to him like "David." Another neighbor, David Nolan, he called "Bubba Nolan."

At about five years of age Earl could not understand the difference between "foot" and "feet." He would point to his left foot and say that's my "put." Then he would point to his right foot and say that's my "peet."

In 1941, (guess what!) we moved yet again, this time a little further north, to a place near Hilton, Georgia. People called the community there "Boozey Bushes" because it was a place where some folks made and drank illegal "moonshine" whiskey. We rented a house from Mr. Madison Freeman, and we lived there for two years.

It was Mr. Madison who gave Darrel the nickname "Pot" because as a little toddler he had quite a chubby belly.

Little Darrel once found a cigarette stub that Dad had thrown aside. My brother put it in his mouth and pretended to smoke it. Mom scolded him, and he defended himself by reminding her matter-offactly that "Daddy smokes." Mom said to him, "But you're not a daddy." Darrel somewhat precociously replied, "I guess I'm a little daddy." From then on Mr. Madison began to call him "Daddy Pot." As time progressed "Pot" evolved into "Potsy," and that nickname has stuck for well over half a century. To this day more of his relatives and close friends refer to him as "Potsy" rather than "Darrel."

Turn Your Radio On

I well remember our first radio. We bought it after we moved to Mr. Madison's place in Boozey Bushes. It was light brown with a rounded top about the size of a small portable TV of today. It sat on a rough homemade table in the corner near the fireplace. I often would lie underneath that table listening to the cowboy dramas or *Amos and Andy*. It was over this radio that we heard about the sneak attack on Pearl Harbor on December 7, 1941.

As an 11-year-old boy whose favorite subject in school was geography, I identified where this new enemy of America was located. On the map it appeared to be a very small nation. Just one day after President FDR declared war on Japan I overheard a bunch of men at Gordon Hall's store talking about it. I told those fellows that Japan was such a small nation the U.S. would whip them in a few weeks. I was wrong. The war dragged on for more than three and a half years.

Our first radio power source was a wet cell automobile battery. A battery would supply power for the radio for about a week before it went dead. Dad would then exchange it with the one in the truck. The dead battery would get recharged in the truck for use in the radio by the following week.

The radio had an antenna wire that was placed on poles about twelve feet high that stretched out into the field outside the house from the radio. The wire collected radio waves that were transferred into the radio in the house. One of our favorite pastimes every Saturday night was listening to the Grand 'Ole Opry, a country-themed music and variety program. I recall taking my normal position on the floor one night under the table to hear the play-by-play description of the heavyweight championship fight between Joe Louis and Billy Conn.

3¢ Stamps, 5¢ Treats, & 12¢ Gas

Hilton, GA had two stores: they went by the inventive names of Gordon Hall's Store and Smith's Store. Smith's Store was about 200 yards down the road from Hall's and stocked about as much as did its rival.

Gordon Hall's store had the added advantage and disadvantage of a room in the back that was the post office for Hilton and the surrounding area. The advantage was that its proximity to the postal service drew customers. The disadvantage was that it was widely thought that Suzy Hall, the proprietor's wife and local postmistress, read everybody's mail, a fact that irritated some and probably lost Mr. Hall some business.

I can recall that a first class postal stamp cost three cents in that era, but sometimes we didn't have a stamp or the three cents handy. We would leave an egg in the mailbox with the letter and the postman would affix the three cents in postage for us.

The stores had groceries, canned goods, vegetables, ice cream, tobacco, soft drinks (no tin cans, all glass bottles) – my favorite was RC Cola because you could buy 16 ounces for a nickel – gasoline, and so forth. The gasoline was dispensed from the old style gas pumps with the glass tanks on the top. A station manager had to pump the fuel up into the glass tank by hand – you could tell how much gasoline was being pumped by the horizontal marks on the glass tank – and then gravity fed the liquid into the customer's gas tank. No self-service in those days. Can you imagine the station employee pumping the gas and charging something like twelve cents a gallon?

The school was a fourth of a mile up from Smith's Store. It had grades from the first through the eleventh. Until about 1949, all schools in Georgia had only eleven grades. The four years of high school were grades eight through eleven. If I had lived there until graduation from high school there would have been about ten students in my graduation class.

In 1942, Daddy's work with the Georgia Highway Department called for him to go 100 miles to east Georgia for a few weeks of work. Because of the Second World War auto gasoline rationing was about to be enforced. Dad penned the first, and probably the only letter he ever wrote, to my mom. It was very urgent. He told her to look in the "backer can" – that was his word for "tobacco can" – in the bottom of the big trunk to find papers that could prove ownership of the truck. She was to get someone to take her and the papers about 15 miles to the county courthouse in Blakely, the Early County seat. All this was to register for gas stamps that would soon be required to buy gasoline for the truck. (Truck owners were allowed more stamps than passenger autos, because they were considered more a priority for work related to the war effort.)

Living Boozey Bushes Style

*O*ur house was more than one half mile from the mailbox and the school bus stop. Our "driveway" was a narrow rutted track through the woods out to the dirt road where the mailbox was located.

Labor Saving Devices?

Boozey Bushes did not have the blessing of electricity for lights or refrigerators, cooking stoves, heating, washing machines, clothes driers, clothes irons, or fans. We had never heard of a vacuum cleaner – Mom swept the floors with a stick broom. Doing our laundry was very labor intensive: clean water was drawn from a well, the clothes were boiled in homemade lye soap, rubbed over a scrubbing board or beaten with a wooden "battlin' board," then rinsed and hung to dry.

We didn't even have indoor plumbing. The first few months we had to carry water several hundred yards through the woods from Mr. Madison's well for drinking, cooking, laundry, or bathing.

Dad later hired my cousin, John D. Lock, to dig a well in our yard by hand. Using a pick and shovel he began with a square hole about five feet by five feet. When the hole got too deep for him to throw the dirt out of the hole with the shovel, dad built a windlass. This was a device for lifting buckets of dirt up out of the hole. It consisted of a cylinder wound with a rope and turned by a crank. John would fill the bucket with the dirt he'd carved out of the bottom

33

of the hole, and Dad would crank the bucket up, empty it, and let it down for John to fill again. This project took about a week. They struck plenty of good water after digging about 20 or 25 feet deep. Later, the windlass was used to draw up water when the well was completed. Needless to say, we rejoiced when we got our very own source of clean water.

Summers in south Georgia could be pretty warm and called for some inventive measures to cope with the soaring temperatures. One such method involved our new well which served as a sort of refrigerator – we would tie a rope to a jug of milk and let it down into the well to keep it cool. Another scheme for beating the heat made use of a long, 12-inch wide board one end of which I put out of an open window with the other end under my bed railing. I slept on the board with my head and shoulders outside the window; the cooler outside air afforded more restful sleep.

A Cherished Gift & a Humiliating Injury

One of my fond memories from Boozey Bushes was a very special gift from my father. Dad thrilled me by buying me a used bicycle for $4. The pedals were worn out and only a bare rod remained where the pedals had been. The fabric had been worn away from the seat – only the metal pan of the seat was left, and it was rusted at that. Nonetheless, I cherished that bike, but I once had a wreck while riding it. The accident caused a deep cut in the lower calf of my right leg. After almost 70 years a scar about two inches long is still clearly visible.

That injury reminds me of another. In those days no one thought of going to the doctor for medicine or stitches. When we were about twelve years old, my cousin, Roy Frank Winget, and I were climbing trees behind our house when a sharp stub of a broken limb pierced through the crotch of his overalls as he slid down the tree. He ripped his scrotum quite badly. Momma simply put him flat on his back, washed out the wound with kerosene – just like she had treated the wound from my bicycle accident – and, without the use of any pain-killer, sewed him up. Anyone need an illustration of humiliation? The pain was severe, but the embarrassment was far worse.

Fishing, Forestry, & Fireplaces

During the 1941-42 rainy season, when the fields were flooded and the ditches flowing into the Sawhatchee Creek were filled with the runoff, fish from the creek would swim up the ditches to the fields to feed on bugs or worms. We built baskets and put them in the ditches to catch some of the fish as they swam toward the fields. Sometimes we could even catch the fish with our bare hands.

At other times we set "trot lines" to catch fish in the creek. This we did by dangling lengths of fishing line – maybe three or four feet long – from branches near the creek bank. We attached pieces of pig liver on hooks at the other end of the lines and submerged them under the surface of the swollen creek. The smell of the bait enticed the hungry fish to swallow the hooks with the bait. We checked the lines often during the night to retrieve the fish and to re-bait the hooks. In this way we were able to enjoy fresh fish with our corn-bread and beans.

In those days the only fuel for the cook stove and for heating the house was wood. Therefore, among our other tasks, Dad and I had to saw several loads of wood each fall. There were plenty of trees not far from where we lived – the supply of wood was never in doubt. Mr. Madison had acres of forest and we were welcome to it.

We kids had chores to do much of the time. We were always to keep a supply of wood by the cook stove. During the winter months we kept wood on the front porch for the fire place in Mom and Dad's bedroom. We tried to remember to have enough wood in the fireplace at bedtime to last all night and to have some hot coals early in the morning. This made it easier to build a quick, hot fire at daybreak. We were careful at bedtime to leave the logs in the fireplace positioned in a way that there was no danger of logs falling forward onto the floor to catch the house on fire.

There was nothing in any Winget house in south Georgia corresponding to what is called today a "living room." We lived in all the rooms and the term "living room" would have been very strange to us. None of the houses we had lived in before I went to college had more than two bedrooms and a kitchen large enough for a stove and a dining table.

We all had our chore assignments but these never included mowing the yard. We never had any grass in the yard to mow. We, however, *did* sweep the yard clean every two or three weeks with a homemade sagebrush broom to clear away leaves, wood debris, or gravel. Occasionally we would have to dig up some grass or weeds because it was difficult to sweep if there was any grass in the yard. Playing marbles was a favorite game and in a clean, smooth yard we could play line marbles or hole marbles. We felt sorry for kids in the cities who had grass lawns in their yards – they had no place to play marbles. Poor city kids!

Pranks & Mischief

*I*n 1943, we moved back to Cedar Springs. Dad worked as a sharecropper on "Miz Annie's" farm. A sharecropper was a poor farmer who didn't own any land but who agreed to work the land owned by someone else. In return the sharecropper received half of the profits from the sale of the crops.

That spring I returned to the school in Cedar Springs. In April or May when the weather was much warmer the classroom windows were kept open. Once, two of my classmates and I played a mischievous prank on our teacher and the class. At recess time while our classroom was vacated we three guys closed and locked all the windows and the transom – that is, the hinged window above the door. We set the lock inside the door to lock behind us when we shut the door and exited the room. The teacher's keys were in her desk inside the room.

The school bell rang ending the recess period, but the locked door prevented entrance into the room. The teacher requested that a couple of volunteers go outside and enter through a window and unlock the door. They discovered that all the windows were locked shut. Someone climbed a ladder to open the transom above the door and found that it was locked also. Finally workers were summoned – not by telephone, of course; there were no phones. Window panes had to be removed in order to get inside to open the door.

Our teacher questioned members of the class one by one to determine who was responsible for the disruptive prank. Only three persons knew who was guilty.

When she called me aside, I could not lie. I "spilled the beans" and three sixth grade boys experienced a painful spanking with a paddle. (All teachers in those days kept just such an implement handy for just such occasions.) In that era none of the parents disagreed with this method of discipline nor ever threatened to sue the schools that practiced this type of punishment. Even parents who were not church-going people were influenced by Bible passages that they were aware of and accepted corporal punishment as proper treatment for overt disobedience or belligerence. Hebrews 12:6 teaches that the Lord's chastening and scourging of his children are proofs of his love. Proverbs 13:24 says, "He who spares his rod hates his son, but he who loves him disciplines him early." Another passage instructs the parent, "Chasten your son while there is hope," (Prov. 19:18). Proverbs 22:15 teaches that corporal discipline produces success. "Do not withhold correction from a child. For if you beat him with a rod, he will not die," admonishes Proverbs 23:13.

Of course, such passages have at times been misused to advocate child abuse, but the Bible clearly calls upon parents to avoid any sort of treatment that would be injurious or harmful to the child. Rather, the father (and mother) are to discipline their offspring in love, and sometimes true love for the child demands stern action. I fear that in many of today's "enlightened" families much of the absolute avoidance of corporal punishment in the name of "loving" the child is, at best, thinly disguised laziness which shirks onerous responsibility, or, blatant disobedience to Biblical instruction, or worst of all, both!

In my generation dads often told their sons, "If you do something in school for which you get a spanking, I'll spank you again when you come home." It was no coincidence, therefore, that the public education system in those days was not overrun with students taking drugs, shooting or stabbing each other, or assaulting teachers.

Student profanity was extremely rare. In our student assemblies and chapel services in the public schools I attended, we daily sang Christian songs and prayed the Lord's Prayer after Bible passages were read. The Pledge of Allegiance to the flag was a regular custom every morning.

The moral decline among the elite of our country which led to court rulings against Bible reading, prayer and corporal punishment in public schools rapidly spread among the general populace. The ACLU arguments about the separation of church and state caused further moral decline. (The ACLU supposedly stands for the "American Civil Liberties Union," but an argument could be made that the phrase "Anti-Christian Liberties Union" more accurately describes this group.) What a shame that so many feel that the Bible and prayer in public schools would cause great and irreparable damage to children.

Initiations at Jakin School & a Blizzard?

The Cedar Spring School had only six grades. Therefore, in September of 1943, I had to ride a school bus twelve miles south to Jakin for the seventh grade. One memorable experience I had during my short term at Jakin was when I was initiated into the FFA club, the Future Farmers of America. The initiates were divided into teams which competed for points. To score ten points for our team we were blindfolded and led up the steps onto an elevated stage. We were led over to a part of the stage and told that to be a successful future farmer we must jump down to the floor below – about four feet lower – and keep our balance and not fall over. Unbeknownst to the new inductees two of the other guys put a big table up against the stage and yelled, "Now jump!" The table made the drop only an inch or so, rather than the expected four feet. I luckily was able to keep my balance, but several weren't able to remain upright.

Next we were shown a cigar box full of white flour into which they dropped a silver dollar and told us if we could get it with our mouths within ten seconds while blindfolded we could keep it and score ten points for our team. After the blindfolds were in place they switched the box of flour for a box of black soot and told us, "Your ten seconds begin NOW!" I did not get the silver dollar nor earn ten points for my team, but I had the evidence on my face that I certainly tried.

The greatest test to determine if we were worthy of admission into the FFA was to prove that we could endure the belt line without a scream or a tear. Two lines of upper classmen were facing each other about five feet apart, and each one had his belt in his hand. We freshmen had to remove our shirts and pass between the lines while belts on our left and belts on our right created large stripes across our backs and shoulders. I don't remember if anybody shed any tears. But I do remember we did scream. The president of the club said the screams were not loud enough to disqualify us, and thus we all became welcome members of the Future Farmers of America.

I remember that the following winter was a remarkable one. The heaviest snow to that point in the century was recorded that year – we got almost a whole inch of the white stuff! For several days patches of snow could still be seen under trees and in the shade of buildings.

Earning Dad's Confidence

In 1944, we moved back to Boozey Bushes into the same house on Mr. Madison's place where we had lived before. This time Dad worked as a sharecropper for Mr. Madison.

I remember many things about that year working on the farm.

Mr. Madison had recently bought two young mules for pulling the field plow. I still remember their names were "George" and "Frank" – George, Frank, and David spent many fragrant hours together under the warm Georgia sun.

Before I relate a bit about that I recall that half of the land that we farmed was across the Sawhatchee Creek from where we lived. (Remember that in rainy seasons the creek would overflow its banks.) The road to the back field went right through the creek and the wagon that George and Frank pulled across the creek in the flood season would float. The water was so deep that the mules would swim across the creek pulling the floating wagon.

Usually young mules were mean and difficult to train to walk between the furrows, but these mules were unusually tame and gentle, so much so, that after only a few hours of training by Dad I was able to guide the plow as they pulled it. In order to signal the mules to begin pulling the plow we would give a lip-sucking sound sort of like what you might hear from a loud kiss. We could also signal them by tapping them lightly on their rear flanks with the plow lines or by saying to them, "Git up." The usual way to get a team to stop was by calling out to them, "Whoa."

Mr. Madison criticized Dad for letting a 14-year-old boy – when he wasn't in school – do most of his plowing while he rode around in his truck. He accused Dad of "getting into his nest" – that was Mr. Madison's term for dad's truck – and "enjoying the country" – his way of saying "roaming around the community." But I was glad Dad had such confidence in me that he would leave me alone with the plowing.

Robert Ward Winget had little formal education. He did not even finish high school, but he knew human nature and how to use psychology. He often would ask me my opinion about certain things. He would say "Son, which direction do you want us to run the rows of peanuts here?" Just think, my dad wanted my suggestion about whether to run the rows north and south or east and west.

To be sure, Dad did remunerate my work after a fashion. Dad bought me a new bike – it was grey with decorative stripes on the fenders. It was one of those sleek models with a smaller front wheel – the kind that grocery delivery boys might have used. In addition, for about six or eight months from late 1944, until July, 1945, he had enough change to give me a whole half of a dollar on Saturdays. I usually took that treasure and rode my new bicycle to see the "picture show" in Columbia, AL. It was about a six mile ride across the bridge over the Chattahoochee River.

As a protective measure I always took care where I left my bike when it was unattended. There was a vacant lot beside the picture show where I hid my bicycle in the high grass while I was attending the movie. I would buy a movie ticket at the window beside the entrance for 10 cents and a 5-cent bag of popcorn. After the movie I often would top off my big weekend extravaganza on the town with a 5-cent "moon pie" and a large 16-ounce bottle of Royal Crown Cola, still only one nickel. I was then left with the princely sum of 25 cents to spend during the week at Gordon Hall's store at Hilton.

Back at the farm, on one particular day, the mules were pulling a walking cultivator in the field beyond the creek when something rather humorous happened. This cultivator was a plow on two wheels which had a "double tree" to which was attached two "single trees" so that it could be pulled by two mules. It had a left side plow and a right side plow which made it capable of plowing both sides of a row of corn at the same time.

I had been able to adjust the two plows perfectly so that when the mules walked exactly in place I would not actually have to hold the plow handles. At some point Potsy, then five years old, came to the field to bring some fresh water.

I asked him if he wanted to operate the cultivator. He answered, "Yeah, if you'll show me how." I instructed, "Just take hold of these plow handles." He then reached up and took hold of the handles. It was comical seeing him grasp those handles which were about the height of his ears. I gave the normal signal to the mules to start pulling.

Within a minute I began to brag on Potsy for the skill he was displaying. He responded by saying, "David, I'm not doing this. You must be doing it." I replied "No. I'm not even touching the plow. See, I'm only walking beside you." He questioned me with emphasis. "David, do you think I don't have any more sense than any other little boy my size?"

The Turtle Hole & Hook Warms:
God's Mercy at Work Again

Sawhatchee Creek flowed through Boozey Bushes and Cedar Springs a few miles further south. We swam often in the creek and, yes, "skinny dippin'" when only boys and men were present, was allowed.

One of the best swimming holes in the whole area was called the "Turtle Hole" near Cedar Springs. At the Turtle Hole the creek was deeper than in other places, and it was safe for diving. Someone tied a long, strong rope to a branch of a tree that leaned out over the creek. We would grasp the lower end of the rope, swing out to midstream, and drop into the water.

My mother was not a very good swimmer, but this didn't keep her from enjoying the Turtle Hole, too. I recall how once she almost drowned in the Turtle Hole before a man rescued her. God's gracious providence had crossed our path once again.

During this sojourn in Boozey Bushes Earl had a serious illness – he kept losing weight and getting more and more skinny. Strangely, this malady caused him to have a strong urge to eat the gray, sandy dirt in the yard. Earl claimed that when he swallowed the dirt it felt good going down. He became so weak he could hardly walk through the house. Mr. Madison repeatedly warned our parents, "If you don't get Earl to a doctor he will die." My brother became so thin that he looked like a refugee child in some newsreel. Bobbie and I, not meaning to be cruel, called him "Quiltin' Frame," a reference to the narrow-slatted, wooden contraptions used to make quilts.

A doctor's examination discovered that Earl had a bad case of intestinal worms called "hookworms." He was too anemic and weak to endure a worm treatment. The doctor gave him medicine to build him up to be strong enough for the treatment that would get rid of the worms. Our merciful God was at work again, and shortly after this Earl became healthy and ate normally once again.

Confronting Two Ladies

Some months later there were some events at Hilton High School that I have not forgotten. I remember well one dear old lady teacher who was about 60 years old and who agreed to teach us one more year in the '44-'45 term. Mrs. Williams was about six feet tall and very strong for a woman. I will tell you how I know of her physical strength.

I am now ashamed of how my two friends and I troubled Mrs. Williams. James, Ralph, and I would violate her class rules, like going up front to the pencil sharpener or going over to put more wood in the classroom heater without getting permission. This may seem petty to some today, but our actions were stubborn and deliberate attempts to distract our fellow classmates and gain their attention. [Note: I later found out that James [Alexander] died in the army, possibly in the Korean Conflict. In December of 2008, I was able to speak with Ralph [Ellis]. He had become a farmer in Early County, Georgia. I was able to give him a gospel witness at that time.]

When we were disruptive in class she would make us stand outside in the hall. If the principal, Mrs. Spooner, should see us we would be taken to the office for a paddling. On one such occasion I had been consigned to the hallway, and I spied Mrs. Spooner coming out of her office. You have to understand that Mrs. Spooner was a rather large woman who kept a correspondingly-sized paddle in her office – at least that's what we had been told. Before she noticed me, I knocked on our classroom door. When Mrs. Williams opened the door I quickly stepped inside and begged for a book that I could read while standing in the hall. You see, said I, "I didn't want to waste my time." Fortunately, Mrs. Spooner went back into her office before I returned to my place in the hall.

On another occasion, James was seen in the hall by the principal and received a good hard paddling. I said to our teacher, Mrs. Williams, "Don't you feel sorry for James because Mrs. Spooner whips hard?" Mrs. Williams detected my impudence and ordered me to make her a paddle so that she could do her own spanking next time.

I made her a paddle with a slight split in the handle so that maybe it would come apart when she used it on one of us. I brought it to school and hid it in my desk. Every time she would ask if I had completed the paddle she demanded I would beg for more time to finish making it. After several days some of the girls told her that I had been keeping the paddle in my desk. Mrs. Williams made me come to the front with the paddle and sit in the front desk. "If you don't behave, I will use it on you," she warned.

I took a seat in the front desk with the slightly split paddle in my hands. When she was not looking in my direction I tried to pull it apart a little more. Gradually, I split it apart little by little, until suddenly it split into two parts. I fitted the two parts neatly together so that the split was not noticeable and placed what appeared to be a perfect paddle on the desk. About that time the school bell rang to end the class period. We students stood to exit the room. As Mrs. Williams picked up the paddle it immediately became two parts in her hand.

"David, you wait here," she said. I replied, "Mrs. Williams, the bell just sounded. It's time to go." She took hold of me with both hands as I tried to advance toward the door. She slung me across the room, I landed on my knees and scuffed up my overalls as I slid almost into the wood heater. The lady was rightfully angry at me because of my behavior and my having tricked her with the split paddle.

Later I was very ashamed for the way I had treated that elderly lady and apologized for my mischief. I was no more trouble for Mrs. Williams. She probably never forgot the events of her last year of teaching at Hilton High School. It amazes me that God's grace would allow such a disorderly pupil later to become a teacher himself.

There was another confrontation with a lady that caused me more physical pain than the one in the classroom.

Confronting a Third Lady

Helen Walton, Mr. Madison Freeman's 14-year-old granddaughter, was a popular young gal in the neighborhood, and I even referred to her as my girlfriend.

I was riding my bicycle down a path through the woods between our house and Mr. Madison's house. Helen and three others stood in the path blocking my way. I had to ride into the weeds to go around them, and this didn't please me one bit. I boldly prophesied, "When I come back through here, I won't ride through the weeds to go around you again."

On my return, they stood their ground, but my honor was now at stake. True to my rather boisterous vow, I rode my bike into them as they stayed in the path. Truth be known, by the time I actually reached them my bike was barely moving and Helen and her friends grabbed the handlebars and stopped my movement altogether. We started arguing with each other, especially Helen and I.

Up to that time she had been the object of my first boyhood crush, but now I was about to become the object of her scorn. She picked up a broken piece of a tree limb about the width of my wrist and a foot or so long. She shouted out at me calling me "Jafus Bailey," the name of a black neighbor that none of us liked.

It was becoming obvious that Helen didn't reciprocate my affections – this, plus her stubborn refusal to let me ride past, inspired me to retaliate with, "If I'm Jafus Bailey, then you are Rose Bailey," referencing Jafus' rather portly mother. Quick as a flash Helen let me have it, and hit me on the side of my head with her weapon. She hit me so hard that it broke the skin on my ear and blood ran down my cheek and chin. No more did I call Helen Walton my girlfriend, but I did meet her again over 60 years later under far more amiable circumstances. We had a wonderful conversation remembering bygone days.

Now Listen to My Story 'Bout a Man Named Dave

*T*he 60s hit sitcom, "The Beverly Hillbillies," lampooned the unsophisticated Clampett family and their backwoods life-style. Though I wasn't raised in the Ozark hills with the Clampetts, much of their backcountry worldview was very familiar to me – I grew up in Boozey Bushes, GA.

Recall that Boozey Bushes was so named because of the making and selling of homemade, untaxed whiskey. By late 1944 the local constabulary had been so successful at arresting the makers of this highly prized commodity that the demand for "moonshine" had increased greatly.

The law officials, or "revenuers," had caught a number of moon-shiners because the process of making white lightning had a normally fatal requirement, a secret place where there was a large supply of water. Most moonshiners put their still – that is, the apparatus for the distillation of beer into alcoholic liquor – in a forest near a river or a creek. It was in such places that the revenuers searched. They would traipse along both sides of the rivers and creeks until they found a still and watched until some men came to "fire it up." The detectives then arrested them on the spot.

Dad knew that we could make a lot of money if we could keep from getting caught by the law. "If we set up a still in the middle of a woods," he said, "a long way from the creek we can fool 'em."

To solve the water problem we dug a well. The water from our well with huge amounts of sugar and ground raw wheat was put into a 60-gallon wooden barrel. This mixture in warm weather fermented in a week into 60 gallons of raw beer. When the barrel of beer was ripe for distillation, we would go to work at the still about midnight. By flashlight the barrel of beer was slowly poured into a metal drum through a three-inch bunghole in the top of the metal drum. When the metal drum was full we would close off the bunghole with a half-gallon can and seal it with an airtight paste of flour and cornmeal. Then we took a three-quarter inch copper pipe about six feet long and sealed it into the side of the half gallon can. The pipe extended from the can through a wooden trough filled with cool water. We then "fired up" the still by starting a fire under the metal drum that contained the beer. Soon the beer began to boil. The steam from the boiling beer ascended up through the can on top of the drum, through the copper piping, and condensed into droplets as it passed through the pipe that was submerged in the trough of cooler water. A thin stream of distilled whiskey ran down the copper pipe and was collected in gallon jugs.

One 60-gallon barrel of beer distilled in about four hours. It produced about five gallons of whiskey and was worth $5 per gallon wholesale. One gallon would fill eight pint bottles which moonshine retailers would then sell for at least $1 per pint. Dad dealt with the wholesale only. It was much more difficult for the detectives to catch wholesalers. The retailers of moonshine made more money, but there was more danger of being apprehended.

Dad and I engaged in an illegal and dangerous business of making moonshine for about seven or eight months in late 1944-45. At that time God "who works in mysterious ways his wonders to perform" stepped in once again.

He moved an insignificant slave, a young female hostage, in 2 Kings 5:1-2, to speak up and bring Naaman into contact with Elisha's life-saving message. In similar fashion God moved my mom, a little woman who was not a Christian at that time, to speak up to move our family towards contact with the soul-saving message of the Gospel. To be sure, it was not her purpose to bring us to hear the Good News. But our coming to the Gospel was the result nonetheless, for it was surely God's purpose and His purposes never fail.

In south Georgia we had never heard a clear presentation of the Good News of the substitutionary cross work of Christ. We heard religious preaching at a few churches we attended infrequently, but we did not hear a clear explanation of the way of salvation by grace through faith alone in the vicarious death and resurrection of the Lord Jesus Christ. There may have been some in our area in those years who did hear a clear presentation of the Gospel, but we did not.

Mom was a submissive wife, but concerning Dad's activity in the summer of 1945, she put her foot down and spoke her mind. "Robert, you *must* quit this illegal stuff before it's too late." She continued, "It will be bad when you get caught, but it will be *terrible* for David to get caught with you."

Dad responded, "Well, I've got to make a living some way." When Dad realized that Mom was determined – he knew she was right – he relented. "I suppose I *could* go down to Florida and talk to Uncle Bob and see if he can give me some work on his dairy farm." (Uncle Bob Jones – not related to Bob Jones, Sr. who started Bob Jones University – was Mom's uncle on her daddy's side.)

Within a few days Dad took a hurried 300-mile trip to Polk County, Florida to talk to Uncle Bob about employment. Though we didn't know it at the time, God was about to move us toward the Gospel. Dad was offered a menial job working for Uncle Bob at the dairy feeding the cattle and cleaning the barn.

With the money we had made through the booze business Dad bought a big truck to haul our things down to Florida. About mid-August of 1945, a few days after President Truman ordered the atomic bombs dropped on Japan and the subsequent surrender ending the Second World War, we clambered up onto that dark blue '38 Chevy truck and left Boozey Bushes and the moonshine trade forever.

Darrel claimed the choice spot in the cab of the truck with Mom and Dad. Bobbie, Earl, and I found a comfortable place among the tools, bicycles, dishes, chests, bedsteads, mattresses, clothes and quilts in the open body of that old ton-and-a-half truck. Some might picture the Beverly Hillbillies, and they wouldn't be too far off target.

Not Beverly Hills But Winter Haven

*A*fter an exciting 18-hour trip – the same drive would take about six hours on 21st century highways – we arrived at our modern rent free house just 100 aromatic yards from the milking barn where we would be working. The temporary housing we now inhabited was the first residence in which we had ever lived to have electric lights, an indoor toilet with running water, warm showers, an electric cooking stove, and painted walls inside and out.

My duties for Uncle Bob consisted mainly of helping him make house to house delivery of the milk. Customers would indicate their desire for more fresh milk by leaving empty glass bottles on the porch. We would exchange the empties for full bottles, and immediately the customers picked up the milk and put it in their refrigerators or ice boxes. If customers weren't home they would leave the money in the empty bottles on the porch and we took the milk inside for them. (Many did not lock their doors because in most localities stealing from houses was extremely rare in those days.)

Electric refrigerators were too expensive for many families. The more economical alternative was the old-fashioned "ice box." This was an insulated cabinet into which a large block of ice was placed. A hundred-pound block of ice could keep dairy or meat products cool for two or three days even during the summer. This would relate to a job I took some years later, so I'll reveal the details at the appropriate point.

Uncle Bob helped Dad get a better job with a plumber friend named Peter. He promised Dad a dollar an hour. We were amazed.

Remember, 50 cents an hour was the best pay Dad ever had for legal work back in Georgia. Even moonshining, with its high risks, only brought a bit more than $1 an hour. But Peter heard that Dad had never been paid anywhere near what he was now offering, so he tried to get by with paying Dad 80 cents an hour. Dad immediately quit – he couldn't stand being cheated. Soon thereafter Dad found a job at the local phosphate mine making 80 cents an hour, but this didn't involve being cheated. In addition, this employment was a steady 40 hours a week.

In September of 1945, I enrolled in my junior year of high school at Summerlin Institute in Bartow, Florida. By this point I had already accumulated two years of high school credits back in Georgia even though I had just finished the ninth grade. (High school credits could be earned there in the eighth grade.)

During my first week we played a game that we never played in Georgia. The game was touch football, and I did not know the rules. After the first play the coach yelled, "Off sides!" and penalized my team. Someone asked, "Who was it, Coach?" Coach replied, "Georgia Boy." That became my name by which my schoolmates addressed me for the last two years of high school.

In early October of 1945, we moved about a mile outside of the Bartow school district to a house on the Rifle Range Road. I did not want to change schools so about sunrise every morning I headed out on my bicycle and rode about a mile and a half back to Uncle Bob's house to catch the big yellow Bartow school bus. Later, I hired a bicycle shop owner to attach a small motor to my bike. This motor bike was my method of transportation to meet the school bus all of my senior year.

The only sports team on which I participated was the track team my last year of high school. I was too small for any other team – I weighed less than 120 pounds – but probably because of my slight stature I had done well at middle distance running in phys. ed. classes my junior year. The coach encouraged me to go out for the school track team the next year, and so it happened that I was chosen to represent the team in the half-mile and mile races. I was quite proud of this, and my performance in the upcoming meets was very important in my thinking.

We Really Weren't Gypsies, But...

In early 1946, we moved yet again. I wasn't yet sixteen and had lived in eleven previous dwellings in three different states. This was the twelfth move, but finally, we were able to afford to buy a house. Before the reader gets the wrong idea it needs to be stated that when the Wingets moved from one dwelling to another it usually didn't take a great deal of effort. The six of us had so few belongings that we could move our entire collection of worldly goods in one trip in one truck.

The house did have electricity and running water by means of an electric pump from the well outside. No drawing water up by hand for us! The house contained one large bedroom and a kitchen with electric stove and refrigerator. That, along with the electric pump, qualified us in our thinking as having "moved on up" into the upper crust of society. We put three beds in that bedroom and the entire family slept there. As I recall Earl and I slept in one, Potsy and Bobbie slept in the second, and of course Dad and Mom slept in the third. Our limited amount of clothes were kept in a chest of drawers or hung on nails that were driven into the bare wooden wall. We had to use an outdoor toilet for the first year, but this wasn't viewed as a great burden because we had used outdoor toilets all the time when we lived in Georgia. (My dad used to say, "Imagine putting a toilet *inside* of your house. But that's how sorry some people have become.") After about a year we added on another bedroom and a bathroom in the back of the house. I guess we were just kind of sorry.

This house was located on the Rifle Range Road, so named because it led to the World War I Army practice rifle range. By the Providence of God our family now lived very close to a Bible-preaching church – only a small palmetto-covered lot separated our house from the Wahneeta Baptist Church. ("Wahneeta" was probably an Indian word, but we pronounced it almost exactly like the Spanish name "Juanita.") Only seven months earlier we had lived in a place where we did not even know of a Gospel-preaching church. Now God's patient and merciful plan brought us within a stone's throw of the site where His grace would be proclaimed in our hearing.

We had not moved to Wahneeta because we were seeking God – we were moved there because God was seeking us. Romans 3:11 says that there is "none that seek after God," and Luke 19:10 teaches that God seeks the lost. While it is common to hear of folks speaking of having "found the Lord," He wasn't lost nor do sinners initiate the search for Him. It probably would be more theologically correct to talk of when "the Lord found me." When Adam sinned in the Garden of Eden he ran from God and hid. On the other hand it was God who came looking for Adam and eventually found him. Only as God sovereignly draws sinners to Himself do they begin to have any appetite or thirst for Him.

The unsaved human being naturally has an inbred blindness toward spiritual things and his distaste for the Gospel, and its requirement of humble acceptance of God's finished solution for sin is something man cannot overcome on his own. In addition to that, man has a spiritual enemy the Bible calls Satan who works effectively to further disguise the truth and keep man in his darkened ignorance. My pride and Satan's strategies were allies warring against God and against my spiritual benefit.

Conviction Without Conversion

Part of what soured my attitude towards Christians and attending church was a previous church experience I had had. A few months earlier some of my friends had persuaded me to go with them to a Pentecostal church revival meeting. The preacher – whom I later came to know as a good friend and co-worker in the same work crew, and whose son later became one of my closest friends and eventually an in-law – proclaimed a hell-fire-and-brimstone doctrine that frightened me a great deal. I knew I was a sinner, and His orations on the horrors of damnation for sinners moved me deeply. However, if the preacher understood the necessity of simple faith in the complete sufficiency of Christ's atoning work, he never made it clear to me. I desperately needed to be informed as to what the Bible said was the only way to obtain God's provided solution. In fear I responded to the preacher's invitation to come to the altar and "seek the Lord," but I didn't have any clear idea what that really meant.

Much like my Uncle Dick's perspective, I thought I needed to beg God for His mercy. I thought that the key requirement was my sincerity and my resolve to change my lifestyle to one that was pleasing to God. The first night I prayed sincerely for God to save me – I honestly thought that I had to persuade God to save me, something that I erroneously thought He was reluctant to do. Nothing happened.

I was still in the dark as to my total inability to *do anything* toward the solution for my sin problem. I was completely ignorant of what God had provided to make that possible. I was totally unaware of the key instrumentality of faith in Christ's completed work at Calvary on my behalf. I resolved to persevere to get God to save me by "living for God" the next day. On one occasion that preacher declared, "The first thing you gotta do to be saved is you gotta quit yo' meanness!" I therefore resolved to obey my parents, avoid using bad language, refrain from smoking, and the like. Thereby I hoped to prove to Him my sincerity.

At the Pentecostal services that first night when I went forward I was counseled to come down to the front again the next night. "God will save you yet," they promised. While I prayed the second night one kind lady whispered in my ear, "Son, you must hold on and pray harder." Another dear lady suggested emphatically, "Son, you must turn loose," by which she meant, "Vow to abandon your sins." It seemed that if I would pray long enough and hard enough, I would finally break down God's reluctance and He would save me, if for no other reason, to get me to quick bugging him. I'm certain that those dear ladies were sincere, but their efforts were not informed by Scripture.

I didn't realize that Romans 8:32 proves that God does not need to be begged into saving sinners. He wanted so much to save sinners that He "spared not his own Son." So eager was He to redeem lost sinners that He sacrificed His perfect Son to make that redemption possible. Yet I continued to beg God for salvation, and still nothing happened in my heart except an emotional stirring.

54

No one explained the Gospel to me, the Good News that God's unique Son took my sins upon Himself and paid the penalty of death in my place. All I needed was to accept that truth by faith and I'd be saved, that is, rescued from the impending judgment I rightly deserved and delivered from the obligation to pay the penalty My sins demanded. Christ has already paid the full pardon of my wickedness.

The words "cross" and "Gospel" may have been used during those days at the church, but no explanation of how they related to getting saved was given. *God's* way of salvation is not clearly presented unless persons are told something to *believe* rather than something to *do*. That's why it's called "the Gospel." It's Good News because my salvation doesn't depend on something I do – praying, or crying, or being good, or quitting sin. Or any other good deed. What the sinner must believe, that is, trust holistically or depend upon totally, is that Jesus Christ's ministry on the cross and His resurrection fully satisfied the just demands of God's righteousness. The sinner must affirm that he can add nothing to what Christ did. He must admit that he can bring nothing to the equation that obtains for him any advantage in the question of his eternal destiny. Solely and only what Jesus Christ accomplished is absolutely sufficient.

The Bible way of salvation is a belief or trust in what God has already done through Jesus Christ rather than something the sinner might do in order to get God to be beneficent toward him. It's a reliance upon God's promise to the sinner rather than a reliance upon the sinner's promise to God. The active agent in man's salvation is God. The recipient is the sinner. God's salvation cannot be had as a trade – the sinner's good behavior in exchange for God's grace. Salvation is not a barter. The sinner's good resolutions, or correct wording, or religious affiliation, or emotional response, or bodily posture garners no benefit in the issue of salvation and cannot result in the sinner being granted forgiveness.

Romans 10:9 does not say "confess your sins." It says that the sinner must "confess the Lord Jesus." It means to "agree with God" about who Jesus is and what He did. It means to "agree with God" about why Jesus died and that God raised Him from the dead to prove that the Father accepted Jesus' death as full payment for the sins of sinners (Rom. 4:25). One noted writer commented, "He who became surety for the sinner's debt could not have been released from the prison house of the tomb unless that debt was paid."

When that preacher said that we must "confess sins" he may have had 1 John 1:9 in mind, but that verse is not addressing unbelievers with instruction on how to obtain salvation. It is speaking to Christians on how to obtain forgiveness and renewed fellowship when it says "If we confess our sins He is faithful and just to forgive us our sins and to cleanse us from all unrighteousness." That this context is addressing people who are already saved and in the family of God is clearly shown by the very next paragraph. 1 John 2:1 says, "*We* have an advocate with the *Father*, Jesus Christ the righteous." God promises His children who confess their sins that fellowship with Him will be renewed if they will "agree with Him" about their sin, that is, have the same abhorrence toward their sin that He does. This passage is not saying that confession of sins brings salvation to them over again.

The preacher told us that there was a baptism scheduled at the lake the following Sunday afternoon and if we felt that we had gotten saved we should be baptized. Someone responded that he felt like he had gotten saved and that he wanted to be baptized. We were not told that assurance of salvation was by faith and not by feeling or by good works. The whole experience left me confused about the whole idea of being saved, and the confusion became part of a web of excuses keeping me from the truth.

Goodner's Gospel Tent

When Mom suggested that we attend Wahneeta Baptist my prejudicial belief that only old ladies and children were religious, my observance of relatives who in spite of their best efforts had "backslid," my focus on doing well in the upcoming track meets, my pride about soon being the first Winget ever to graduate from high school, and my earlier disappointments at the Pentecostal church all conspired to make me very reluctant to consider having anything to do with the church next door. But God arranged something to whet my appetite and heighten my curiosity about the church across the vacant lot.

Pastor Cumby of the Baptist church invited Evangelist Paul Goodner to bring his tent down from south Alabama and set it up in front of the church for an evangelistic crusade. It was the tent that God used to get my attention. I had heard of a circus tent or a skating rink in a tent, but I had never heard of church services in a tent. The fact that my mom and sister and brothers had planned to attend the meeting – Dad, as yet, had no interest in spiritual matters – coupled with my curiosity caused me to decide to go and sit in the back of the tent to observe what might happen.

That first night, for the first time in my life, I heard what I had never before heard in all of the churches I had attended. From the Bible Evangelist Goodner, a tall man with a clear voice, communicated clearly the Gospel of Christ. Such a clear explanation had been sadly wanting a few months earlier at the Pentecostal meeting. Using simple Scriptures Goodner showed that the need for the Gospel was caused by human sin. The remedy of our sin was the cross, and that remedy must be accepted by faith by each sinner.

At the end of the service each night there were some who eagerly stepped forward to indicate that they were trusting in Christ and his death for the salvation of their souls. Several of my family were among those who answered the invitation to accept Christ's offer by publicly expressing their faith in Him, but not I.

Powerful Portrayal

Friday night was the climax of the meetings. The sun had set, and the bare electric bulbs hung from wires strung from one tent post to the other cast a stark glare through the warm spring night. There may have been a hundred or more in attendance, and I maintained my vigil from the back row, as the tall, animated speaker in a long-sleeved, white shirt and tie gave the clearly enunciated message. My attention was riveted on the speaker, and it was as if the message was meant for me in particular. It was in that service that the evangelist did something that God used to convince me of my desperate need and of the sufficiency of Christ's death as the only solution for my sin.

Evangelist Goodner strode down from the front platform to the middle of the tent. With him he brought a plaited leather horsewhip and proceeded to lash the center post of that tent just as Jesus was lashed across his back with the "cat-o'-nine-tails." As he struck the post Goodner counted aloud, "One...! Two...! Three...! Four...!" and then quoted Scriptures related to the crucifixion: "We esteemed Him stricken, smitten of God, and afflicted... He was bruised for our iniquities... The chastisement of our peace was upon Him... and with His stripes we are healed," (Isa 53:4-5). "Five...! Six...! Seven...!" My attention was totally captivated and the Holy Spirit was doing His work of convincing me that this was the Truth that I had been avoiding.

Goodner paced back to the front, but he wasn't finished. The tension only increased as he hefted a heavy-timbered cross to his shoulder and stumbled awkwardly back down the center aisle depicting how Jesus was made to bear His cross on His bleeding back up Golgotha's hill. Goodner quoted, "Christ, His own self, bore our sins in His own body on the tree..." (1 Pet. 2:24), as he continued down the aisle all the way to my back row. As he reversed his steps dragging that cumbersome load to the front he cited, "He suffered, the just for the unjust, that He might bring us to God," (1 Pet. 3:18).

The evangelist summarized many Bible verses and emphasized the truth that the death of Christ was the central event in God's plan of salvation for sinners. He pointed out that Acts 2:23 taught that He, Jesus, was "delivered to the cross by the determinate counsel and foreknowledge of God." Goodner used 1 Peter 1:20 to show that Christ's death was "foreordained before the foundation of the world." He pointed my attention to Isaiah 53:10 which stated that although Jesus was sinless, "yet it pleased the Lord to bruise Him. He put Him to grief." Unfortunately, today, some use the expression "God's *plan* of salvation" who do not really believe God *planned* the death of his Son as the only satisfactory remedy for human sin, but not Paul Goodner on that evening in April of 1947. The cross of Christ was central to God's program for history, and that night when I heard and saw that message, it was to become the central pivot of my life, too.

About 700 BC Isaiah predicted that the Lord would lay on Jesus "the iniquity of us all," (Isaiah 53:6). Because "all have sinned" (Rom. 3:23) and "the wages of sin is death" (Rom. 6:23) it is abundantly clear that the only thing that pays the penalty of sin is death. Only death, and always death.

For God to construct a way for the sins of mankind to be paid and men to have forgiveness, a Sinless Substitute *had to die*. For God to construct a way for the sins of mankind against an infinite Judge and His Law to be remitted an Infinite Sacrificial Death Penalty *had to be imposed*. Only Jesus Christ could be that Sinless Substitute and bear that Infinite Sacrificial Death Penalty. And, all glory to Him, He *was* the Sinless Substitute and He *did bear* that Infinite Sacrificial Death Penalty on the cross.

Good works, giving to the poor, reading the Bible, reading the Bible *many* hours, even longer hours of prayer and doing penance – none of these things will pay the debt of death. But guilty, hell-deserving sinners who will accept God's promise that any sinner who agrees with God about His Son, the Lord Jesus – Who He really is and what He has already accomplished at Calvary – and trust in his heart what God's raising Jesus from the dead implies – namely, that God the Father was totally satisfied with the finished payment that Christ had paid – then that sinner shall *surely* be saved (Rom. 10:9).

Private Reception

I did not respond to the invitation to go forward for counseling that night. I stayed in my seat. But that compelling explanation of what Jesus suffered in my place and stead to pay for my sins by his death gripped my heart for the next several hours. I couldn't get it out of my mind, and I returned home pondering my sin and an overwhelming realization of my guilt before a holy God.

That night sleep alluded me. I could think of nothing else but the truths of the message I'd been given. Finally, sometime well after midnight, in all sincerity I told God that I could no longer reject a Savior who suffered such physical pain and such mental shame for me. The prayer I prayed was not a begging kind of prayer like I had prayed at the religious services before I had heard the gospel. I said something like this: "Dear God, I admit that I am a sinner, and I cannot do anything to earn salvation. But I have learned this week that Jesus paid for all of my sins. I right now with all of my heart accept Him as my Savior and trust His death alone as the remedy for my sin. By faith I accept Your promise and I thank You for saving me."

At that moment my burden of sin rolled away. I experienced a new peace with God, and while I didn't comprehend all that occurred in that instant, I entered into an eternally safe relationship with the Creator of the universe. God became at that moment my Heavenly Father because I had just been born again into His family (Jn. 3:3-8). The sovereign God had about 21 months earlier moved a little south Georgia mother to issue an ultimatum concerning the making of illegal liquor which set in motion a series of events that culminated in the transformation of a guilty, good-for-nothing sinner into a grateful and a joyful saint. God gets all the glory because He planned it all and carried it out by His sovereign grace and power. It included the supplying of the remedy for my sin, bringing me into contact with the Gospel, and convincing me to take Him up on his offer.

Sometime later I came to know of a couple of songs that so well captured my attitude on that night:

> My sin, oh the bliss of this glorious thought,
> > My sin, not in part but the whole,
> Is nailed to the cross and I bear it no more.
> > Praise the Lord, praise the Lord, oh my soul.
> And when I think that God his Son not sparing,
> > Sent him to die, I scarce can take it in;
> That on the cross my burden gladly bearing,
> > He bled and died to take away my sin.
> *Then sings my soul*, my Savior God to Thee,
> > How great Thou art, how great Thou art.
> *Then sings my soul*, my Savior God to Thee,
> > How great Thou art, how great Thou art.

Petulant Rejection

Many years after my salvation I witnessed to a man who had spent time in prison and who challenged my message. He said "Suppose my best pal and I are the same age, same size, live on the same street, we're guilty of the same sins and you tell both of us these same facts about Jesus' death. He believes this message and asks Jesus to save him, but I refuse to believe and I never do trust in Jesus. Do you mean to tell me that even though my pal and I are the same in every way except he accepted what you call the Gospel and I did not, that he will enjoy the bliss of heaven with all its joys forever while I will suffer in a place of torment forever?" I replied, "That is exactly what the Bible teaches." The man set his jaw and stomped his foot and yelled at me, "If that is the way it is I will just go on to hell! I'm not about to worship such a God as that!"

To that man I should have said, "Even if you are an upright, honest and kind man who does not use profanity, who does not get drunk, nor take drugs, but lives the best you can and performs good deeds, your eternal destiny will be the same as just mentioned if you refuse Jesus and his Gospel offer." Jesus Himself said "I am the way, the truth, and the life; no one comes to the Father but by Me" (Jn. 14:6). Throughout all eternity Jesus' statement will never be proven false.

Metamorphosis

*N*ot many days after my conversion our track team took part in the Polk County Track Championship down in Lake Wales. Coach Ausley, who was nicknamed "Brick" Ausley because he was a big man and a strict disciplinarian, had scheduled me to compete with others from all over the county in the mile run. He changed his mind a few minutes before the meet began and put me in the half mile which was scheduled to take place about an hour earlier than the mile run.

I found some privacy behind the stadium and communed with God in prayer. I promised Him that if He would enable me to run a good race and score points for my team, I would give Him all the glory.

The P.A. system crackled to life and called all participants in the half-mile run to the starting line. Under the lights a dozen runners responded to the summons in the stadium that night. The starter's gun set us off, and I ran the best time of my life. My teammate, Claude Thompson, won the race, but I finished second, only three or four paces behind him. I can't remember for sure, but I think our team may have won the meet, due in small part to the combined points Claude and I accumulated in that race.

Only a few days earlier I had been in the habit of using my participation in track as an excuse to avoid spiritual things. But things were changing in my entire outlook. Now, in my spiritual infancy, I was attempting to employ my activities as means of highlighting the greatness of God. *Soli Deo Gloria!*

Fledgling Steps of Discipleship

After salvation I was faithful to all the church services, but I did not immediately submit myself for baptism or request church membership. I was not yet aware of the importance of either.

I did not realize how crucial it was to obey the Savior's command to publicly proclaim my testimony of His work for me on the cross and my new direction in life through the symbolism of baptism. Christ's first public act was to submit to public baptism and His final words to His followers included a direct command regarding the importance of all believers undergoing this symbolic rite.

The New Testament views the act of baptism as a means of identification – followers of Christ are called upon to identify themselves with Him and His Church by means of, what may appear to modern observers, as a rather quaint and peculiar ceremony. The new child of God mimics Christ's death and resurrection by being immersed in water and then raised up out of his watery "grave." In a secondary symbolism the medium of water also depicts the spiritual cleansing provided by Christ's death and resurrection.

That every believer should submit to the accountability of membership and faithful participation in a local assembly of committed believers follows from the importance that Christ and His apostles placed upon local churches. Jesus predicted the building of His spiritual Body, the Church, and the apostles risked their lives to bring into being local manifestations of that Body. Those local congregations were the recipients of most of the letters of the New Testament, and what few letters weren't addressed to local assemblies seems to have been addressed to leaders of those local churches. The New Testament knows nothing of a purely private Christianity lived in isolation from other believers. Believers are viewed as a flock of sheep, as parts of a body, and as sections of a building. By virtue of our human nature and the fact that no individual is sufficient in and of himself to fully live out the implications of the Gospel by himself, the necessity of local church membership is clear. The New Testament commands believers not to "forsake the assembly" but rather to "encourage one another" to faithfulness and following after the Master (Heb. 11:25).

Pastor Cumby, the man who had been used of the Lord to invite Evangelist Goodner to Florida, resigned as pastor a few months after the tent crusade. Shortly afterward, Pastor May took leadership of the congregation. He remained in this capacity for more than a year.

It was during Pastor May's oversight of that small congregation – attendance on any given Sunday was probably no more than sixty or seventy – that I became convinced that I should obey the Lord in baptism and join the church. The morning I joined the church the pastor nominated me to be superintendent of the Sunday School. It seemed that all who were present that day were in agreement. Therefore at a chronological age of 18 years and a spiritual age of less than two years old the first Winget to complete high school became the first Winget to hold an official position in a local church. A few days later I, along with several others, were baptized in the open air in nearby Lake McLeod.

The primary responsibility of the Sunday School superintendent was to present a Bible devotional each Sunday morning. I enjoyed selecting and studying various passages of Scripture during the week and then taking 10 or more minutes each Sunday at the start of the assembly to explain those verses to my fellow church attendees. I am sure that the Lord taught me far more through these exercises than anyone else, and it was one of the means the Lord used to affirm His gifting. Occasionally different members of the congregation would tell me that the explanations I had offered helped them to understand the truth of the verses. My sovereign Father, in these meager ways, was beginning to prepare me for a lifetime ministry in the exposition of His Word in a number of churches, a Bible college, and ministerial seminary. At the time, however, I had little or no concept of what God was doing in my life, nor what was in store for me.

First Adventures in Capitalism

Bag Boy, Fruit Hog, Etc.

*A*fter graduation from high school my first job was as a bag boy at the checkout counter in a local supermarket. I worked five days a week, eight hours a day, and earned $25 for those 40 hours. I only kept that job a short time – I realized I could make more at other employment. One such opportunity involved doing odd jobs for a dear Presbyterian lady, Miss Jane Currie. I pruned the trees in her citrus grove before the fruit was ready to be harvested. I later came to understand that this employment relationship with Miss Currie was one of the providential appointments that God designed to further His purposes in my life, but more about that later.

Yet another opportunity presented itself: I worked seasonally – October to May – as a "fruit hog" or citrus fruit picker. With only one other exception, this was the most lucrative type of employment I ever had as a young man. Our crew worked for Snively Packing Co. out of Eloise, FL.

Our crew members would sometimes drive their own vehicles to an assigned citrus grove before dawn, but more usually we would all go together on the tarpaulin-covered bed of the crew truck. The crew truck driver was a local country preacher named Snipes – "Preacher" is what we always called him. Other crew members included "Preacher's" son and one of my best friends, Raymond "Buck" Snipes; Buck's two brothers, Tom and Ike; "Pappy" Gladney (more usually called simply "Pappy G") and his son, Bill;

66

Ralph "Lightered-Knot" Toole; Arlo "Nose" Conley; and Ivan Adelbert "Cooter" Kirby. (You might think that Adelbert's name rhymes with Englebert, but you'd be mistaken. We pronounced his name Ay-DEL-bert with the emphasis on the 2nd syllable.) Another member of the crew we dubbed "Strick," an abbreviated form of his last name, Stricklin. I don't think I ever heard his real first name. There were also a half dozen or so others whose names I don't recall.

It was exhausting labor. Each "hog" would have his own heavy wooden ladder, maybe twenty feet long or longer, which would lean up on a citrus tree. The picker would wear cotton gloves to partly protect his hands from the little thorns that were often growing on the trees. He would lug a large bottomless, canvas bag slung by a cotton strap over his shoulder. The bottom of the bag was folded shut and held closed by a simple rope-and-hook mechanism which, when the bag was full, could be opened to allow the fruit to tumble out the bottom into collection boxes.

Up and down the ladder, and up again, we would haul those heavy bags. Hour after hour we stretched and strained to right and left to reach the fruit and twist it away from each branch. To be sure, some trees were small enough to have their fruit collected from the ground without the use of ladders – this was a bit easier – but as much as 75% of the fruit required the use of ladders. Cramps from loss of fluids was common, and all of us were deeply tanned, at least on our faces – no one wore short sleeves because of the brambles.

"Come on down, Men. Next man down strikes oil!" was a commonly heard cry in the groves. It was the foreman's code for encouraging workers to pick the fruit of their present tree as quickly as possible because the next tree in line was heavily-laden and would be a very productive tree to work on.

Each worker was assigned numbered tickets which he would attach to the boxes that he was working to fill. By attaching his tickets to the boxes he would be given credit for that fruit and at week's end would be paid according to the number of boxes he had filled during the previous week. We were usually paid fifteen cents per box. At that rate it took 67 boxes to make $10 plus one nickel. The fastest workers picking in very productive trees could harvest 134 boxes in

10 or 12 hours. Therefore a diligent worker could potentially make the princely sum of $20 in a single day's labor.

This employment was not only lucrative and arduous, it was also quite colorful, perhaps mainly due to the personalities of our crew members and the simple rural perspective we shared. It didn't take much to make us laugh or amuse us. For instance, someone might shout out, "Cooter, would you 'put 'er 'neath the clay'?" and then someone else would almost always request, "And be sure to put a tail to it!" You see, "Cooter" Kirby, a good 'ole country boy from Rocky Branch, AL, was the song leader at a local church, and was considered by some to have a rather melodic tenor voice. He was famous – at least among our crew – for a homely ballad about a young man's love who had tragically died and was buried "'neath the cold, cold clay." At the close of his renditions Cooter would often yodel or otherwise extemporize some coda ending – what we called a "tail." We never tired of Cooter's musical entertainment, and Cooter never tired of entertaining.

Already in his 50's by this time, "Pappy G" was one of the elder members of the group. He was quite diminutive, maybe five feet six and 120 pounds, but his most striking physical characteristic was the prominence of two rather large ears, one on either side of his head, of course. On the other hand, Arlo "Nose" Conley, at about six-four, towered over most of the rest of us. His most noticeable feature was his protruding nose. Even today I can picture in my mind a curious habit he had. With a partly-smoked cigarette cradled between his right index- and middle fingers – especially while deep in thought – Arlo would flick the right side of his prominent nose with his right thumb. Arlo might occasionally cry out with his southern drawl, "Preacher, who do you think of when I say, 'Ears'?" Instantly, Pappy G would respond, "Preacher, who do you think of when I say, 'Nose'?" Likely, one or the other would repeat the joke an hour or so later. Such simple banter never failed to elicit laughter all through the grove and helped pass the tedious hours.

Sometimes, a heavy dew in the morning (or a rain shower early in the day) forced a temporary pause in the work because we couldn't pick wet fruit. (If the fruit was damp and was dropped on the sandy soil of the grove, it would pick up a gritty coating and that would scar

Buck and Bobbie figure prominently in another later incident which I'll relate here. June was the time of the year when all the oranges and grapefruit had been harvested and the cherries in Michigan were about to be ripe for picking. Many of the local fruit hogs would migrate north to find work. Bobbie and Buck had been married for more than a year and Buck needed to make a living for his wife and new baby, Barbara. I needed to save money, and Pappy G and his son Bill needed work also.

The three other men agreed to pay for the gasoline if we could use Dad's car. So six of us – Buck, Bill, Pappy G, Bill's wife with her young baby, and I left after church one Sunday night. We were in for quite a ride.

Through the night we traveled north through the flatlands of southern and central Georgia. It was still dark as we began to traverse the rolling hills of north Georgia. To those of us who had spent our entire lives on the tablelands of south Georgia and Florida, these hills were something we had never encountered.

By mid-Monday morning, traveling up old Highway 41, we had made it across the Tennessee state line and were approaching Chattanooga. The tunnel through historic Missionary Ridge was blocked for some reason, and we were forced to wind our way up and over the ridge. To that point, I had never been on such a high mountain, or so I called it. As we crested the top of the ridge and caught a first glimpse down into the city we were dumbstruck. We looked across the valley at the town which stretched out below all the way to the Tennessee River and Lookout Mountain. We could hardly believe our eyes. I exclaimed, "Looook! at that town in a hole! How in the world do they get down in there and get out?!" As soon as I found a place to stop we got out and just gaped. Little did I know – how could I know? – that that "city in a hole" would play such a major role in my life in coming years.

We knew we had to push on, and by noon we were about to ascend Monteagle Mountain – remember that this was in the days before the interstate system had been built – when we were hit by a rain storm. The six miles of winding road up the mountain were being widened, and in some spots the wet clay surface was as slick as a wet bar of soap. Pappy G fussed, "How in the world could they

make roads such as this up on the side of these God-forsaken hills!"
It was so slippery that even when the car engine was idling in its
lowest gear it would spin the wheels. The three other fellows had
to get out and push several times to make any progress at all up the
mountain. We were all exhausted by the time we reached paved road
again.

We got to within 28 miles of Nashville by midnight and we were
all so tired that I stopped beside the road. The other three men slept
on the grass near the road. I slept in the front seat, and Mrs. Gladney
with her baby slept in the back seat. A very tired carload of potential cherry pickers arrived in Benton Harbor, Michigan by Tuesday
night.

Scientists, who study such matters, tell us that our sense of smell
leaves more deeply-ingrained memories than our other senses. I
don't know whether or not that is always true, but one of the most
prominent of my memories of that trip revolves around Bill's baby.
At fairly frequent intervals the baby produced some quite memorable evidence that his digestive system was functioning as it should.
His mother was behooved to change the baby's diaper, but this was
also before the days of disposable diapers. She needed to keep the
soiled diapers with us in the car. We didn't want to take time for
her to clean out the diapers. Pappy G had his own method of taking
care of the pungent residue – he would surreptitiously roll down the
window and drop the used diaper overboard. Thus, upon arrival at
our destination the baby had a much smaller wardrobe of diapers
than when we had left Florida.

Unfortunately for us, the cherries weren't yet ripe enough for
picking, but we were offered a job thinning peaches. When peaches
grow too thickly on the branch they don't develop properly. They
need to be thinned back with a long-handled instrument to at least
three inches apart. Our job was to reach up and knock off some of
the small green peaches. The problem was that this operation filled
the air with itchy peach fuzz, and this suspended particulate irritated
our eyes and skin. It was very uncomfortable.

The fatigue and lack of sleep and the irritating conditions made
all of us begin to wonder if this had been such a good idea after all.
In addition to this, the presence of Bill and his wife and baby caused

Buck to begin to pine for his own wife and baby. By afternoon he was completely disgusted with all that itchy peach fuzz and determined to find a way to head home immediately.

The problem was that the price of a bus ticket back to Florida was more than all the cash he had with him. The rest of us offered him all the money we could spare, but still he didn't have the price of a ticket to Winter Haven.

I then remembered that our family was visiting old friends that very week up in Boozey Bushes near Hilton, Georgia. Buck found out that he barely had enough for the bus ticket to Hilton. He boarded the bus for the ride down to Hilton, but didn't have any money left over for meals en route. All he had with him was one pack of crackers. Some 32 hours later a very hungry eighteen-year-old daddy had his baby girl and his very surprised wife in his arms.

The rest of us stayed in three different migrant worker camps in Benton Harbor, Shelby, and Hart, Michigan for about two weeks and picked cherries and other fruit. We earned a little more than our expenses to and from Michigan. Afterwards, Bill and his family traveled to Pennsylvania where his wife's people lived, and Pappy G and I came back to north Alabama where I left him with some of his relatives.

I started for Florida early the next morning before anyone else got out of bed. By late that night I had crossed the state line into Florida. In spite of my best attempts to stay awake I fell asleep at the wheel and was speeding straight toward a bridge abutment. Suddenly, something – maybe a guardian angel (Heb. 1:14; Matt. 18:10) – awakened me. I was able to steer back on the highway safely. The gracious hand of God had once again intervened. To Him be the glory!

Ice Man

In 1949, Dad began to work part time delivering ice to homes in the Lake Wales area of Polk County, Florida. The ice was used in ice boxes for the refrigeration of food because electric refrigerators were too expensive for many people in those days. Ice boxes varied in size, but the average-sized ice box had a compartment in the top third of the unit that could hold a 100-pound block of ice. This block of ice would last about two, sometimes three, days depending on how well the unit was insolated and how often the ice box was opened. About two-thirds of the inside volume of the unit was for meat, vegetables, fruit and other things that needed refrigeration.

That summer I often helped Dad load the ice truck at the ice plant in preparation for deliveries. The water had been frozen into huge 300-pound blocks of ice in large tin buckets. It was easy to slide the large blocks of ice into the truck. We would cover the ice on the truck with a huge tarpaulin to retard melting.

Some customers would buy only 25 or 50 pounds at a time. Using ice picks we could break the 300-pound blocks into 100-, 50-, or 25-pound pieces – we would chip a line along the big blocks at the appropriate place and then strike a harder blow which would break the ice block at the right point.

When I began helping with deliveries I would use ice tongs to carry the 25- or 50-pound blocks into the houses with the small ice boxes, while Dad would use tongs to tote the 100-pound blocks into the houses of customers who owned the larger ice boxes.

Many paid for their ice in advance and requested the same-sized block of ice every delivery. The people left their houses unlocked and we deposited the ice into their ice boxes in their absence. Others paid for their ice upon delivery.

About the time I started helping Dad, the ice company bought a new green ton-and-a-half Chevrolet delivery truck. By this time I was eighteen years old, and Dad let me drive the truck. It was an easy vehicle to maneuver. In a short time Dad even let me make the deliveries alone. I weighed only about 130 pounds, but I learned how to lift even the 100-pounders up to my chest and slide them into their places in the ice boxes.

A number of times I performed a task called "pulling ice." Huge rectangular tin buckets about the size of a filing cabinet containing 300 pounds of water were frozen into solid ice in the freezing bins. I would use a machine to lift each bucket of ice up out of the freezer bin. After laying the bucket on its edge and running a little water over the bucket to loosen the ice, the ice would slide out of the bucket. Then, with ice tongs, I could stand the big block of ice back up and easily slide it into the storage freezer.

Occasionally Dad gave me some spending money for doing his ice deliveries and his pulling ice duties at the ice plant. However, my greatest sense of satisfaction was that Dad trusted me enough to let me do his work in his place. In September I went back to citrus picking until all the citrus was harvested in the spring. Part of the summer of 1950, I worked for Miss Currie pruning her citrus trees until I went away to Tennessee Temple College in late August.

Harvesting Spiritual Fruit

*A*bout this time my dad purchased a 1946 Chevrolet four-door sedan. It was a beautiful dark blue that I really liked. Dad agreed to let me use the car while I paid him back, and eventually he signed the title over to me. Many times on Wednesday nights or Sunday nights after church I would take several friends – often a group of four or five girls because there weren't any teenage boys who faithfully attended our church during those days! – the five miles up to Winter Haven for ice cream or hamburgers. These weren't really dates in the normal sense. It was just a group of friends getting together, or so I told myself. (I'll have to admit that at least one of those young ladies did eventually become more than a passing acquaintance.)

I remember that once a waitress gave me back too much change. Before we left I got her attention and gave back the extra money. As Sunday School superintendent I had opportunity to enunciate Bible principles, but here was a tailor-made opportunity to "practice what I had been preaching."

During those days I attempted to witness to friends and encourage them to attend church with me. I was able to bring two daughters of a pastor of a church that did not emphasize the Gospel to the services a few times. Both of these girls subsequently trusted Christ, and I had the joy of taking part in some discipleship with them.

Polly & Her Mom

At this stage in my life I had had a few dates – usually to church. One such date involved a cute little blonde named Polly Watson. After the service we drove over to Lake Wales to see the stadium where I had won second place in the half mile at the 1947 county championships. There, with my New Testament open, I explained the Gospel in detail, and she eagerly received Christ. Shortly thereafter Polly became my steady girlfriend.

Within a few weeks Polly persuaded her mother to go to church with us. The Gospel was clearly set forth and Mrs. Watson seemed to listen. At the conclusion of the message an invitation was given, and after a stanza or two of the invitation song Polly began to cry and to beg her mother to go forward to receive Christ. Her mother firmly refused.

After the service was dismissed I took both of them home and sat down on the couch between them. I began, "Mrs. Watson, Polly and I have been praying for you to trust Christ as your Savior. We thought tonight after such a clear sermon about how to be saved that you would go forward and accept Christ. Mrs. Watson, why didn't you?"

That little lady of no more than 100 pounds set her jaw and answered slowly, "Because... I... think... I'm... all... right... just... like... I... am!" "May I read some Scripture with you?" I asked. She nonchalantly replied, "I don't care. You may if you want to."

I had developed the habit of carrying a small black pocket New Testament. I brought it out and began reading slowly from Romans 3: "As it is written, there is none righteous, no not one. There is none that seeks after God. There is none that doeth good, no, not one," (verses 10-12). Then I read the last part of Romans 3:19: "...that every mouth may be stopped and all the world may become guilty before God."

At that key word "guilty" the Spirit of God, Who is the Author of the Word of God, answered Polly's prayer and shot an arrow of conviction into the heart of her self-righteous mother. Mrs. Watson burst into tears and exclaimed, "I'm *not* all right, am I?" Since she saw her guilt, she only needed to be reminded that Jesus took upon Himself her guilt and paid her debt of death. Although she was a sinner at war against God, He had demonstrated His love for her through His Son's death in her place (Rom. 5:8). We then read Romans 6:23 which tells us that eternal life is the gift of God through Jesus Christ our Lord. It is eternal and it's a free gift to us, but it cost God's Son a very painful, bloody agony.

With her head bowed Mrs. Watson told God that she was accepting his Son as her Savior and trusted His death as the payment for her sins. After that I did what I subsequently have done many times through the years after someone received Christ. I put my fingers on Romans 10:9 and read the part where God promises, "If thou shalt believe in thine heart thou shalt be saved."

I turned to her and, tapping myself on the chest, said, "Notice. This is not David making the promise." I emphasized, "This is the promise of God – a God who cannot lie – to you and all who believe in Christ and receive Him with all your heart as you just did." I put my finger on the words "thou shalt be saved" and said, "Right now, Mrs. Watson, are you saved?" With a smile she replied, "Yes, I am." After a prayer of thanksgiving I left the two rejoicing ladies.

I enjoyed a good friendship with Polly and her mother for a few months until their family moved back to Alabama.

Key Mentors & Benefactors

*D*uring the winter of 1949-50, Millard Branson became the pastor at Wahneeta. Standing only about five feet, nine inches tall, Pastor Branson was not physically very imposing, but he was a keen student of the Word of God and a devoted shepherd to the flock which the Great Shepherd had placed in his care. Though he had no formal theological training he did his best to make up for that lack by diligent personal study. He was an energetic preacher, and I later came to view him as a key mentor in my early spiritual development.

Immediately after taking charge of the church in Wahneeta, Pastor Branson began to urge the congregation to visit relatives, friends, and other acquaintances to invite them to attend the services of the church. He promised that if everyone would get enthusiastic about building up the Sunday School attendance, when we reached 100 in Sunday School the pastor and the Sunday School superintendent would sing a duet. This caused a bit of interest in the congregation because everyone knew that neither of us could "carry a tune in a bucket." To the surprise of us all the very next Sunday the attendance was 125. It was suggested that the two of us should sing *Heavenly Sunshine*, the theme song of the nationwide radio program, *The Old Fashioned Revival Hour*.

We did not have the sheet music for the song, so, to the amusement of everyone, we made a miserable attempt to sing it *a cappella*. That performance by the pastor and superintendent was the subject of considerable conversation, and it sparked new interest that helped Sunday School and church attendance.

Pastor Branson urged me to consider becoming a preacher of the Gospel as my life's vocation. He encouraged me to go to a Bible college to prepare for such a ministry. Not only did he express interest in career planning, but he offered me opportunities to develop skills in ministry. Besides my weekly devotionals Pastor Branson also gave me the assignment of speaking at one of the monthly services the church held at the county old folks home in Bartow. Whether anyone else profited from those early homiletic exercises, these opportunities proved very helpful to me.

Pastor Branson invited his former pastor, Victor Sears, to come to Wahneeta for a series of Bible conference messages at our church. One of the messages was on the doctrine of the security of the believer. His teaching was so helpful to me because many of my friends were heavily influenced by the kindred views that believers could "lose their salvation" or a doctrine of perfectionism which argued that true believers achieved in this life a level of spiritual purity in which they do not sin. I asked Mr. Sears if I could talk to him privately about some of the passages that my friends had used to attack the doctrine of security. One such passage was 1 John 3:6, 8-9: "Whosoever abided in Him sinneth not: whosoever sinneth hath not seen Him, neither known Him...He that committeth sin is of the devil...Whosoever is born of God doth not commit sin..."

As we sat in his car before the service one night I ask him, "How do these verses relate to what you taught the other night about 'once saved–always saved'? Pastor Branson has taught us the same way, but my friends are always using this passage to back up *their* view." Mr. Sears patiently instructed me that when John wrote these verses in Greek he used the present tense which means *continuous* or *habitual action*. "The apostle," he explained, "wasn't talking about someone who commits an act of sin, but of someone who continually or habitually lives a sinful lifestyle." His excellent explanation was so beneficial. I came away from that encounter thinking about how wonderful it would be were *I* to be able to study Greek so that I could understand and teach the Bible so much more effectively.

The Lord was planting seeds of desire in my heart to bring me to see the need of formal education and advanced preparation for ministry.

In the spring of 1950, Pastor Branson took three of us teenagers with him to the annual Bible conference at Tennessee Temple College in Chattanooga, Tennessee. This happened to be the first year that the conference was held in a large new auditorium on the school campus. The superstructure for the auditorium had been erected using steel girders from a war surplus airplane hangar. It seated almost 2,000 listeners for the services. I had never been in such a massive auditorium.

Every year that conference featured some of the era's most powerful preachers such as Jimmy Johnson, James McGinley, Fred Brown, Bob Jones, Sr., Fred Garland, Bill Rice, John R. Rice, and R.G. Lee. I was overwhelmed to hear some of these great preachers. I had a passing thought – perhaps the seed of which had been planted deep in my heart by the Holy Spirit and now enunciated in my thinking – that could it ever be possible that *I* could one day be privileged to preach at such a gathering.

On our return to Florida we left Chattanooga immediately after the Sunday morning service. We stopped at a country Baptist church near LaGrange, Georgia just in time for the evening service. There were about 25 people present, including us four. The preacher's message that night was the same kind of message that is too often delivered in churches across the land. It did not contain the Bible plan of salvation. It seemed to say persons could be saved by living right, by keeping the commandments, by going to church, by reading the Bible, and so forth. That night I told Pastor Branson, "God sure needs some preachers that can at least explain God's plan of salvation. I am no preacher, but I could do that."

Miss Jane Currie, the kind lady for whom I occasionally did odd jobs, played her part in God's tugging me in a new direction. She would often plead with me to go to college. My response had always been, "Miss Currie, I'm not college material. No Winget has ever attended college." She probably began to tire of my lack of confidence in what God could accomplish through me. Finally one day she turned to me and challenged my lack of faith with these memorable words: "*You* could be the *first* Winget to go to college, and I will *help* you."

For some time I had been thinking that *just maybe* God was leading me to surrender to the Gospel ministry. He had been using various people and events to whet my appetite for studying to teach the Word. I was approaching a crucial crossroads.

Blinded to See the Light

*I*n the late spring of 1950, a crisis event took place that brought about a turning point in my story. Next to my conversion and my marriage it was the third most significant crossroads I ever encountered.

The citrus groves were under constant attack by various fungi, parasites, and diseases. Powerful chemicals were employed to try to combat these enemies to our livelihood. These chemicals were sprayed onto the trees as a white liquid which quickly dried into a dusty white powder. It was nearly impossible for the pickers to avoid getting the powder in their eyes, but normally one could counteract the effect of the stinging powder by rinsing the eyes with evaporated milk.

One day the inevitable happened and some of the "spray dope" – that's what we called the chemical spray – got in my eye. This time was more serious because, instead of a single grain of the dust, what lodged in my eye was a white flake of the chemical. The problem was compounded by the fact that the white substance was almost invisible against the white of my eye. That night my mother tried to cleanse my eye with the normal procedure, but without success.

The next day the stinging flake of "spray dope" had eaten into my eyeball and for the first time that I can remember I had to go to a doctor. An eye specialist had to be called to remove the particle. The doctor put medicine in my eye, bandaged it, put a patch over my eye to hold the bandage in place, and ordered me to stay away from light and in a dark room for a week.

During that week I had time to spend in meditation and prayer concerning God's will for my life. I reviewed how my sovereign Lord had used my little mother's ultimatum to my dad to quit making illegal whiskey. I remembered how the Lord used her courage to move us towards the Gospel. He had brought us to a house next to a Gospel-preaching church. He had brought an evangelist with a tent to bring me an understandable message of the Gospel. And He enabled me to receive the salvation his Son had purchased for me by His substitutionary death and resurrection. He put it into the heart of Pastor May just minutes after I presented myself for baptism and church membership to give me the privilege of weekly public ministry which whetted my interest in Bible exposition.

God had moved Pastor Branson to encourage me toward Gospel ministry by taking me to the Bible conference at Temple and giving me opportunities to preach at the rest home. God caused us to stop at the country church in Georgia on our way home to show me the need for trained Bible preachers. The Lord moved my boss lady, Miss Currie, to offer me financial help to go to college. My Heavenly Father in that dark room that week shined a light on all these indications of what His plan was for my life. He secured my surrender to Him to be his ambassador for life in any capacity wherever and whenever He would choose.

And my injured eye? The Lord mercifully allowed my eye to heal completely.

Sometime about midsummer, I made application to enroll in Tennessee Temple the following September. I still had some doubts as to whether I was ready for the challenge of higher education. "It may be," I half-expected, "that for some reason my application would be denied." The answer came so quickly I was a bit surprised. I had been accepted and was due to begin my studies in less than two months.

Miss Currie was overjoyed that I had been accepted and gave me extra summer employment pruning her citrus trees so that I could save more money for school. However, there was another, much younger, lady – a teen-aged brunette named Margaret Davidson – who was not so excited about my plans to go away to far away Tennessee.

Margaret had been saved in a revival meeting at Wahneeta Baptist and was a maturing young Christian. She attended the services at WBC regularly. We had grown to like each other quite a lot, and we both wished that she could go to Temple also. But she could not. Her mother had died a few years earlier, and she lived with her dad who was not able to help her with college finances. Margaret also had the responsibility of keeping house for her dad.

Leaving home, my parents and family and friends, the church home that had nurtured me spiritually for over three years, Pastor Branson, and especially Margaret was tough. It was also difficult to say goodbye to that blue Chevy that I liked so much. But some months earlier the issue was settled when I surrendered to my sovereign Lord for full time ministry for His glory. I knew a major part of His plan involved me going away to get academic training to proclaim His Word. My Lord Jesus had had to leave his heavenly home and his Heavenly Father and the angelic choirs to do his Father's will to pay the penalty for my sins. The Father's assignment for me was hundreds of times easier than his assignment for his own Son, Jesus.

How could I do less than follow the path that He was tracing ahead of me?

Where God Guides, He Provides (In Various Ways)

*W*hen I said goodbye to Miss Currie before departing for Chattanooga, she gave me a sealed envelope. "When you get to school give this to Dr. Roberson," she instructed me referring to the school president. Mom then took me, with a single suitcase in hand, to the Greyhound bus station in Winter Haven a little before noon. As I was about to board, both of us choking back tears, Mom hugged me and said, "Son, you study hard." "I will, Momma." And that was that.

I spied a vacant seat near the last row on the bus and settled in for a long ride. The trip up to Chattanooga would take about 24 hours because the bus seemed to stop at every small town and hamlet along the way to pick up or discharge passengers. Because I slept a good deal of the way, I remember little about the trip.

Upon finally arriving in my new home town, I took a shuttle bus for the short ride from the station to the campus. Soon afterwards I found myself in the school business office. Interestingly, I saw Dr. Roberson there. I approached him and introduced myself. When I handed him Miss Currie's envelope he opened it.

He looked at me with those piercing eyes of his and asked, "Do you know what is in here?" I replied, "Yes, Sir... money. But I don't know how much." He pulled from the envelope a check made to the school in the amount of $500. To say the least, I was surprised. (A check of that amount would surely be worth close to $5,000 today.) Seeing my astonishment, Dr. Roberson said something that I later heard him repeat numerous times. My guess is that he had had more than a few similar conversations with students who had been taken aback by the Lord's providential supply. "Son," he said to me, "where God guides, He provides."

Miss Currie's gift covered a good deal of my room, board, and tuition, but there were still books, clothing, and other financial needs that had to be met. The following day, as unlikely as it might seem, I talked with Dr. Faulkner, the vice president of the institution, about the possibility of employment at the school. He arranged for me to have a job in the kitchen washing dishes... by hand. The pay was 30 cents per hour. This job averaged between 20 and 25 hours a week. There were no automatic dish washers in those days, at least not at Temple. I was learning that God's provision sometimes came in the form of checks from friends and at other times in the form of dishpan hands. I was also about to learn that the dishpan-hands form was the better of the two.

Early in the first semester, while playing touch football with some of the students and faculty, I collided with Dr. Charles Mashburn, one of the professors, and sustained a broken wrist. At the hospital my wrist was put into a plaster cast. That put my dish-washing career on hold for a while, but it also affected my class schedule. Mrs. Dykes, my typing teacher, saw me with my wrist in a cast and understood why I could not complete the typing course. Some ten years later I learned that she had turned in an "F" for me in that course to the registrar's office. I had not known that I was supposed to officially withdraw from the course. It was the only failing grade on my college record.

Size Seven and a Half, Please

In addition to my new profession as Tennessee Temple's top "culinary utensil hygiene engineer" I worked on Saturdays at Baker's Shoe Store selling women's shoes. The manager told us always to use a certain shoe-sizer gadget before we selected a shoe for any of our customers. A particular lady came in with a friend and, as I proceeded to do as the manager instructed, she told me confidently, "You don't need to use that thing to find the size I wear. I wear a seven and a half. Please get me a seven and a half of that black shoe there on the display." The sizer indicated that she really needed an eight, and that's what I put on her foot. She took a few steps, stood before the mirror, and said, "This is the most comfortable new shoe I have ever tried." Her friend commented, "Sue, that one sure looks good on you." Sue agreed. "Yes, it *is* a pretty shoe and this is the one I want." As I began to write out the charge ticket Sue looked into the shoe and saw "size eight." Immediately she stood up and yelled at me, "I told you to get me a seven and a half. I have never worn a shoe that big because my foot is not *that* big." The two ladies stormed out vowing never to buy shoes at Baker Shoe Store because of the faulty shoe-sizers that were used there.

Bobbin Stripper

Yet another means of employment came at the end of second semester in the form of a 3:00-11:00 shift job at the Peerless Woolen Mill in Rossville, Georgia, only five miles south of the campus. The Lord provided transportation to this job when my dad transferred to me the title of that blue Chevrolet that I liked so much. At the woolen mill, for three years, I had many wonderful opportunities to learn patience "stripping bobbins" and operating a thread-tying machine.

Before my first paycheck from Peerless I had very little money even for food. To make matters even more critical the college dining hall was closed because school was out. I lived off pork and beans for one whole week. Each day I had only three 10-cent cans of beans. For those seven days I ate one can of beans in the morning, one at noon, and a third can in the evening. I'll admit that, while I like pork and beans, twenty or so straight meals of pork and beans was a real test of endurance, but again, it was yet another way that the Lord was teaching me how to empathize with people who experienced the paycheck running out before the month ran out. We'll talk about the woolen mill more later on.

Though I was training to be involved in vocational ministry those experiences before and during school years working at "regular jobs" helped me understand the outlook of people whom I would later be responsible to shepherd, teach, and lead in various ministerial roles.

Trickery

Tennessee Temple Schools had a liberal arts college, a Bible school, and a seminary. I had planned to attend the Bible school because I wanted to prepare to preach the Bible. History, literature, math, and psychology were of no interest to me. God had called me to a Bible ministry, and the Bible was what I wanted to learn. However, I didn't realize that such a curricula would not allow me to pursue graduate studies.

My sovereign Lord used the trickery of my roommate to cause me to make an academic decision that resulted in changing my plans. He brought a schedule of classes to our room and pointed out to my surprise that the liberal arts college program seemed to have more Bible courses than did the Bible school. Actually, my roommate tricked me by pointing to subjects listed on the college schedule: Old Testament Survey, New Testament Survey, Gospel of John, Epistles of Paul, Synoptic Gospels, Acts of the Apostles, Romans, Hebrews, the Epistles of Peter, the Book of Revelation, and so forth. He showed me the Bible school schedule that had certain courses listed such as Synthesis, Analysis, Hermeneutics, Homiletics, and others. Those certainly weren't Bible subjects that I'd ever heard of. A cursory comparison of the two schedules, although it was puzzling to me, *seemed* to show that the college taught more Bible than the Bible school. Therefore I registered for the college and pursued a baccalaureate degree which in the Lord's sovereignty more readily suited me for being accepted a few years later into seminary.

College Days

"Distinctively Christian" was Temple's motto. From the outset I found that motto to be descriptive, and my college experience was really enjoyable. Most of my classes were like being in a Bible conference every day. I never smelled tobacco smoke, never heard profanity nor dirty jokes. The fellows in the dormitory participated in

Bible reading and prayer before lights out every night. The students alongside whom I attended class and with whom I worked in the kitchen and dining hall were godly young people.

The teachers were godly examples and desired that their students learn self-discipline, industry, and the ability to think for themselves. In one instance it may have been that I exercised my "thinking-for-myself" skills a bit too much.

As a part of an exam on the Book of Acts under one of my very favorite teachers, Dr. Mashborn, we were given ten "true or false" questions. One statement read, "Simon was saved and traveled with Phillip." I answered "false," but the professor said that the correct answer was "true." My reasoning was that Acts 8:13 states that the man "continued" rather than "traveled" with Phillip. The professor responded by saying "continued" is the same as "traveled."

By the next class period I had researched the Greek word used in that passage, *proskartereo*. I reported in class that it was used to say "*continued* in one accord in prayer" in Acts 1:14, "*continued* in doctrine and fellowship" in Acts 2:42, and "*continued* with one accord in the Temple" in Acts 2:46. Therefore, Simon "continued" with Phillip in the sense of "continued in agreement with Phillip and in support of Phillip's ministry," not that he traveled from place to place with Phillip. My arguments didn't dissuade the professor, but I'll let the reader determine as to whether I pressed the point too far.

Some years later when Dr. Mashburn preached in my church in Florida he used this incident jokingly to prove that I was a contentious student. I interpreted his tone that he later came to accept my point.

Washing Dishes Pays Off

Early in the semester an attractive, slender waitress in the dining hall caught my attention. She was a junior in the college from Rock Springs, Georgia, and we chatted casually at various times. She seemed quite friendly, and I enjoyed the few chances I had to get to know her.

About the mid-semester point Norma – that was her name – came into the kitchen where I was busy washing the dishes after a meal.

She said, "David, would you like to have some help with washing those dishes?" I understood that she was offering her help, but I thought that I would play along a bit, so I flirtatiously responded, "It all depends on who wants to help. If such a one broke one of these dishes I'd be responsible." She picked up on the game immediately and replied, "Well, I had a lot of experience washing dishes for my large family before I came to college." I turned and tossed her an apron saying, "I do believe you qualify – put on this apron and we'll get this job done in short order."

The dirty dishes were soaking in hot soapy water in a huge sink. As we neared the bottom of the stack of dirty dishes, I reached for another plate and discovered another hand reaching for the same plate. I "accidentally" grasped the hand instead of the plate. In that there did not seem to be any resistance, I held it for a brief moment and even felt it safe to squeeze slightly. That started something in my heart that continued for more than 56 years.

Courtship Days

Shortly after the hand-holding-in-the-sudsy-water caper we were talking together, and I somewhat timidly suggested the possibility of attending one of the church services together. (No one ever accused me of being overly aggressive in the dating category.) Norma commented that usually when guys and gals went to church together the guy would come to the gal's dorm and escort her to church. Still a bit unfamiliar with the protocol for this type of appointment, I replied, "I'm not sure if I know where your dorm is." She eagerly explained how to find her dorm, and I proposed a time to pick her up. Thus, our first date was set. It was the first of a half century and more of romantic rendezvous that were to follow.

We became much better acquainted during the next several weeks. I learned that Norma had been born in Chattanooga on June 23, 1930. Her family had later moved several miles south of the city to a little country hamlet called Rock Springs, Georgia, and during her teen years, through the ministry of Pea Vine Baptist Church, had come to Christ.

During the second semester there was an open house one Saturday when the male and female students were allowed to visit each other's dormitories. (Remember that this was a day when schools were much more circumspect and realistic about not allowing students of the opposite sex to freely visit one another in their dorm rooms, so this event was both esteemed as a special occasion by the students and rigorously chaperoned by the administration.) Most of the fellows put out their high school trophies and pictures of their parents and girlfriends as decoration on their dressers or chests of drawers. I had nothing to put out except one eight by ten picture of Margaret Davidson. Although Norma and I were going steady by that time, I naively set out the photo without thinking through the possible repercussions. When Norma and her friends visited my room she quickly put Margaret's picture inside my dresser. That picture was never displayed again.

Soon after school was out after my freshman year I went down to Florida for a few days, and Pastor Branson invited me to speak in the morning service at Wahneeta. I chose for my subject "The Cost of Discipleship." To illustrate that true discipleship demands total dedication to God I told of a young lady at Temple from Rock Springs, Georgia. Her dad had promised to pay her way through beautician school if she would choose that career. She explained to her father that she felt it was God's will for her to attend Temple College to prepare for full-time Christian service. Her dad was adamantly against her going to a Christian school and vowed not to help her at all.

On the morning she left for college her dad even pulled out a gun insinuating that he might shoot her if she persisted in her plan. One of her brothers quickly took the gun away from him lest some accident should occur. I told the church that upon her arrival at Temple Dr. Roberson, as a precaution, required her not to go to class but to stay in the dormitory for a couple of days. I mentioned that at times she had to work two jobs to pay her school bill in order to continue school. Though she did visit a few times, she never returned home to live. I did not include in my illustration that day the detail about this young lady helping me wash dishes in the dining hall.

My mother and some others, including the pastor, could tell that I must have had more than a passing interest in that Georgia girl. And they were right. By this time Norma and I had talked in general terms about the possibility of marriage before the end of the summer, but because of financial reasons we postponed any plans until after the spring term of the following year.

We both knew that if there was any chance of getting married then, we both needed to get jobs for the summer and save some money. Norma and her fellow student, Mavis Sims, took jobs serving as waitresses at Lake Louise Bible Conference Center near Toccoa, Georgia.

At least three times during the summer of 1951, I made the 4-and-a-half-hour drive through the north Georgia mountains to Lake Louise to see her. I left Chattanooga after getting off work at 11:00 p.m. on Fridays, and I would drive as far as I could before getting too tired, then stop at an all-night service station for a nap. I stretched out on the bench seat of my car and set an alarm clock that I'd brought along to awaken me after a few hours. I'd get to Lake Louise about breakfast time, and then we'd have a portion of the morning together before Norma had to go back to prepare for serving lunch. We would be able to spend a good deal of the afternoon together and then also the evenings after supper until her curfew at around 10:30 p.m. I repeated the process on the return leg so as to be back in Chattanooga for church on Sunday morning.

Norma had begun college immediately after high school, but I did not enter college until three years after I finished high school. In her senior year, my sophomore year, we were in two classes together: "Biblical Greek" with Dr. Cierpke and "New Testament Survey" with Dr. Mashburn. In Greek class we learned how to say "I love you with all my heart" in mangled Greek: *agapao se sun halos cardia mou.* This we whispered to each other often. It was grammatically incorrect, but lover's don't normally analyze such finer points.

Two fellow students who worked with me at the woolen mill and I were on our way to work one day in the spring of 1952, when a lady traveling west on Bennett Avenue in a red Oldsmobile ran the stop street at Orchard Knob Avenue. I was driving south on Orchard Knob, and our car collided with the passenger side of her vehicle. Fortunately no one was hurt, but both cars were extensively damaged. The other driver and I were summoned to court. After a brief rehearsal of the particulars the judge handed down his verdict. He pointed to my insurance agent and, motioning toward the attractive woman driver, said, "You fix this lady's car." And that was that. I needed immediate transportation so I traded my damaged 1946 Chevy to a mechanic for a 1939 Chevy. But that dark blue '39 Chevrolet was a good 'un!

Royal, uh... Loyal Love

We were married on Memorial Day, May 30, 1952, one week after Norma's graduation from college. It was a Friday.

For financial reasons we planned a simple house wedding in the home of her best friends, Bob and Bobbie Jean Lowery, in Chickamauga, Georgia. With marriage license in hand we left Chattanooga about 3:30 p.m. with my best man, L.B. Thomason, and Norma's maid of honor, Christine Griffith. Norma wore a new, white, knee-length dress with matching white shoes. I wore a brand-new, navy blue, double-breasted suit and matching tie. We arrived at the Lowery's house about 4:15. The ceremony was held in the living room with about six or eight other friends in attendance including Norma's mother, Eva Mae Hicks. Unfortunately none of my family were able to make the trip up to the wedding. Leon Riddle, pastor of Norma's home church in Rock Springs performed our ceremony.

After a short charge from the pastor and a brief explanation of the significance of marriage we came to the vows. Pastor Riddle turned to me and said, "David, place the ring on Norma's finger and hold it as you repeat after me." Not having any experience at repeating wedding vows and under the pressure of placing a ring on the hand of the one I so adored, I had some difficulty repeating correctly. He continued, "With this ring I thee wed." I said solemnly, "With this ring, I thee red." The pastor proceeded, "With loyal love I thee endow." The nervous groom repeated, "With royal love I thee endow." I wasn't even aware at the time of my having misspoken.

Later, when Norma brought the *faux pas* to my attention we listened carefully to the tape recording. I had indeed misspoken. I declared, "Well, OK, royal love it is, Queen Norma." From that time on, my favorite pet name for her was "My Queen."

After the vows only one song was sung: "Savior, Like a Shepherd Lead Us." That was truly the prayer of our hearts, and we watched in amazement over the decades how our God continually answered that prayer.

Following the service we drove back up to Chattanooga with L.B. and Christine. The four of us celebrated with a sumptuous meal at Gulas Restaurant on McCallie Avenue. I remember that we feasted on shrimp (Norma's favorite), chicken, and steak. After taking the other two home to the dorm, I took my new bride to our honeymoon suite, a tiny, flea-ridden apartment on Kirby Avenue, near the campus.

We stayed at home Saturday.

Newly Weds

My new bride and I had decided to wait until later in the summer to take what we called our "honeymoon." The woolen mill closed every year for the week of July 4th so the employees could have a week of vacation. We went to Winter Haven by way of St. Augustine, Florida. When we got to Winter Haven I was proud to introduce my queen to her new in-laws for the first time.

When our first Sunday as man and wife rolled around, I took Norma down to Larkinsville, Alabama, eighty miles south of Chattanooga, to a little preaching station that was one of the small branch churches of Highland Park Baptist, the mother church that had oversight of Tennessee Temple Schools. Though I had visited once before, this was my first official Sunday as pastor there. For about three months during that summer break from classes we and L.B., who led the singing, drove down every Sunday morning and stayed all day ministering together in that little rural church. Those dear country folks provided a lavish home-cooked lunch for us that came fresh from their gardens and fields. More importantly, they provided a great way for Norma and me to start off serving the Lord together.

For the first month of our marriage we lived in that small, apartment on Kirby Avenue in Chattanooga. It had one connected kitchen-bedroom and a bathroom. The most memorable thing about that first dwelling was that it was infested with seven and a half swarms of fleas. The way we knew that there were that many swarms was that each day of the week a new swarm of the little critters would take turns alternately nibbling at our ankles or crawling up our legs, and when we returned from Larkinsville each Sunday night there was the normally assigned swarm for that day plus half of another visiting swarm they had invited over. We weren't expecting much in the way of luxuries, but the situation was intolerable and we had to find other accommodations.

We found another place not far away, so we packed up and moved. To our dismay, this second residence, though a bit bigger, was not much better. For the next eleven months we traded in our flea friends for a somewhat larger tribe of rather territorial roaches who evidently felt that *we* were encroaching upon *them*. I suppose that you could agree that they had a point – we found roach tombstones on the premises that dated back to the early 1800s! We did have one advantage at that second domicile, however. They say that misery loves company, so we rented one of the two bedrooms to my best man, L.B. Thomason. I've felt ever since we owed him an apology, but he has graciously refused to admit any regrets for accepting our invitation to board with us. [Note: Leon Baxter Thomason, "Dad Leon," went on to have a fruitful ministry in the pastorate for 38 years in Florida. He, and his wife, Ethelyene, are retired, but at this writing L.B. is serving as a hospice chaplain.]

By then we were ready for a clean, comfortable home, and living and sacrificing as we had, we had saved up a little money. We already knew way back then what Dave Ramsey has been preaching for the last several years. We shopped around until we found something we could afford and bought it. It was a fully-furnished, 21-feet-long Nashua mobile home for which we paid $1,500 cash. We parked it in a mobile home lot on Main Street about five blocks from the college campus. We were home-owners, and our Nashua seemed a palace to us.

A New Brother

A very significant event took place in that little mobile home that I would like to relate to you. It was the conversion of Richard Kay. Richard, a former military policeman, stood six feet, four inches tall and weighed 260 pounds, and his bulky physique dwarfed my small frame. We had worked together at Peerless for two years and had become good friends. Whenever there was a spare moment's opportunity I talked to him about the way of salvation. One day he grumbled about the unfair treatment we faced on the job. Seizing the opening to turn the conversation away from complaint to something far more profitable, I asked him, "Richard, do you know what's worse than working in a woolen mill *all* your life?" He replied, "No. *What* could be worse?" He had taken the bait, and I sought to set the hook: "To work *all* your life in a woolen mill and then... *miss heaven*."

Later one Saturday morning he came to our mobile home to help me fix something on my car. Within a few minutes after his arrival the Lord sent a rain shower, and we had to go inside. God kept the rain coming in order for me to explain more clearly to my buddy God's purpose for the death of Jesus. Finally, I asked him if he would like to trust Christ as his Savior. With tears brimming in his eyes, he immediately responded "Yes, I would, *right now*." Of his own accord he fell on his knees by the chair on which there was an open Bible. Just like a little child that big man accepted Christ by faith and trusted Christ's death as the only payment for his sins. I don't mean to insinuate that Richard's physical posture or tears were crucial; it was the humble posture of heart that was so important.

Richard Kay became a new creature in Christ according to 2 Corinthians 5:17: "Therefore if any man be in Christ, he is a new creature. Old things are passed away. Behold, all things are become new." At the same instant he was also "delivered from the power of darkness into the kingdom of God's dear Son" according to Colossians 1:13.

I later learned that Richard grew in the Lord and became a deacon at Peavine Baptist Church in Rock Springs, Georgia, the church where Norma had accepted Christ and was a member before leaving home for college. Richard went to be with the Lord in 2007, and I look forward to seeing my old friend again one day.

Turning Points

*T*he last twelve months or so of our time of study at Tennessee Temple were full and fruitful. This period saw several formative developments introduced into our lives and I would like to relate them at this time. I'll begin with a rather humorous incident that set the stage for an important conversation.

Thy Word Have I Hid...

Sometime just before the close of my junior year evangelist Lester Roloff (pronounced "ROLL-off") spoke to the assembled student body in a chapel message. Brother Roloff operated a home for former addicts, runaways, and otherwise troubled youths. He and his staff were successful in changing the lives of people who had repeatedly faced failure in similar attempts at renovation elsewhere. One of the key components of his method was that he required those under his charge to commit extended portions of the Word of God to memory. In his absolutely inimitable style Roloff challenged us to memorize a chapter of Scripture every month. I reasoned that if those former junkies and alcoholics who came to his homes could memorize Scripture, then so could I. I decided to accept the challenge.

The Lord had arranged that I had a job that allowed me opportunity at various times to study while I was "on the clock." This was nothing clandestine or against the rules of my workplace. While I waited for some process at the mill to be completed I could sit alone with my New Testament for extended periods and work at hiding away into memory portions of the Bible. It took a lot of hard work, but twelve months after my decision to take Roloff's challenge, I could quote twelve key chapters perfectly. The memorization of key Bible passages did more to prepare me mentally and spiritually for a life of teaching and preaching the Word of God than anything else.

Ever Had a Bad Taste in Your Mouth?

During the Christmas holidays of my senior year we decided to visit my folks in Florida. We phoned Granny Bama Jones, by then a widow, and invited her to go with us. We picked her up about midnight at her home in Phoenix City, Alabama, and with Norma and me in the front seat and Granny in the back, we struck out for Winter Haven.

Granny Bama was a dear Christian lady, but she had one objectionable habit – she enjoyed her snuff. Before too many minutes past she had begun to savor a pinch of her favorite brown powder. As everyone knows, a byproduct of this habit is the juice produced by the snuff. The user is required to spit out the excess juice periodically. The window in the back seat couldn't be rolled down, so she was obliged to ask me to roll down my window. I would lean forward so that she could stretch and spit out my opened window. After a couple such requests she apologized for the trouble she was causing and promised, "I won't take any more snuff until we get to Vera Mae's place." She slumped over and went to sleep for a few hours, but about sun up she tapped on my shoulder and motioned for me to lower my window again, and I complied.

Soon after the noon meal that day at my parents' house, Granny left the table. She was not aware that all of us watched as she put a dip of snuff into her mouth. I told the others present about Granny's promise the previous night, and how she'd fudged. As I was finishing and the others were chuckling a bit, Granny returned to the table, just a little embarrassed for having broken her promise. She offered an excuse, "Well, I did not *plan* to take any more snuff, but I went to sleep, and when I woke up, I had such a bad taste in my mouth, I needed something for the bad taste." As quick as she said that, everyone burst into laughter. Granny also laughed, spraying snuff dust from her mouth all over the room.

Much more to the point, this visit was the occasion for a formative conversation with my former mentor, Pastor Branson. Due to some serious denominational issues he felt compelled to tender his resignation as pastor from Wahneeta Baptist Church. Many of the congregation agreed with him and saw it as necessary for them to leave the church as well. They began to hold services in Pappy Gladney's front yard, but soon the group bought a vacated church building in town. They organized the First Bible Baptist Church of Winter Haven, but some of the members who lived outside of town on the Rifle Range Road wanted to start a church in their area. During our Christmas visit Pastor Branson asked me to preach, and after the service suggested that I consider leading the effort to plant an independent church out in the Rifle Range Road area. Norma and I began to pray about that possibility.

Important Milestone

In May of 1954, I graduated with a BA in Bible. I was ranked sixth in a class of about 70 graduates. I was glad that Mom and Dad were there to witness my graduation. I remember little about this auspicious occasion, but I do remember that before Dad and Mom left Chattanooga to return home, we were all shocked to learn that their house in Florida had just burned. The house and all their belongings (including all our family photographs and records) was a total loss. Upon their return home they bought a little house on First Street in Winter Haven which had an small adjoining grocery store that they operated for a few years.

Still more important, we had become convinced that we should indeed move to Winter Haven and help establish an independent congregation on the south side of town on the Rifle Range Road. If we had only known what God was going to do...

Planting a Church in Sandy Soil

*F*ive weeks after commencement we sold our Nashua trailer home. We both resigned our jobs at Peerless [Note: Norma had joined me working at the woolen mill over a year earlier.] the first week of July, loaded all our belongings into our '39 Chevy, and went to Florida. Norma was three months pregnant.

As soon as we arrived in Winter Haven we found a 32-foot mobile home, but neither of us had a job to qualify for a bank loan. Uncle Bob Jones took me to his banker in Bartow and signed a pledge to pay if I failed to make the $40 per month payments.

There we were: expecting a baby, facing a monthly mortgage of $40 and a $10 per month rent owed to the mobile home park, and neither of us employed. Our situation caused us to recall what Dr. Roberson had said to me the day I had first stepped on the Tennessee Temple campus: "Where God guides, He provides." The statement had been proven true then, and the Lord showed Himself faithful yet again in this situation. In addition to Uncle Bob, He brought a number of other people into our lives in those days to provide for our needs.

Before our first week had ended Bernie Fowler, another member of First Bible Baptist, helped me move our mobile home to a rent-free location. Miss Currie, my benefactor from years earlier, gave us permission to park our house trailer near her orange grove at no charge. A water line and an electric line were connected to Miss Currie's garage, and I dug a septic tank hole and lined it with concrete blocks. We enjoyed that quiet spot underneath the shade of a

103

large oak until the church was established and purchased property several months later.

Walter ("Junior") Hoover was a hard-working brick and block mason who headed up a local construction crew. Within a few days of our arrival in Winter Haven Junior offered me a job on his crew. My job was to keep that crew of masons supplied with mortar and bricks (or blocks as the case might be). It was exhausting work, but it was the means of God's wonderful supply of our needs. What's more, Junior later proved very zealous for the cause of Christ and invaluable in the effort to plant a church in that area. The skills I picked up working with his crew also proved very useful in the years to come, but I'll hold that part of the story until a bit later.

Under the auspices of the First Bible Baptist Church of Winter Haven we proceeded to work toward the establishment of a daughter church on the Rifle Range Road. Mr. Upchurch, a Presbyterian believer, who lived nearby, had offered to donate a half acre of land with frontage on the highway. Mr. Waters, a member of First Bible Baptist Church, had offered to donate trees from his property for material to construct an open air shelter. Before the end of July some of the men borrowed a truck and cut and hauled several logs of various sizes to the building site. Different folks helped as they could and an open air shelter about 30 feet by 60 feet with a simple tar paper roof was constructed in short order. Only one corner where we placed the piano had walls. The dirt floor was covered with a layer of saw dust. We did have a professionally painted sign out front which read "Rifle Range Baptist Chapel."

I was ordained to the Gospel ministry on August 6, 1954, at First Bible Baptist Church, and the following Sunday afternoon the first service was held under the open air shelter that had just been completed. The Scripture for my sermon was "A prophet is not without honor but in his own country," (Mk. 6:4).

A two-week crusade was scheduled for the next two weeks with a friend from college days, evangelist J.B. Buffington, doing the preaching. Slight of build but possessing the heart of a lion, J.B. had been a B-17 pilot over occupied Europe during World War II. He was a dynamic and passionate preacher of the Gospel, ministering as an itinerant speaker as well as a much loved pastor for many years. [Note: After a long and debilitating illness J.B. laid aside his armor in 2009, and went to meet his Captain in glory. His faithful wife, Betty, cared for him throughout his extended infirmity. She still resides in Lakeland, Florida.]

At the time, my dad was still unsaved. Though he did not make a decision at that time, Dad attended a number of those meetings.

It was about that time that we began to advertise a special organizational meeting to be held on the last Sunday afternoon of September at 3:00 p.m. By the time that meeting was held we had received a gift from another church – they had installed new pews, and we had inherited their old ones. Every pew was filled at the organizational meeting.

Dr. Luttrell of Bradenton, Florida delivered a challenging message to those gathered under that temporary shelter. Afterwards the Rifle Range Baptist Church constitution and bylaws were read aloud by another visiting pastor. As I was about to issue an invitation heavy rains tested the roof of the shelter. It did not leak but the rain was hard enough to cause water to run inside and float the saw dust we had spread for flooring. I invited any who had previously received Christ as Savior and had been baptized into a Baptist church, and who agreed with the constitution and bylaws just read, and who desired to join this new congregation to step forward to sign the church membership roll. In that way we organized the Rifle Range Baptist Church with 18 charter members. [Note: Some 50 years later the church voted to change its name to "Redemption Baptist Church."]

Within a few weeks we rejoiced that two new converts had professed their faith in Christ as Savior: a teenage girl and my dad! I had the privilege of baptizing both of them not long thereafter in Lake Winterset near where our mobile home was parked, and we now numbered 20 members. The irony was that not only had a Presbyterian brother, Mr. Upchurch, donated the land for our new Baptist church, but the young pastor and his wife were living rent free and our first baptism took place on the property of the dear Presbyterian lady, Miss Currie, who had funded much of my first year of college studies. Such was the interdenominational goodwill that the Lord gave us during those days.

This all took place during the Korean War, and the military draft was still functioning. For a minister to remain with his congregation he was required by law to be a fulltime employee of his church. I told the congregation that Norma and I could live on $40 per week; thus a letter, signed by the men of the church, was sent to the draft board stating that the congregation would fully support me financially.

In November the weather had gotten too cool to hold services under our shelter so we began to hold services in our members' homes. I preached in Mr. Chaney's home once on the question, "Can one know for sure that he is saved?" My answer was based on 1 John 5:13: "...that you may know that you have eternal life." During the course of the sermon I exclaimed, "I *know* that I'm saved. I *know*, n-o, *know!*" Everyone laughed. When I realized my mistake, I was embarrassed and extemporized, "If 'n-o' does not spell 'know,' what *does* it spell?"

In December we obtained an additional half acre of land from Mr. Upchurch. Mr. Goodman, a good friend of Pastor Branson, drew a set of blueprints for the church building. We took the blueprint to the bank and got a written commitment that when the building was completed the bank would loan us 60 percent of the appraised value. When the bank commitment letter was shown to the lumber and block companies they agreed to furnish material for construction on credit until the bank issued the loan.

Members of the church did most of the labor. I dug the foundation footing by hand and put in steel and poured concrete. Mr. Chaney, one of the charter members who owned well-drilling equipment, drilled a well for us. My former employer, Junior Hoover, another charter member, paid his crew of block layers to help him erect all of the concrete block walls. Some of the other men of the church were able to do carpentry work. A friend in the community who was not a believer did the electrical wiring without charge.

I believe that the only cost we had for labor was for the plumbing installation. The plumber, Shirley Newberry – yes, "Shirley" was *his* name – was not a Christian at the time, and I tried to explain to him the Bible way of salvation. There on the building site I quoted to him: "By grace you're saved through faith, and that not of yourselves, it's a gift of God, not of works, lest any man should boast,"

(Eph. 2:8-9). I also added, "Not by works of righteousness," (Tit. 3:5) and "to him that worketh not, but believeth on him that justifies the ungodly, his faith is counted for righteousness," (Rom. 4:5).

Shirley stopped me and said, "What Bible are you coatin' from?" That was his word for "quoting." He probably had been taught that one must do good works to be saved. The verses I was quoting that said "not by works" made him wonder if I was referring to some strange modern Bible. "I am quoting from the same kind of Bible you have in your home," I told him, "I am quoting from the King James Version." Then the plumber explained, "That is not the Bible I use. I only use the Old Holy Bible." Although he was not convinced of the truth at that time, the Holy Spirit later opened Shirley's eyes and he did receive Christ sometime later.

Junior Hoover and I were laying up some decorative brick on the front of the building when Norma and his wife, Betty, returned from a trip to Norma's doctor. Norma was told that our first child's birth was imminent.

That night about midnight I had to take Norma to the hospital. In those days husbands were not allowed to stay with their wives in the labor room. I waited on a couch in the hallway with hopes that our child would be a boy. At 5:00 a.m. January 11, 1955, a nurse appeared holding a 30-seconds-old baby and called out to me, "Mr. Winget, you have a baby boy." I leaped to my feet and shouted, "Praise the Lord!" at my first sight of that little fellow. I was overwhelmed with a sense of awesome responsibility to protect him and to raise him for God's glory. We named him "Steven Lee Winget." His first name we took from the courageous hero in the Book of Acts, and his middle name corresponded to his mother's middle name.

Shortly after Steve's birth the church building was completed. It had an auditorium that would seat about 125 people, two average-sized Sunday School rooms, two restrooms, and a pastor's study. A well-attended special dedication service was held the last Sunday of February, and Dr. Luttrell came again to give the dedicatory sermon. I remember that that day was unusually cold, and the building didn't have any heat, but this did not dampen our spirits on such a meaningful occasion.

Only a few months after the church had been formed we hosted the first missionary we considered for support. George Wisner was planning to go to Brazil with ABWE, the Association of Baptists for World Evangelism. Brother Archie Ford strongly opposed the idea of supporting Wisner. When he voiced his opposition before the congregation, I asked him why he was opposed to helping this missionary. He said, "I'm opposed because that organization promotes false doctrine. It is postmillennial and our church is premillennial. They believe that they are going to win the world to Christ and bring in the millennial kingdom." I said to him, "What makes you believe that ABWE is postmillennial?" He replied, "Their very name, Association of Baptists for World Evangelism, suggests a postmillennial viewpoint because they believe that the world will come to Christ."

I explained to him that "world evangelism" did not mean "worldwide salvation." Rather, the term spoke of "taking the Gospel to all the world." ABWE was not, nor is now, postmillennial. They did not expect to win all the world. Jesus' command in Matthew 28:19 was to go to "all nations" and Mark 16:15 says, "Go, ye, into all the world." ABWE simply tries to get the gospel to the far corners of the earth in obedience to Acts 1:8 which says, "Power will come upon you, and you will be my witnesses both in Jerusalem, Judea, Samaria and to the uttermost part of the earth." Archie was embarrassed, but to his credit he apologized and dropped his opposition. After that he supported everything that I promoted.

It is rather interesting that roughly 30 years later that first son of ours would take his family to the country of Hungary to serve as a missionary, and a short time later our second son, David, would likewise go to the Ukraine with his family, both under the auspices of ABWE.

Go West, Young Man

*I*n August of 1956, I became convinced that more formal education in seminary was God's will for me. My most effective professor in college, Dr. Howard Vos, was a graduate of Dallas Theological Seminary, and because of his influence, I chose to go to that seminary. I could have gone to a seminary where the basic course took only three years leading to a Master of Divinity degree, but I chose the school of my favorite college professor even though it did not offer a three year degree. At Dallas I had to register for the four-year program that led to a Master of Theology degree. Among other requirements the degree demanded four years of Greek and three years of Hebrew.

To some who sarcastically refer to seminary as "cemetery" it may seem somewhat prophetic that for several weeks prior to moving to Dallas I had earned a bit of supplemental income by selling burial lots – excuse me, "cemetery property" – for Glen Abbey Memorial Gardens. It paid better than picking oranges in those days, and we certainly needed the additional income.

Norma and I had traded our faithful old '39 Chevy for a 1946 "straight eight" Pontiac station wagon, and with it we pulled our mobile home to Texas. We planned our three-day trip to Dallas so that there was a trailer court near the state highway where we could park each night. Upon our arrival in Dallas we parked in a trailer court about 15 minutes from the seminary just inside the city limits on Highway 80.

When I began studying in the seminary the first of September Norma began working in the records department of Baylor Hospital to support our family. After a few days I found part-time work to pay for my tuition and books. Steve was about 20 months old at that time and was tended five days a week by a lady who lived in the same trailer court. After visiting three or four Baptist churches we joined the recently established Grace Baptist Church located on Fitzhugh Avenue in east Dallas. It was my privilege to teach the young married couples class for almost three years. I was also invited by the pastor, Pastor Ausburn, to preach several times.

At that church we became close friends with a number of people, including Mr. and Mrs. Birkhead, who owned a life insurance company. Years later after I finished my master's degree, the Birkheads were instrumental in helping fund a trip that Norma and I took to visit missionaries in Mexico and the Pacific islands. Some years later these dear friends learned about Tennessee Temple Schools when they visited us in Chattanooga in the early 1960s. Brother Birkhead put Temple in his will – his gift was memorialized when the building that houses the Temple Baptist Theological Seminary was named the "Birkhead Building."

At the start of my second year of seminary we rented our "Pacemaker" mobile home to a seminary couple who had no children. We rented it because Norma had become aware that in a few months a visitor was coming to stay with us, and we needed a bigger place. We moved into a government-subsidized, two-bedroom apartment in West Dallas. That visitor turned out to be permanent – our second child, David Earl, was born on February 24, 1958, in Baylor Hospital after Norma endured almost 24 hours of labor. He was given my name and the name of my brother, Earl. This began somewhat of a tradition in our family such that the second son is given the middle name of a brother of his father.

The couple who had been staying in our mobile home moved out within a few months. Without that source of income we moved back into the trailer. By that time Norma had gone back to work at a much better job as a secretary at Grove Hill Cemetery. I had worked two jobs the previous summer: one was in the day time at the John E. Mitchell Company making auto air conditioners and cotton gin equipment, and the other was from about 4:00 till 9:00 each afternoon at the Boys Club operated by the Salvation Army.

During my third year at seminary we traded our 32-feet-long mobile home as a down payment on a new 42-feet mobile home. This trailer had a front and a rear bedroom. We had it set up in a good shady spot on the back side of the trailer court. One bad thing about that trailer space was that the rear bedroom was very near the back fence, and just beyond the fence was a railroad track. Steve and Dave slept in the rear bedroom and the first night we spent there we heard the train coming. We were certain that the boys would be frightened to death. Norma and I leaped out of bed and rushed back to their bed to check on them, but we were pleasantly surprised, for they both had slept right through all the noise and vibration.

Childhood Prayers & Aspirations

As Christmas approached Steve, only four years old at the time, began an interesting prayer campaign during family prayers – he prayed for a football uniform. Our finances were such that we had no means of fulfilling such a request, so for weeks we tried to divert his attention towards something else. Not to be deterred, every time he prayed Steve would thank Jesus for the football uniform he was going to get for Christmas. We came to realize two important lessons: God can answer the prayers of children (even big ones), and He can do so without the assistance of parental "help."

During the course of a conversation with a colleague at work Norma told Mrs. Hearn about Steve's prayer. Unknown to us, Mrs. Hearn's brother, worked at a sporting goods store. When he heard the story he arranged to give his sister a football uniform for her to give to Steve at Christmas. Steve thanked Jesus for answering his prayer. So did his parents.

Some months later we held a boxing tournament at our Boy's Club. Physicians came to examine the applicants as they were to register for the boxing tournament to determine if they were physically fit to box. Mr. Hatter, the club director, filled out a questionnaire for each boy. One little Mexican lad about seven years of age came to register. His name was "Hector," and Hector was loved by all our staff. Mr. Hatter said, "Hector, I need to know if you have ancestors." He replied, "No, sir, Mr. Hatter." Then the question was, "Have you ever had ancestors?" His answer was, "No, sir. I am sure that I have never had ancestors." Mr. Hatter told him, "Okay. Let the doctor check you over." On another occasion I saw Hector put two nickels into the candy machine in the lobby of the Boy's Club to buy two candy bars. I called to him with a concerned tone of voice. "Hector, do you know if you eat those two candy bars at one time they'll both go to your stomach?" He asked, "Would it be okay if I eat just one of them?" I assured him, "Yes, that would be okay." He played in the gym a few minutes and then came to me asking, "Mr. Winget, do you think I could eat my other candy bar now?" I responded, "Yes, you may eat the other one now."

There was a classification in the tournament for five year olds. Since Steve was now five, he wanted to compete. I borrowed a pair of boxing gloves from the club for him to use for practice. I got on my knees before him a few times and let him hit me on my face and head. Norma and I tried to build his confidence by telling him he was a good boxer. He felt that if he did so well against Daddy, any little guy his size would be a pushover. What a big surprise he had in store! A little Mexican about his size landed three or four solid blows to his face and head within five seconds. Steve began to bawl loud enough to drown out the cheers of the Mexican fans who were yelling for their boy. Immediately the umpire stopped the contest. That ended Steve's pugilistic aspirations, possibly the shortest boxing career in history.

For part of my four years in seminary our mobile home was parked behind the Grace Baptist Church Sunday School building. A high-body garbage collection truck crewed by a driver and two men who loaded the garbage came down the alleyway beside our place twice a week. One man on the ground threw the full cans up to another on top of the load who would empty them and trample the garbage down. In part, because they spent time talking to him, Steve admired those men. When anyone asked him what he wanted to be when he grew up he would answer, "A garbage man." Which one of those garbage jobs did he prefer? It was a terrible dilemma: on the one hand the man up on top of the truck must surely have discovered amazing treasures every day, but on the other hand, the man on the ground who threw the full cans up to the man on top of the load had to be very strong. Besides this, he got to jump onto, and off of, the *moving* garbage truck. The real appeal of the latter position, however, was that this man – *without even putting his fingers to his lips!* – could make a loud, shrill whistle to signal the driver when to stop or go. This had to be the absolute epitome of virility and manliness. Fortunately, Steve never realized his high ambition.

What Does "Believing in Jesus" Mean?

While employed at John E. Mitchell Company I worked with a young man one summer who was a sophomore in a local college. Norman was the president of a youth group in a local church that he attended faithfully. We talked at length about salvation and related subjects. We both used such terms as "being saved," "believing in Jesus," "accepting Christ as Savior," "trusting Christ," and the like. Because of something Norman said I became concerned as to whether or not he was truly born again.

I probed, "Norman, tell me what you mean by 'believing in Jesus' or 'trusting in Christ to be saved.'" He replied, "One must make a decision to turn himself over to the Lord; to trust Him to take care of him in every situation. He just believes that in sickness, and accidents, and everything Jesus will just be with him and help him." I responded, "Is that what one believes about Christ to become a Christian, to be saved and go to heaven when he dies?" He said "Yes. Is that not correct?"

During our lunch hour he allowed me to show him some verses from my pocket New Testament and to explain the Gospel and why people needed to be saved. I went on to expound upon the basis of salvation, Christ's substitutionary death and resurrection, and the means for becoming a recipient of salvation, faith in the total sufficiency of Christ's Person and cross work in our stead. I tried to make it clear that sin was the problem, death and separation from God was the penalty, and Christ's death paid that debt for us. I emphasized that these basic truths had to be accepted by faith alone.

His exact words are very vivid in my mind: "I have *never* heard this before in my *whole* life." I think Norman understood that day the truth of the Gospel and how one appropriates the benefits of the Gospel for himself. The whistle sounded to end our lunch hour and also ended our conversation. I do not know whether he ever embraced by faith Christ's death as the basis of eternal salvation – it is matter that I had to leave to a sovereign Holy Spirit.

Appreciating Grace & Anticipating Further Studies

It was a distinct honor of mine in my fourth year to have been chosen as one of four members of my class to preach during senior chapel week. This involved a competition for the annual H.A. Ironside Expository Preaching Award. I spoke on the theme of grace from Ephesians chapter two. In my introduction I stated, "Our greatest failure is not in our inability to define grace, nor in our inability to tell what the Bible says about it, but in our failure to truly appreciate grace." I outlined my remarks thus:

Part I – Our Gratitude for Grace Will Be Increased By Taking a Backward Look at a Picture of Our Past (verses 1-3)

Part II – Our Gratitude for Grace Will Be Increased By Taking an Upward Look at the Person of Our God (verses 4-6)

Part III – Our Gratitude for Grace Will Be Increased By Taking a Forward Look at the Purpose of Grace (verses 7-9)

I do not know whether I was second, third, or fourth, but I was not voted number one for the award.

One major task during that year was completing research in writing my master's thesis, *Fulfilled Prophecies Concerning Judas Iscariot*. In addition to writing my thesis I spent many hours – I can say, *hundreds* of hours – of hard work to finish in the top ten percent of my class. Because I attended classes during the day and spent five hours at my job each afternoon and evening, it was necessary for me to spend many Saturdays studying twelve hours in the library. I would arrive at the library early in the morning equipped with my study materials and a sack of food for lunch and another for supper. Around lunchtime I would take a brief break by going outside for a few minutes to walk around as I nibbled on a sandwich or piece of fruit. Around suppertime I'd repeat my recess routine. Otherwise I was inside grinding away at the books.

Being listed among the top ten percent of the master's degree graduates made me eligible to enter the doctoral program. It was a victory just to qualify to continue studying towards the higher degree, and I had harbored aspirations to do so. However, the Lord's timing intervened.

There arose a pressing need for a professor at Temple Baptist Seminary in Chattanooga. Dr. Cierpke, the co-founder of Temple Seminary and chair of the Theology department had fallen ill. Dr. Roberson called on me to take over the Greek and theology classes that Dr. Cierpke had taught for a decade. He offered to pay me $275 a month. After praying about it I determined it was God's will for me to accept that teaching opportunity beginning in September of 1960. Therefore we began to make plans to move to Chattanooga.

Chattanooga Choo-Choo (Sort Of)

*I*t had been difficult to pull our 32-foot trailer from Florida to Texas in 1956, and for sure we did not savor the idea of pulling our 42-foot mobile home to Tennessee. We tried our best to sell it, but to no avail. We prayed and searched and searched and prayed for someone to whom we could *give* this two-year-old mobile home if they would simply assume the monthly payments. No takers crossed our path. The Lord had always proven faithful at our point of need, but what was He doing now?

We finally admitted that we were going to be forced to haul our trailer over those hundreds of miles from Texas to Tennessee. It was therefore necessary to have professionals outfit the trailer and our Chevy station wagon with heavy equipment for pulling the mobile home to Chattanooga. This was expensive and time consuming. "What was God doing?" continued to preoccupy our thoughts.

About August 15 Norma, Steve, Dave and I, climbed aboard our *Chevynooga Express* and pulled out of the station bound for Chattanooga. Behind us was hitched our mobile home heavily laden with all our household goods plus a sewer pipe and a heavy metal fuel drum. The trek took three and a half days traveling over mostly two-lane roads. Because of the extremely heavy load the brakes on the trailer carriage were ineffective. As a result the car brakes alone were used to slow or stop the trailer. I had to anticipate at great distance any need to slow down or stop. A sudden attempt to stop would have caused us to jack-knife and totally lose control.

The Chevrolet had sufficient power to move the load as long as we could maintain even a slight momentum. However, pulling away from a dead stop came near to over-taxing the transmission. Starting up an incline was next to impossible. Therefore I tried never to stop still at traffic lights on any upward slope. Whenever I saw a traffic light in the distance I would try to count the seconds the light would stay green and time our approach so as to catch the green light. If I stopped I would have to back up and go another way. A few times I went through red lights blaring on our car horn and praying that the on-coming traffic would yield.

On one occasion I encountered just such an incline and was forced to stop. We had no choice but to try to back down the hill and try another route. God sent along a kind gentleman who saw our dilemma from a gas station across the street – he strode out into traffic and stopped the flow of cars in both directions long enough for me to back up and angle the trailer into a side alley that was *just* wide enough for us to pass. That this man understood our need and was willing to help, that the alley was *just* wide enough, and that I was able to back into it *on the first try*, was incredible. Our God was teaching us again that He was in the business of supplying needs to those who followed His leading.

The tension was hard on all of us – after several hours on the road that first day around nightfall Dave began to whimper and said, "I want to go home." Norma tried to reassure him, "Look behind there; that's our home." He said, "I know, but I want to go home." Sometimes, though, simple humor lightened our anxieties – when we crossed the Mississippi River one or both of the boys thought it was a big swimming pool, but they called it a "thim pool."

By the third night we had reached Birmingham, Alabama where we spent the night with Norma's older brother, Lawrence, and his family. The next day marked the final stage of our "Tour de South." We made it to Chattanooga sometime in the afternoon, but we still had some 20 miles or so to Rock Springs, Georgia, where Norma's parents lived. We finally pulled into Granny Hicks' gravel lane sometime before dark. We had traveled almost 900 miles, and under the circumstances, that we had made the trip without incident was purely and simply a testament to God's safe-keeping and care over us.

Ever kind and gentle, willowy Granny Hicks greeted us with a brimming smile and open arms. I don't remember whether Poppa Hicks' belligerence toward his eldest daughter's commitment to Christ allowed him to even acknowledge our arrival or not. He hardly greeted us at all for several weeks. George Hicks was well-liked by his acquaintances and industrious, but as long as I knew him, this burly, hard-working brick mason was antagonistic toward the Gospel. This was a continual burden to us, especially to Norma, and we prayed for him regularly. I attempted on numerous occasions to speak to him about his need before God, but he never indicated anything but a stone-hard refusal to heed my entreaties.

After two days, Joe Hicks, one of Norma's unmarried brothers who lived alone in a brick home that he had recently built a few hundred yards from where Norma's parents lived, made us an offer that seemed too good to be true. He offered to take our mobile home as a down payment on his three-bedroom house with its six acres of land. He allowed us $3,000 for our equity in the trailer – the trailer that a few weeks earlier we couldn't give away. His property was valued at $10,000, and thus we were in debt to him for $7,000. But we had no credit. He therefore borrowed $7,000 from the bank against the house before he signed it over to us. Then we went to the bank with Joe and signed an agreement to make the monthly payments to pay off the $7,000. Yet Joe was responsible for the thousands of dollars if we defaulted. Now we saw what it was that God had been doing in not answering our prayers for a buyer for the trailer. It was a stunning example of the fact that sometimes God answers the prayers of his people with a "No, not now," because He has in mind something far better. Those confused prayers back in Texas asking the Lord to send a buyer, those costly days of packing and outfitting the vehicle for the trip, and those tense days dragging that load cross country to our new brick home all made sense now!

The story of God's wisdom became even more astounding. In a little over a year we sold that brick house for $10,500. This resale cleared us $3,500 which we used as a down payment on another place much closer to my work at Tennessee Temple. The trailer that we couldn't give away in Texas netted us a total of $6,500 in equity and cash one year later.

To God be the glory.

Teaching, Trinity Church,
& Tall Tales

I met Boyd Dickey on the first day of registration for the fall semester of 1960. He was a sandy-haired student from Harriman, Tennessee, some eighty miles north of Chattanooga on Highway 27. He was married to Betty, in his early- to mid-thirties, and compared to me, quite tall. He served as a deacon and Sunday School teacher at his home church. Ever the one who struggled with people's names, I had a hard time not referring to him as "Dickey Boyd," especially in those early days of what proved to be a long and warm friendship.

Boyd invited me to go with him to Harriman that Wednesday evening and preach. Of course, I was glad for the opportunity. After the service that evening I was asked by the church to return on Sunday to speak morning and evening. That was the beginning of eight months of interim pastoral ministry at Trinity Baptist Church in Harriman, Tennessee. [Note: Boyd Dickey and his faithful wife went on to have very fruitful pastorates for nearly 40 years in Texas, Florida, Georgia, and Tennessee. Boyd later wrote a book named *The Country Preacher* which he dedicated to his wife referencing Solomon's words from Proverbs 12:4: "A virtuous woman is a crown to her husband." He went to be with the Lord in 2006. At the time of this writing Betty is still living in the house that Boyd built in 1958 before I met them.]

Those first few days as a new faculty member at Temple were the occasion of another providential meeting. Sitting on the front row of my very first class was a gentleman I deduced to be several years older than I. (I found out later that we shared the same calendar day as our birthdays, September 22nd, but he was seven years older.) His name was Wymal (rhymes with "primal") Porter. He was about my height, prematurely bald, and gladly bore the remnants of his Arkansas-Louisiana upbringing. As the years rolled by he became one of my very closest friends and colleagues in the ministry, and those days traveling up to Harriman afforded a solid foundation for that relationship. Many times we and our wives celebrated our mutual birthday by going out to a favorite restaurant together. This dear couple were "friends indeed," and through the years they proved it by demonstrating gracious, New Testament *koinonia* when we really needed it. I trust that we were as faithful in return.

For three years he enrolled in almost every course I taught and earned an "A" each time. The same year that Wymal graduated from the seminary, Dr. Carl Greene had just resigned from the Bible faculty to accept a position at another school. I asked Dr. Roberson to consider Wymal as a replacement for Dr. Greene on the Bible faculty at the college – I knew that Wymal was an excellent Bible scholar and effective Bible teacher. Dr. Roberson immediately hired Wymal. In addition, Dr. Greene's vacated office immediately became assigned to Wymal and me.

Because we shared an office together we had opportunity to discuss biblical and theological issues. We usually saw eye to eye on most major issues, but sometimes we sparred with one another on finer points. On one occasion we disagreed on the meaning of a theological term, and he read the definition from a dictionary that supported his view. Immediately I responded, "you can't trust that dictionary – it's obviously an old Arminian dictionary."

Dr. Roberson's faith in Wymal was validated over the years, and he later received an honorary doctorate from Louisiana Baptist University in recognition of his many years of effective teaching – his ministry at Tennessee Temple stretched over three decades and more. At this writing he still is active in teaching and preaching at various Bible conferences across the country.

Our first ministry partnership, however, was at Trinity Baptist in Harriman. The same 1948 Chevy station wagon that had pulled our mobile home from Texas made two trips per week, 99 miles one way, from our home in Rock Springs. Whereas I made the trip alone on Wednesdays, a total of eight souls went to Harriman every Sunday morning in that station wagon: Norma, Steve, Dave and I; Boyd and his lovely wife, Betty; and Wymal Porter and his wonderful wife, Evelyn. These were the days before compulsory seat belt use – indeed, that vehicle didn't *have* seat belts – so we had three adults in the front, three adults in the second seat, and Steve and Dave rode in the cargo area in the back.

I was responsible to preach in the main morning and evening services on Sundays, and Boyd and Wymal taught Sunday School classes in the mornings and "Training Union" classes in the evenings. On Sunday afternoons following an excellent meal provided by the church, Wymal, Boyd, and I held a Gospel service at a local jail.

The Difference Between Teaching & Preaching

One man quit coming to the church soon after I became the interim pastor, and Brother Porter and I visited him with hopes of encouraging him to return to church. He informed us that he was attending his preacher friend's church that he liked very much. He explained that his appreciation for the other church had to do with the fact that he felt comfortable there and wasn't intimidated by the preacher. He told us, "Why, he don't know no more than I do." We asked, "Does he teach the Word of God?" He replied, "Yes. He teaches the auditorium Bible class every Sunday and he preaches too." Brother Porter's curiosity was raised a bit. "What would you say was the difference," Wymal inquired, "between his teaching and his preaching?" The man responded, "There's a *world* of difference. When he teaches you can understand what he's saying." His intended distinction was, of course, that when this fellow was preaching his listeners could *not* understand what he was saying! It is sad to say that this type of "preaching" is fairly common, but I must admit that the memory of that gentleman's differentiation between teaching and preaching has been a private source of considerable laughter by some of us for almost a half-century.

In that same church one of the deacons and Wymal were chatting one day. The deacon quizzed Brother Porter, "Wymal, do you know that you can see the wind?" Wymal responded, "What are you talking about, 'you can *see* the wind'?" "Well," explained the deacon, "Peter *saw* the wind. If you don't believe that Peter saw the wind, you just don't believe the Bible. It says, 'Peter saw the wind boisterous.'" I rehearsed that conversation in one of my classes the next week, and a student quipped, "Well, if Peter 'saw the wind,' it's not too far-fetched to say that voices have feet because the Bible says, 'Adam heard the voice of the Lord walking in the garden.'"

'Ole Mick

One Sunday Brother Porter and Evelyn were not able to travel with us. I invited another couple, John Greene, and his dear wife, Norma, to go and serve in place of the Porters. The Greenes agreed. They were a gracious couple and have remained fast friends all these years.

While driving home after church that night Boyd, as was the custom, volunteered another of his many homespun anecdotes. The boys were thrilled, and if the truth be told, so were the rest of us. He began to spin an interesting narrative about trying to sell his favorite bird dog, "Mick," to one of his college teachers, Dr. Carl. Boyd said that he took Dr. Carl and 'ole Mick bird hunting one Saturday to show off what a good dog Mick really was. They took their shotguns out into a large field and turned Mick loose to stir up some birds. Inexplicably, Mick began to race around the field in a large arc. Boyd was embarrassed that he had spoken so highly of his well-behaved dog, and now the dog seemed to be totally out of control.

Mick continued to circle the men, but they realized the radius of the dog's circuit was rapidly becoming smaller and smaller. Though Boyd yelled repeatedly for Mick to come to heal, the dog refused. Boyd apologized, "Dr. Carl, I don't understand what's wrong with him. He's always been a very obedient dog." Mick kept running around in smaller and smaller circles, refusing to obey his master. Then suddenly Mick came to a complete halt and laid down on his belly in the middle of that field with his front paws stretched in front of him.

As the two men approached the place where Mick had suddenly stopped a bird flew up from the high grass near where Mick was now resting. Boyd quickly raised up his shotgun and felled the bird. Another bird flew up, and Dr. Carl shot that one. One by one several more birds flew up just in front of the hunters. Both took turns shooting the birds one at a time.

Boyd concluded his tale by relating that they then discovered what had happened. Mick had, in his racing around, herded all the birds in the field into a hole. With his front paws covering the hole, he would let one bird fly up at a time!

In that split second before any of the rest of us could chuckle at Boyd's outlandish exaggeration, Norma Greene exclaimed incredulously, "My! What a *smart* dog!" The rest of us in the car erupted with such loud laughter that I almost drove off the road! To this day the mere mention of "'ole Mick" never fails to bring a broad smile to our faces.

Three Bears

Our sons always looked forward to those long drives, primarily because of Mr. Dickey's animal stories, especially his "bar" (bear) stories. After Trinity Church called a full-time pastor we no longer saw Boyd and Betty on a regular basis, but Dave especially missed Mr. Dickey's entertaining narrations. When he was about three years of age, Dave asked me to tell him a bear story like Mr. Dickey used to tell.

I began to extemporize a story about three bears. "There once was a Papa Bear, a Mama Bear, and Baby Bear," I began. I was inventing this story line by line. I proceeded to tell how Papa Bear climbed a hollow tree with a beehive in it to get honey for Baby Bear. He was about to put his paw into the hive to get some honey when a bee stung him. He screamed and quickly slipped down the tree and ran away. Mama Bear, the tale continued, said, "I'll go up and get some honey for you, Baby Bear." She climbed up the tree and was about to put her paw into the hole when two bees stung her. She screamed and quickly slipped down the tree and ran away. I looked at Dave and said, "Then Baby Bear decided to climb the tree and get honey for himself." Just as I related that Baby Bear was about to put his paw into the hole, Dave yelled out, "No, no, stop, Daddy! I don't want him to get stung, too."

I See It – That's It!

Before moving on I want to share an account relating to John and Norma Greene. A decade or so later John invited me to speak in a Bible conference in his church in Anderson, Indiana. During the course of the meetings John pointed out a certain member of his flock and shared with me that the man had been having difficulty with the matter of assurance of his salvation. Brother Greene had counseled with this parishioner on at least two occasions about the issue, but the gentleman was still troubled over the matter.

In one of my sermons I preached from Isaiah 53 about Christ's death. I talked about the "Source of His Death," the "Substitution in His Death," and the "Satisfaction with His Death." The Father planned the death of His Son, His Son's death was intended as a sub-stitutionary replacement for sinners, and the Father was completely satisfied with the work His Son had accomplished in His death.

The next day I had an opportunity to speak with the man John had mentioned earlier. I inquired as to whether he was saved. He responded in the affirmative. I pressed a bit further by requesting details: "When did you become a believer?" Without hesitation he replied, "Last night." My first thought was that Pastor Greene had met again with him and had finally settled the question, but the man continued, "While you were speaking last night I saw it, and I said to myself, 'That's it.'"

In class I used this incident several times as a teaching tool to emphasize a key pastoral point. I asked, "Should I have said to that gentleman, 'Sir, I didn't notice you kneeling down by your seat, nor did you come forward at the altar call. Why don't we nail it down right here and pray to God for salvation?'"

I answered my own question: "Of course I should not have said any such thing." To do so would have suggested that salvation is a matter of posture or a certain pious act like walking to the front of the church or perhaps repeating certain phraseology in prayer. Salvation is not obtained by such religious acts. It comes to the sinner by an acceptance and affirmation and trust in the finished work of Christ at Calvary as the only solution for his spiritual problem. That's the only way salvation comes to a sinner.

Another Move, Another Church, & Another Victory for the Gospel

Missionaries to Resaca

*T*he brick house in Rock Springs was almost twenty miles from the Temple campus, a long commute in those days. Though we loved the quiet of the country and the comfort of that nice house near Norma's relatives, we decided to move closer to school. In much the same way that our move years earlier from south Georgia to central Florida placed us near the church where I later came to hear the Gospel, so this move set the stage for Steve's conversion. But I'm getting a bit ahead of myself.

Shortly after we moved to our home on Union Avenue near the Temple campus, the Corinth Baptist Church, in Resaca (pronounced "Ree-SACK-ah"), Georgia called me to be their pastor. The time was September of 1961, and this little country church, fifty miles south of Chattanooga, would provide numerous opportunities for us to serve, to learn, and to be humbled.

The congregation had an adult lady's Sunday School class which was led by a 40-year-old public school teacher. That winter, following the denominational Sunday School curriculum the church used, the teacher was dealing with the Christmas narratives. At one point she commented that Joseph, though engaged to the Virgin Mary, had had a previous marriage when he was in bondage down in Egypt. Unconsciously Norma let out a sigh of surprise and said "No, that was a different Joseph in Egypt, and that was hundreds of years earlier." The rest of the class had not caught the teacher's historical error, but there was no mistaking the fact that this still suspicious newcomer was correcting their beloved and veteran teacher! This was only one of many instances where we were completely shocked at the spiritual immaturity and Biblical illiteracy of folks who had been in that church all their lives.

Wymal Porter went with us to Resaca each Sunday and taught the men's class. During one lesson he told the men that in reality there was "only one devil" but "many demons" mentioned in the Bible. Mark Holden – he always went by "Mr. Mark" – the oldest deacon in the church, later brought copies of Bible references that employed the word "devils." He gave copies to all of the fellows in the class to prove that Porter was wrong. There had been growing skepticism toward these two guys, one a teacher and the other a student from Temple Seminary – a school not recognized by the Southern Baptist Convention. Now here was proof positive that these folks from Chattanooga didn't know what they were talking about.

Wymal tried as gently as he could to explain that the New Testament was originally written by the apostles in Greek and that the Greek word for "devil," *diabolos*, is always singular. That's why he had said there is only one devil. He went on to clarify to the men that the word "devils" in the plural is found in the English translation of the New Testament, but this term was a rendering of the Greek word *diamonia*, which literally means "demons." Therefore the Bible speaks of only one "devil" but of many "demons."

While there were a number of teachable people in the pews of Corinth Baptist, quite a few folks in that church weren't receptive to Biblical teaching at all. They doubted anything or anyone that was not strictly Southern Baptist, and they resented the fact that this new pastor had graduated from a seminary that was not run by the Convention. What's more, that he was presently a professor at Temple Baptist Seminary, another school not affiliated with the SBC was equally irksome. (I want to make it clear that there were independent churches scattered all across the country with Biblically illiterate and carnal, hard-hearted people in positions of leadership. It is also true that there were many SBC churches where the Scriptures were taught and in which Godly leaders ministered. The two statements remain true today. The problem arises when people revere their denominational affiliation – or their independence therefrom – with higher regard than they do the Bible and the God of the Bible.)

To make matters worse, this new pastor had ordered children's literature from a Baptist publication company that was not under the auspices of the SBC. One 30-year-old Sunday School teacher noticed a statement in one of the children's booklets that said that Jesus had helped God His Father create the world. She quickly phoned another teacher and reported what she had just read from the booklet. The second teacher responded, "There's no way that that can be true! Jesus wasn't even born then."

At church they later cornered Mr. Padgett to show him their evidence of the "heresy" in the new children's literature that the pastor had ordered. Brother Padgett, one of the cluster of members that appreciated my teaching, told me later that he looked into the faces of those two ladies and said, "Ladies where *have* you been?" He went on to explain Jesus' pre-existence to them using John 17:5 where, in His prayer to the Father the night before He was crucified, Jesus prayed, "Now, oh Father, glorify thou Me with thine own self, with the glory which I had with thee before the world was." "Jesus," he continued to explain, "had existed before He was born. He existed before the world was created."

These two ladies illustrate the doctrinal ignorance of many who attend church regularly, even churches where the Bible is held to be the Word of God. They did not understand the truth of the deity of Jesus Christ, that He has all the attributes that God the Father has, including eternality. He is as old as the Father and the Father is no older than He. He is absolute deity. He always has been. He is, and always shall be. Sadly, this type of thing is true of many churchgoers in our day. One of the biggest lessons the Holy Spirit impressed upon us through our time at Corinth was that the teacher of Scripture must not take anything for granted when he teaches the Word of God.

I invited Freeman Googe, a zealous missionary to the Caribbean Islands that had been supported by that church for many months, to preach a series of evangelistic meetings. Red-headed Freeman was the person who had recommended me as pastor a few weeks earlier.

Before the special week of meetings had begun, the minutes of the Gordon County Baptist Association's annual meeting had been published. Freeman had become aware of a heretical doctrinal statement that appeared in that publication: "We believe that man is able to save himself by his own good works."

Freeman emphatically disagreed with that statement and publicly declared it heresy citing such passages as Ephesians 2:8-9 ("For by grace are you saved, through faith, and that not of yourselves, it is the gift of God, not of works, lest any man should boast.") or Romans 4:5 ("But to him that worketh not, but believeth on him, it is counted to him for righteousness.") or Titus 3:5 ("Not by works of righteousness which we have done, but according to his mercy he saved us by the washing of regeneration and renewing of the Holy Spirit."). Some of the church, led by Mr. Mark, defended the statement. If forced to it, Mr. Mark and his band strongly preferred the statement of the denominational publication as opposed to the opinion of some missionary to black folk.

Two weeks later a representative of the county association appeared at the front door of the church just as the morning service was beginning. I invited him to come to the pulpit for a greeting or other comment he might like to make to the church. He admitted to the church that it was a great embarrassment that a serious printing error had appeared in the recent doctrinal statement. He said it should have read that "We believe that man is *un*able to save himself by his own good works," and he apologized for the terrible confusion it may have caused.

Other illustrations could be given to point out the Biblical ignorance of even some of the leaders of that church, but even more telling was the level of mean-spiritedness and un-Christlike attitude displayed by some in the congregation. For example, the custom of the church was that the Sunday morning offering was given to the pastor and the Sunday night collection went to the church for utilities and other expenses. As time went by and we were forced to confront one area of misinformation or sinful attitude after another the amount of the offering each Sunday decreased. Theoretically, one might grant the benefit of the doubt and suggest that the decreased offering reflected a temporary downturn in earnings or some other explanation. But the following incidents hardly allow such generosity.

Shortly after beginning my pastoral role at Corinth Wymal and I planned to encourage the congregation to memorize a verse of Scripture each week. We would choose a key verse, usually rather short, and spend a few moments each service drilling the congregation by various means so as to help in the memorization process. A few weeks later, one of the more spiritually mature men of the church, Marvin Blackstock, remarked to another, "I've learned each verse so far. How 'bout you, Brother?" The second man, who we know was a practicing Masonic Lodge member and who had committed reams and reams of their dogma to memory, boastfully snorted, "I ain't learned n'er a one yet!"

Yet another appalling comment had to do with how much of a waste it was to send money to that missionary (Goodge) who was using it to preach to those black n_____! "After all," the disgruntled church member mumbled, "those n_____ got their own religion. Telling 'em all this stuff will just confuse 'em! If we hadn't wasted all that money we could pave our parking lot and have indoor toilets."

Such was the confused mission field to which I had been called.

The custom at Corinth was to hold a vote every August as to whether to keep the pastor for the coming year. In August of 1962, those who were embarrassed that they had a "man-taught" pastor instead of a "God-taught" pastor – that was their terminology – contrived a way to vote their "man-taught" pastor out of the pulpit.

On the night of the vote they brought in several folks who had not come to church all year (some who were not even members of the church!) and thus secured the majority they wanted. Soon they got a pastor who was more to their liking.

It would seem that the Scripture had been proven true: there would come a time that certain ones having "itching ears" would not accept sound teaching, but would only choose to listen to those who said what the people wanted to hear (2 Tim. 4:3).

God Planned This Before He Ever Made the World

Our move from Rock Springs to Chattanooga also set the stage for a very meaningful event in the history of our family. If we had been living 19 miles away in Rock Springs I would not have insisted that Steve allow me to take him to see a children's evangelistic film on that special night in September of 1962. Steve really didn't want to attend, but I insisted. The film, produced by Child Evangelism Fellowship, gave a clear explanation of the Good News. At the close of the film, even though there were a number of other children who responded to the invitation, Steve refused. My son and I walked home that night, and I went to my study. In a few minutes Steve came back to the room that I used as my study area and just stood near my desk.

I detected that he was still thinking about the film and the invitation that he had ignored, so I reviewed for him several salvation verses from Romans. When I asked him if he wanted to receive Christ, he again shook his head "No." I then said, "I'm going to my bedroom, and if you want to talk to me anymore about this you may follow me there." He slowly walked behind me to my bedroom, and I asked him to kneel with me, which he did. I said, "Are you ready to accept Jesus?" He replied "No, daddy, not now."

I told him I was going to pray and thank Jesus for dying for me. I added that I would express my thanks that Jesus was willing to suffer all the pain and torment and shame that He sustained for me on Calvary. "When I finish," I instructed him, "it will be your turn to pray. You tell Him that you're *not* thankful that He did this for you." At that point he burst into tears and said "No, no, Daddy, I can't tell Him *that*."

"Well, you only have two choices. Tell him the opposite, that you *are* thankful that He died to pay for your sins and you want Him to be your Savior." The Holy Spirit clearly showed Steve what his refusal really meant, and at that point Steve relented. In his own words he accepted by faith God's offer as given in Romans 10:9, that "if you will confess with your mouth the Lord Jesus, and believe in your heart that God raised Him from the dead, you will be saved."

Steve's attitude changed completely, and he began asking all kinds of questions about the Bible and spiritual things. I said to him, "Who's the first person you want to tell about this." "Mama," he answered. So we rushed into the kitchen where his mother was, and he boldly told her the good news. Then as he sat in Norma's lap, he looked with a sudden light of insight at her and then at me, and said emphatically, "Just think... God planned this before He ever made the world."

New Car, New Daughter, New Church

*1*962-63 was a big year for us. Not only had Steve come to Christ, but several other red-letter dates mark that part of our family calendar.

On May 29, 1962, I had the joy of officiating at my younger brother's wedding. Darrel married Mildred Selman at Phillips Chapel on the campus at Tennessee Temple. It was a doubly joyous occasion for our family because Norma and I were also celebrating our tenth anniversary the next day.

Not that it qualified as big of an event as a child's commitment to Christ, or the acquisition of a new sister-in-law, but I do remember that a few weeks before I was mercifully released from our labors at Corinth Baptist, I traded our old Chevy station wagon in on a new car. It was a 1962 Volkswagen "Bug" that cost us $1,790 less the $275 the salesman allowed for our Chevy. That gray VW was my first new car, and I never have enjoyed another car as much. If the Lord allows us to drive in heaven, I think I'll request a 62 VW Beetle!

Of much greater import is the fact that on July 27, 1962, God blessed Norma and me with a beautiful baby daughter. Dave had expressed his desire several times for a baby sister. When Norma called him from the hospital and told him the good news over the telephone he dropped the phone and ran through the house shouting, "It's a girl, it's a girl, I have a baby sister!" Norma finally made use of the name she had wanted to use for her previous children, but they had turned out to be boys. Finally, she was able to name a daughter, "Joy Lynn." You'll read a lot more about our darling "Joy Lynn" as the narrative unfolds.

The very night that the Corinth church voted to get rid of their "man-made" preacher, many of those who had supported me expressed their deep disappointment. A number said I was the only pastor that church had ever had who really taught the Bible. They invited me to teach a home Bible class on Wednesday night in one of their homes. (Corinth had their midweek service on Thursday evening, and we, at least at first, attempted not to appear to "compete" with the older congregation.) We called our home Bible class "Maranatha Bible Class." "Maranatha" is a Greek word that occurs in 1 Corinthians 16:22; it was a greeting the early believers used to encourage one another. The term means "our Lord comes." Within a few weeks we began to hold Sunday services in different homes – we were beginning to think of ourselves as functioning as a new local church even though formal incorporation was still a few weeks away.

One Sunday afternoon, in late September before the weather turned too chilly, we held a baptismal service from the shoreline of the nearby Conasauga River. Those gathered on the river bank sang a song, and I gave an explanation of the significance of Scriptural baptism. Someone led the group in a prayer before I waded into the muddy river with Steve, Gwen Wood, and two other girls, one of which was named "Patricia." Each had given testimony that they had trusted Christ as Savior and that they wanted to obey Him in baptism. Steve, as the youngest, was the first of the four to be baptized. As I raised him up out of the water, from the sandy bank a few yards away an amazed four-year-old Dave called out loudly, "Steve, does that water taste good?" That solemn crowd burst into laughter while an embarrassed pastor's wife tried to shush her inquisitive little boy.

In mid-October the class voted to officially organize the Maranatha Baptist Church and drew up a church constitution and bylaws. On Wednesday night October 31, 1962, – I remember that somewhat strangely, it was Halloween Night! – we met in Paul and Marie Woods' home on Highway 225 near Calhoun, Georgia. Evangelist Milton Kerr delivered a Bible message to about 25 people. As I had done eight years earlier in an open-air shelter on the Rifle Range Road outside of Winter Haven, Florida, so here I read the proposed church constitution and bylaws and invited all who had accepted Jesus Christ as Savior and had obeyed the Lord in believer's baptism, and who wished to participate as members of this new church to step forward and sign the charter membership roll. The Maranatha Baptist Church of Calhoun, Georgia, was thus organized with 18 charter members. Ironically, it was the same number as had chartered the church in Florida!

My youngest brother Darrel, and his wife Millie, were among the charter members of Maranatha. Darrel led the congregational singing that night at that organizational meeting. I had performed their wedding ceremony about four months earlier. They were both attending Tennessee Temple College at that time.

Margaret Tally, one of our charter members, worked as a secretary for a lawyer in nearby Calhoun. She and the lawyer drew up the official papers for Maranatha Baptist Church to be recognized by the State of Georgia as a legal corporation.

I can recall at least some of the other charter members: Gilbert and Minnie Wood, Paul and Marie Wood, Mr. and Mrs. Claude Padgett, their son, Wayne, and three younger Padgett sisters.

We soon bought a parcel of land on Highway 225 near where a majority of the members lived. Gilbert and Minnie Wood contributed most of the $1,500 which we paid for the land. A building contractor, Brother Wood bought the material and paid his crew of carpenters out of his own pocket to build the church. The work began in November. A number of the men and women of the church helped as they could with the labor. In January of 1963, the church borrowed $6,500 against the building and reimbursed Gilbert for most of the material he had bought. I have for years praised God for that godly man because, without his many contributions in money, labor and material, Maranatha Baptist Church might not have been built.

On Sunday, February 20, 1963, we rejoiced in God's rich blessings as we dedicated our completed church building to the service of Christ and His Gospel.

Surprise! Another Move

In the fall of 1963 we needed to move out of the coal dust and sooty smog of the valley where Chattanooga lay. The suspended particulate in the local atmosphere had given us, especially Norma, pretty serious allergy problems. During the winter when one breathed the thick smog one could actually taste the coal soot. (Within a few years the situation greatly improved because the city government initiated measures to reduce the amount of smoke caused by the burning of coal.) After we modernized the kitchen we sold our Union Avenue house for $7,600. We used the equity for part of the down payment on a new house outside the valley just across the Georgia state line. This is how the Lord brought that purchase about.

One day while looking for a house outside the city we saw an expensive-looking house on State Line Road just across from East Ridge, Tennessee, about eight or nine miles from Tennessee Temple. At least, it was expensive in relation to our finances. It was a three-bedroom, brick house with hardwood floors and an inside garage, something that none of our previous houses had. It was an all-electric house in a good neighborhood with a level yard, nice shrubbery, and a green lawn in both the front and back yards. To me it looked totally out of our price range.

Norma pled with me to call about it nonetheless. I told her that there was *no way* we could afford that house, but she was "the queen," so I called the owner, Mr. Wells. He said the price was $13,900. I said, "I told you so." Norma, however, insisted that we go to see the house. With Mr. Wells we worked out a deal by which, after a minimal down payment, the monthly payments would be $90 for 30 years. Up to that point our largest mortgage payment had been $60 per month. How could we pay $90 every month, especially in light of the fact that Norma had quit her job at the business office at Temple when Joy was born. Norma promised to do child care in the new house to help make those high payments. You already know that we did indeed buy the house.

As a way to help with the new house payment my wife volunteered to start up a child care business in our home. For the next decade or so Norma cared for as many as 14 young children at a time. She loved those kids, and they loved her, many of whom called her "Mama Winget." One little lass named Melissa – everybody called her "Missy" – once said to her mother, "If you will take all my clothes to Mama Winget's, you would not have to take me and get me from her house every day."

By July of '64 Maranatha had grown to an average Sunday School attendance of between 40 and 50 people, and it became clear to me that the church needed a pastor that could minister daily in the community. Because we loved those folks dearly, the thought of leaving the church was something I struggled with for quite some time. Another development, however, settled the issue.

There developed an undercurrent of disagreement over music styles and some matters in the Maranatha church charter documents. The church constitution had a strict statement against the use of tobacco by anyone who served in any public ministry of the church including, teaching and musical ministry. In that many churches in the South do not take a position on this matter, this stipulation inevitably created some fairly heated discussion. Some of the members felt that this provision limited the church to an overly narrow position which effectively hindered the potential growth of the church in the community. Because of our deep affections for this dear congregation, and desiring to avoid being a long-term cause for contention, I tendered my resignation at Maranatha in late summer of that year.

Maranatha Baptist is now over 45 years old, and at this writing they are still supporting a number of missionaries including our two oldest sons who serve in central and eastern Europe.

Within the month of my resignation I was asked to accept the pastorate at another church, this time in Chattanooga, Foust Baptist Church.

Chapel Challenge

Foust Baptist Church was actually one of several scores of "chapels" or preaching points under the auspices of Highland Park Baptist Church scattered across the tri-state region (Tennessee, Alabama, and Georgia). Foust had been in operation for approximately ten years and was located about two miles from Tennessee

Temple's campus and the main auditorium of Highland Park. The previous pastor had been Ben Byrd, a teacher at Temple, who had resigned to accept another ministry opportunity in South Carolina.

A substantial list of folks associated with Tennessee Temple, many of whom had been in my classes, attended the chapel over the years, and this provided a wonderful opportunity for further teaching, this time in a local church setting under more informal conditions. While I'm certain that I will omit some names due to my poor memory (and I hope that those not mentioned will be gentle toward me), I want to list some of those dear folk:

Bill and Lalanne Barber, Johnny and Gina Barker, Scott and Denise Caroll, Larry and Connie Cloud, Bill and Pansey Combs, Curtis and Cathy Fitzgerald, John and Norma Greene, E.C. and Carolyn Haskell, Wayne Haston, Jim and Karen Hock, Mark and Janey Hollingsworth, Gary and Brenda Hunter, Mike and Jenny Jennings, Jerry and Bev Johnson, Ferrell and Barbara Kearney, Bob and Brenda Kinzel, Ken and Carol Korns, Mike and Carol Layne, Bob and Linda McCabe, Gerald and Marguerite Pauley, Bruce and Nancy Peters, Greg Peterson, Bill Poole, Jim and Diane Price, Ray Pritchard, Floyd and Diane Rinehart, Frank and Tamara Roe, Stephen and Sue Schrader, David St. John, Ray and Sandy St. John, Ken and Pat Thomas, Aaron and Denise Webb, Jack Whitley, Darrel and Millie Winget, Dave and Penny Winget, and Steve and Cheryl Winget.

Among this group of folks there were a score or more who earned master's degrees and at least 14 who pursued doctoral studies. Still more significantly, virtually all of them went on to vocational Christian ministry in pastoral work (at least 18), theological education and teaching ministries (at least 15), missions (at least 11), counseling (at least 5), and various other fields of Christian service. I look back on those years of ministry at Foust and the relationships nurtured there with great fondness.

German Squarebacks, Poodles' Presents, & Swimming Pools

*I*n the mid-60s – I think it was in the summer of 1965 – I asked a contact I knew in Germany to arrange a purchase of a blue Volkswagen "Squareback" from a German dealer and have it shipped to New Orleans. (The VW Squareback looked like a small station wagon.) The total cost of the purchase and shipping was less than buying from a dealer in the States. I flew to New Orleans to claim the car at the boat dock and drove it back to Chattanooga. You might think this a somewhat extreme means of saving some money, but this kind of frugality was a significant part of my upbringing.

A humorous situation transpired in connection with this car that I'd like to relate. Wymal and I were invited to speak in a Bible conference in Ocala, Florida, and we drove down from Chattanooga together in that blue Squareback. During our week in Ocala, he and I stayed in the pastor's home. The accommodations were very comfortable, but there was one little fly in the ointment: the pastor had a couple of pet poodles who were quite obviously very jealous of the attention their owners were paying to these two visitors. At breakfast on the second morning the dogs were causing such a nuisance that the pastor did not allow them to stay in the dining room. We continued eating and chatting for quite some time and ignored the two poodles. When we concluded our conversation I went to the bedroom and noticed on the bed what I first thought were some leaves that had blown in the open bedroom window. Upon closer inspection it became clear just how jealous the dogs were. The dark objects that I had first thought were "vegetable" in nature were, in fact, "animal." The poodles knew where those pesky intruders slept and had left each of us a fragrant "calling card" to let us know how they felt about us. Those dogs were at least as smart as Boyd Dickey's "Mick," but I had two witnesses to prove *my* story.

After one year I sold that VW for what I originally paid for it and immediately ordered another Squareback from Germany. This time our two-toned, black and white VW was delivered to Jacksonville, Florida. This second Squareback is memorable for another incident.

We were driving that second VW to Florida for Christmas holidays when we met with an accident on a rain-soaked road near Griffin, Georgia. Only one person was injured in that crash, my daughter, Joy. In the collision she was thrown against the back of the seat in front of her. We were afraid that she had sustained serious broken bones in her face, but the doctors at the emergency room concluded that she had only been severely bruised.

Our car was damaged too badly to continue the rest of the way to Florida, so our family made its way to the local VW dealer. From the dealer's show room I called my banker in Chattanooga, told him our situation, and asked how he could help. My banker told the dealer that any check I would write for a car would be honored by him personally. I therefore bought a third Squareback then and there. On our return trip through Griffin we picked up our crippled car and limped back to Chattanooga. We were able to sell it (at a substantial loss) and thus recovered some of the cost of the new car.

In 1968, when Steve was thirteen years old, he and a much bigger neighbor got into an argument while playing in our front yard. Steve climbed a stepladder that was leaning against the six-foot tall fence in an attempt to jump over it onto our back patio and escape his pursuer. As Steve got to the top of the ladder the boy grabbed Steve's foot. As a result Steve plummeted head first, landing on his outstretched right arm onto the concrete patio. Steve suffered a dreadful compound fracture of his right arm about halfway from his wrist to his elbow. The bones of his forearm stuck out through the skin, and the back of his hand lay against his elbow.

I came home from school just after the accident and saw Steve on his back on the concrete patio writhing in pain. Norma's motherly instincts came to the fore – she was so mad at the big boy that she slapped him and kicked him in the seat of his pants so hard that she broke her toe.

An ambulance took Steve to the hospital. He lay in bed in much pain for a week with his hand and arm in traction. Special doctors took exceptional measures to keep him from losing the use of his hand and arm. One specialist commented that he had never seen such a badly broken arm. There was considerable doubt as to whether Steve would be able to use the arm as before. We were amazed over the coming months to see how God completely repaired the bones and nerves of his arm – about the only significant results of the injury were that it forced Steve to use his left hand and arm while the right was healing. This increased dexterity greatly helped in his athletic endeavors in years to come.

Through the insurance settlement we netted about $500 – we decided to apply this money toward a small swimming pool. I knew how to build concrete block walls because of my work with Junior Hoover when we built the Rifle Range Church in 1954. It occurred to me that I could dig a hole and build a "box" out of concrete blocks inside the hole and fit a water-tight, vinyl liner inside the box. I asked a pool builder if he thought that my idea would be successful. He said, "I have never known of anyone building a pool in that way – we always use those vinyl liners inside a heavy wooden frame above the ground – but it may be worth a try." He agreed to sell me the materials I would need.

I measured the exact spot for the pool hole and marked it off with spray paint. One of Norma's brothers owned a backhoe, and he dug a hole exactly 12 feet by 24 feet by four feet deep. The finished hole had hard clay walls and bottom. In order to be sure that my first layer of blocks would be perfectly level, I ran water into the dry hole until the water was about two inches deep. I then drove metal stakes into the floor of the hole until the top of each stake was level with the surface of the water. When the water evaporated enough for me to start laying the blocks I began the work. Actually, the only tools I had were a couple of trowels, a level, and a hammer.

It took me almost three months, but the pool was finished in early May. The kids begged to go swimming immediately, but I told them we would wait until the day the weather was 80 degrees. About a week later on a Sunday in the middle of May when we came home from church it was 80 degrees. And we all celebrated in our very own pool.

Within a few days someone asked me to help him build a pool for his family. Later a man who was too busy to help with the labor paid me to do the whole job. You guessed it. My upbringing in the aftermath of the depression and our family's entrepreneurial spirit came to the surface yet again! For the next thirty years I augmented our family income by building pools. Almost every year I built at least one pool. A number of times during the '70s and '80s, I built from two to five pools each spring and summer and sometimes into early fall. Each succeeding attempt was a slight improvement over the previous one.

Except for the backhoe used to dig the hole and most of the block work, I did the majority of the labor. Norma, Steve, Dave, Phil (a son born in 1973) and Potsy helped occasionally. All through those years I continued to teach fulltime at Temple. Some years I earned almost as much by building pools as by teaching.

I suppose that one downside to my pool work may be that it might have contributed to a serious medical difficulty I later experienced. I developed a double hernia that had to be repaired by surgery. The surgeon had to make an incision almost all the way from one hip bone to the other. However, this surgery healed fast and caused me less difficulty than the appendectomy I had a few years earlier.

My wonderful wife also worked hard to augment our family income. We refurbished the indoor garage area in that house into a finished combination child care area and play room. Her child care business expanded to the point where she looked after as many as 14 children from a few weeks old to school age. She loved them and they loved "Momma Winget," too.

Surprise! Surprise! Yet Another Move

In 1968, we bought a building lot one block east of our house on Stateline Road. The new lot was on the corner of Stateline and South

Prigmore Roads. I believe we paid $3,000 for that building lot. We hired Norma's brothers, Buddy and Harry, who were building contractors by trade, to build us a larger house. We put a garage on the ground level as well as a room for Norma's "adopted" kids. The style was called a "tri-level," and it cost us – in addition to the lot – $21,000.

We sold the house at 5320 Stateline to Harry Hick's brother-in-law, Jack Silver. Jack agreed to pay us for our equity and take over the $90 monthly payments. He signed an agreement to pay back our $6,800 equity for an additional $40 per month at seven and a half percent interest. A few days later we were notified by the lawyer that the initial agreement was improper because under the stated terms the buyer would never be able to pay off the principle. An adjustment had to be made so that some of the principle was being reduced each month. I agreed to reduce the interest to 7 percent and Mr. Silver agreed to increase his payment to the collection firm from $40 to $45 per month.

That Mr. Silver had such a small amount invested in the house concerned me a good deal – he could have walked away at any time at very little loss. To lessen this possible temptation, I offered to pay $500 on the principle if he would as well. This he was glad to do. About a year later I offered him the same kind of deal again, and again he agreed. In the long-run we actually ended up with $5,800 equity. Even 40 years later Jack continued to thank me for the generous terms to which we had agreed so that he could buy the house.

Lost Balls & Long Distance Shooting

The new place, as I said, was situated at the corner of Stateline Road and South Prigmore Road. At that intersection Stateline Road stopped, though of course the state boundary line did not. Actually our driveway sat in line with Stateline Road, but it was not a part of the public right of way which ended at our property – the public thoroughfare took a ninety degree angle there. Steve was very interested in playing basketball so we built an outdoor court on our driveway. Since the boundary line between Tennessee and Georgia ran through the middle of the basketball court the free throw line was in Georgia and the basketball backboard was in Tennessee. I've heard sports commentators speak of someone taking a shot "from downtown" or "from the next county," but in this situation the boys often shot "from the next state!"

Our boys liked to play various athletics, especially if a ball was involved. This love of balls was the context for an argument that arose between them. Steve accused Dave of losing a favorite ball of his. Dave denied it. Steve insisted, "You *did* lose it. You were the last one to play with it, and you don't know where it is." Dave replied, "I did not lose it. I just dropped it in the grass and couldn't find it."

This house had a good-sized back yard that lay adjacent to a large open field of several dozens of acres. It was a wonderful place for the boys to roam and explore, but the summer after we built the house we felt the need to put up a fence around our property because we had built another pool beside the house. We were concerned about the liability an unfenced pool area might incur.

This second pool was bigger and better than our previous one. (One particular improvement was the fact that I had installed a 6-foot-tall, curved water slide next to the pool.) Our family, the bigger kids Norma watched over, as well as some of our friends swam in it often. Once, Wymal Porter even enjoyed a dip in the pool.

Do Rabbits Go to Heaven?

I remember an interesting story having to do with our daughter, Joy. I had built a couple of things in the backyard that she particularly enjoyed. One of these projects involved a "playhouse." It was a miniature cottage just the right size for her. I remember that we even covered the sides of the playhouse with some of the leftover siding that we had used on the "real" house and we even stained the playhouse the same color as the big house. The other project Joy appreciated was a rabbit pen for her two pet rabbits. Did she ever love those rabbits! Unfortunately, one night a couple of big dogs climbed the five-foot tall chain link fence and made short work of the defenseless rabbits. We heard the rabbits shrieking in terror but before we could come to the rescue the dogs had done what their natures demanded and scurried back over the fence. We were all sad about the rabbits, but especially Joy. Through her tears that night my seven-year-old, grief-stricken little girl asked, "Daddy, did my rabbits go to heaven?" After a brief pause I answered, "Darling, one thing we can be sure of; your rabbits certainly did not go to hell." This seemed to ease her sorrow, and she had no more questions about the destiny of her rabbits.

Though it may seem childish to some, Joy's question probably reflected a recent heightened spiritual sensitivity because she had recently accepted Christ as her Savior. This wonderful event occurred as a consequence of a children's lesson at Foust. I later had the marvelous privilege of baptizing my only daughter and new sister in Christ in the baptistery at Highland Park Baptist Church. At that time Foust did not have its own baptistery, but since Foust was so close to Highland Park, we would always use the main church's baptistery in the afternoon after the Highland Park's services had been dismissed.

Travels:
Across the Waters & Otherwise

*O*ne of my former students, Ferrell Kearney, attended Foust Chapel with his young wife, Barbara. After completing their studies at Temple, they joined Baptist International Missions, Inc. with a view to ministering as missionaries in Iceland. Our church assisted them by helping to purchase a ministry vehicle, a black VW "Beetle," to use on deputation. After completing their fund raising they took the car with them to Iceland. When the car that the church had helped purchase was paid off we had planned to continue to send them monthly support. Ferrell asked us to send that money to some other missionaries because they were adequately supported without it. It is a known fact that not all missionaries have had that kind of integrity.

Atlantic Waters

In August of 1970, Foust Church sent me to Iceland to visit the Kearney family and encourage them in the ministry. I recall that on my way to Iceland the Reykjavik airport was fogged in, and we had to fly to Luxembourg, Belgium. We spent the night there and flew back to Iceland the next day. My first trip to mainland Europe, including hotel room and two excellent meals, was at the expense of Icelandic Airlines. We returned to Iceland the next day without difficulty.

During my visit in Iceland Ferrell took me in that VW every day to interesting sites. When I was there the temperature was 50 degrees in the early morning and 55 degrees in the early afternoon all five days, but since I have such a tender head and am prone to headaches in even mild weather, I almost always wore my overcoat, hat, and ear muffs when we were outside.

In Iceland in 1970, beef steak cost more than a dollar a pound, but whale steak was only ten cents a pound. At least one time while I was there Mrs. Kearney served us both whale steak and beef steak. Contrary to what I had expected, whale steak was not fishy in texture. The texture and color of whale meat was close to that of beef steak, but rather strong in taste. We visited Whale Bay to see part of the process of bringing whale steak to market. It was quite interesting. (I, in my overcoat and earmuffs, watched bare-chested men skinning the whales. It was hot weather to them. They must have been amused at the crazy guy dressed for winter.) The workers stood on top of the whale carcass which was nearly as long as a basketball court. Their task was to skin the giant beast using sharp-bladed tools with broom-length handles. That whale must have produced hundreds and hundreds of pounds of whale steak.

I was amazed to learn that houses, stores, schools and so forth in Reykjavik, the capital, were all heated by natural hot water that was channeled from the hot springs in the mountains through huge pipes, some of which may have been 36 inches in diameter. This volcanically heated water was then circulated through radiators in the different buildings. It was also used to heat the local swimming pools which Ferrell, his two young sons, Dennis and Lee, and I enjoyed while I was there.

Pacific Waters

In May of 1971, Norma and I made a trip to visit missionaries in the Hawaiian chain. This was the trip that I mentioned earlier as having been financed primarily by Brother and Mrs. Birkhead, our good friends from Grace Baptist Church in Dallas.

On our flight to Hilo, Hawaii, a lady sitting next to us was quite agitated and expressed her fear of flying. She gladly listened to my testimony as to why I was not afraid if the plane should crash. I told her that, should our plane meet with misfortune, I was sure of heaven. The lady received Christ as her Savior, and I even had a good deal of time on that flight to give her a crash course in Bible doctrine. As we landed in Hilo she said to me, "Thank you, for telling me about the Lord. You have made my day." I'll mention this lady again a bit later.

We first visited a missionary working on the island of Maui. It was the local custom to remove one's shoes before entering a home or church. On the front porch outside the church were scores of shoes lined up along the wall and doorway. That marked the only time in my life that I preached with no shoes on my feet.

We also were privileged to visit my youngest brother and his wife, Darrel and Millie, who were missionaries on the island of Molokai. I can still remember taking a drive up to the top of one of the highest mountains on the island. From that vantage point we could see a historic leper colony on the coast below. Potsy and Millie remained on Molokai from 1969 until 1973.

As an interesting sidebar I need to relate to you that our son, David, so very much wanted to go see his uncle and aunt on Molokai that he decided to make enough money to take his own trip to Molokai by collecting old cola bottles and turning them in for the deposit at the local grocer. He did indeed collect a good number of thrown away bottles from the brush along the roads near our house, but he also collected a rather severe case of poison ivy.

Chili & Peppers

On the return leg of our trip we also visited another missionary for whom Foust had purchased a car: another BIMI missionary, and another Volkswagen, and another brother. My brother and his wife, Earl and Rachel, lived in El Paso, Texas, and did their missionary ministry across the border into northern Mexico. We were there to observe their work among the poor of Juarez, Mexico. Earl took us to the small house in which they held Gospel services, and we visited in the homes of some of the people.

I can recall a particular couple with four small children who lived in a tiny one-room hovel made of scrap plywood, cardboard and rusty sheets of tin. The dirt floor was covered with scraps of dirty carpet and cardboard, and the family slept on the floor. I remember looking carefully at the size of that lean-to that was only a bit larger than our bathroom back in Georgia. I tried to figure out how six people could find space enough to lie down without lying on top of one another.

They had to fill gallon jugs with water at a public faucet and carry the jugs about 200 yards up a long dusty hill to their shack. Earl told me that if the family stayed there for a certain number of years on that plot of ground, they would be given a deed to the land. The man had placed rocks the size of baseballs on the border around his 75 by 75 foot prospective homestead. He happily anticipated that within a few more years he would become the owner of that piece of real estate.

Earl resigned from BIMI after a few years, but he continued for a time to do some missionary work among the Mexicans across the Rio Grande River in northern Mexico under the auspices of the First Baptist Church of El Paso.

BMA & Crippled Glee for God's Glory

In August of 1971, I was invited by the president of Bible Memory Association, Dr. Woychuk, to once again teach an adult Bible class at the BMA Camp near Albany, New York. He had invited me twice before to teach at other BMA camps: once at the camp near Cleveland, Georgia, and once near Shelby, Michigan. We rented a motor home to take our family to New York and to live in at the Bible camp.

BMA offered a free week of camp for any who would complete a prescribed course of Bible memorization during a given period in the previous year. The morning schedule at the camp included two, 45-minute classes for all those attending the camp. Each youth camper was required to be present at a class assigned according to age to study the passages that had been recited earlier in the year. The adult campers attended a class on a particular book of the Bible.

In my class in New York there was a gentleman afflicted with cerebral palsy who was always in his place at class time. This crippled fellow, his shriveled limbs confined to a wheelchair, didn't weigh more than 110 pounds, and he had to depend on someone to push him up the slight hill to the shelter where we had our Bible class each morning. One morning we chatted before class. He was a bit difficult to understand because his condition would not allow him to speak without terrible tremors, but his spirit was strong and his love for the Lord clear to all who knew him. He spoke in his slow, halting manner: "Bro-ther Win-get,... Why... do... you... think... God... al-lows... peo-ple... to... be... like... me?" I called him by name, and I said, "I don't know, but it may be that God allows people to be like you to cause people like me who have all our faculties and have good health to thank Him for those gifts." I'll never forget that dear fellow's joyous reaction. With a massive grin spreading across his contorted face, he began clapping his withered hands. "That's... what... I've... been... a... think-ing...!" he exulted. He seemed truly glad that in some way, more glory would accrue to God because of his condition.

After the week of camp our family took a short tour in the motor home through New York and Canada. I remember that we saw a lot of gorgeous early fall foliage and the magnificent splendor of Niagara Falls.

Minor Heroics

Our first son, Steve, graduated from high school in the spring of 1973. He had been voted "most valuable player" of his soccer team and "most outstanding athlete" at Tennessee Temple Academy. He had also claimed All Dixie Conference and all-state honors in soccer.

There was an interesting high school basketball game in which Steve and his good friend, Steve Faulkner, Dr. Faulkner's fifth son, participated. It was in the fall of 1971.

It was the first year that Temple Academy had been in existence, and they were having a hard time competing with the public high schools around them. The newspaper headline read: "Winget pulls impossible feat, to lead Temple to a 53-52 win." I'll quote the article:

Steve Winget scored two foul shots in the closing moments Friday night to lead underdog Tennessee Temple High to a close 53-52 victory over Sale Creek capping an almost incredible comeback in the last 12 seconds. Sale Creek had a five point lead with but a dozen seconds on the clock and had possession of the ball. But little Winget stole the show and the ball game.

He first stole a pass and hit a driving layup to cut the deficit to three points. Teammate Steve Faulkner stole the inbounds pass and fed to Winget, cutting the Panther's lead to only one point. And luck was again on Temple's side. As they recovered a loose ball, but, guess who, Winget was fouled in the scramble. The talented player missed, however, on the first of a one-and-one situation, but grabbed the rebound and again was fouled. This time, however, he made good on two free throw shots and gave Temple the victory, their first of the year...

Top Crop

Two years later Steve found himself a freshman in college. As with most first year college students he took "Fundamentals of Public Communication" with an assignment of giving a "Demonstration Speech." In such a speech the student is expected to demonstrate some skill they had learned and explain the process to the class.

When it came time for Steve to stand before the class he introduced his talk rather cleverly. He went to the front of the class with a large brown paper bag in hand. He faced the class with a somewhat sober expression and began, "Several months ago my mother had to go to the doctor. During her examination the physician discovered an abnormal growth in her abdomen. Over the course of the next several months the growth got increasingly larger, until, just a few weeks ago, she had to go to the hospital to have it removed." Reaching into the paper sack Steve withdrew a doll and said, "It turns out that when they removed the growth they named it 'Phillip

Mark Winget,' and today I'm going to demonstrate how to diaper a baby."

That Norma was 43 at the time of Phillip's birth (August 17, 1973) caused us some concern about his health and the possibility of Down Syndrome or other genetic abnormalities. We prayed and trusted God, and He responded by giving Phillip the best health of any of our children at birth. We have thanked God many times for such an answer to prayer. Not only did he not have even a fever as a little tyke, he has seldom been sick through the years.

My daddy had a peculiar term he used for a couple who had an unexpected birth later in their marriage. He called such a child "top crop" referencing the final crop to be harvested in a particular year, and with Phillip the Lord surprised our family with just such a "top crop."

One of my favorite preachers, Dr. Fred Brown, had his own way of speaking of our situation: he once quipped from the pulpit, while looking somewhat slyly in our direction, that certain Temple faculty members reminded him of Abraham and Sarah. In a similar vein, one of our older children requested prayer for his mother in his Bible class at Temple Academy. It was reported that he had commented, probably jokingly, that his mom was "too old for that sort of thing."

Dr. Faulkner, vice president of Tennessee Temple, later commented that if mothers would take care of themselves they could "remain fruitful" for many years. His wife was well into her 40s when her youngest child was born.

I'll say a good deal more about Phil a bit later. Oh, by the way, I think Steve got an "A" for the speech.

Demon Oppression

The Foust church sent me on a missionary visit to the Virgin Islands in the West Indies in June of 1973. Norma was unable to accompany me on that trip because it was only two months before Phil was born. I had the honor of preaching at Bluewater Bible College that had been established by Dr. Ray Thompson after he and his wife, Jean, as newlyweds went there as missionaries in 1956. Ray and I were members of the same graduation class at Temple in

1954. Bluewater Bible College was so named because it was located on a high precipice overlooking a harbor of amazingly blue water and the gorgeous capital city of Charlotte Amalie. Probably no college in the world has a more spectacular view than does that college. At least five former students of mine served at the school in faculty or administrative roles: Dennis Bellew, Heath Charles, Les Warren, Ken Guth, and Calvert Dixon.

During my time there with the Thompsons I enjoyed the opportunity to preach in a Bible conference at Calvary Baptist Church, a strong active church established by Dr. Thompson some time before the inception of the school. In addition to these opportunities Dr. Thompson also invited me to speak on their weekly radio program while I was visiting with them.

One of the more remarkable things I recall about the Thompsons was that, in their home over a period of four years, they served as parents to a total of six girls from the islands. The girls ranged in age from three to fourteen years. At least one of the girls, the oldest, was plagued by demonic oppression during those days, and only through the Spirit of God and the message of the Gospel was she relieved from the tyranny of darkness and torment and translated into the kingdom of light. This young girl later became a very effective Bible teacher.

For nearly 50 years the school has educated several hundreds of dedicated West Indians for the proclamation of the gospel of Christ.

For more than a decade Dr. Thompson, with the loyal support of his godly wife, has had an effective ministry as vice president of Baptist International Missions with headquarters in Chattanooga, Tennessee. He has been called upon by leaders around the world to speak at missions conferences in promotion of missionary ministries.

My maternal grandparents, George & Bama Jones, with their children (L-R)
Harvey, Henry, Raymond, & Vera Mae (c. 1917, probably near Dothan, AL).

My dad & mom, Robert Ward & Vera Mae, on the porch of our house on
Rifle Range Road in Winter Haven, FL (c. 1946). On the R is my Whizzer
motorized bike that I rode to Summerlin Institute. The house later burned
along with many of our family's photos and documents.

My original birth certificate

Program for my high school graduation ceremonies

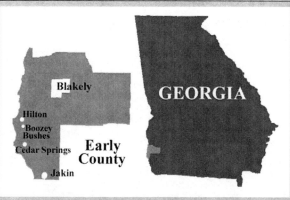

Early County in SE Georgia where my family called "home" in my younger years

My school pictures from grades 4, 9, & 10.

Earliest known photo of the 4 Winget kids (L-R: Bobbie, Darrel, Earl, me; c. Dec, 1939, in Boozey Bushes, GA). I think the car might be Uncle Clarence's '36 Ford. The children are playing with the famous red wagon.

Mom & Dad, Robert Ward & Vera Mae Winget

A Florida boy enjoying his first snow at college

**Easter, 1952, shortly
before our wedding**

**It was Memorial Day, May 30, 1952,
and what a memory it was!**

**Norma, carrying our first child, standing in front of the open shelter
where Rifle Range Baptist held its first services in the fall of '54**

**Dallas Theological Seminary Class of 1960
I'm on the front row 2nd from the right.**

Receiving my Th.M. degree from Dr. John Walvoord

A family tradition -- not sure who got the bigger thrill, a proud poppa or the little ones -- L-R (top to bottom) Steve, David, Joy, Phil

Maranatha Baptist Church Building Dedication - February, 1963

Our 25th wedding anniversary at Foust Baptist - May 1977

It's a long way from Boozey Bushes to the Alps & barrios of northern Mexico...

to the pyramids of Egypt & the Sea of Galilee...

to teaching in the Caribbean, & fishing with missionaries in Alaska...

to snorkling in Hawaii, to sightseeing in Budapest.

(L-R) Our oldest son, Steve, his wife, Cheryl, their son, Joel,
and daughter, Karis, and her husband, Joe

Our second son, David, and his wife, Penny (middle), with their sons,
Nathanael, and wife, Bethany (left), and Andy, and wife, Kara (right)

Our third child, Joy, and her husband, John Smotherman, with
their sons, Josh (back) & Zac (right), and daughter Brianna

Our youngest, Phil with his wife, Amy, and their children (L-R)
Josh, Daniel, Wilson, & Mia

Some of the friends that have touched my life: (L-R) Wymal Porter, Norma, me, Oswald Summers, Evelyn Porter, Barbara Summers, Sophie & John Economidis

Boyd Dickey  Doug Griffin

Bruce Lackey  J. B. Buffington

My Queen & I

Our Golden Anniversary

Various family members at Norma's home-going (L-R) "Buck" &
Bobbie, Barbara & "Lucky" Snipes, Darrel, Millie, Tammy, and
Earl Winget

Our offspring at their mother's home-going (L-R) Phil, Joy,
David, Steve, and me -- this was surely a joyous occasion
because of the hope we have in Christ!

Footsteps of Christ (& Moses & Paul)

Ancient Sights & Restless Nights

*I*n August of 1974, several Temple teachers, along with about thirty others, took a trip to Europe, Egypt, Jordan, Israel, Lebanon and Greece. The teachers included John and Sophie Economidis, Mr. and Mrs. Henley, Bruce Lackey, Wymal Porter and me. From New York we flew first to Amsterdam, then to Cairo, Egypt. There we saw the pyramids up close, and had our pictures taken sitting astride camels with the pyramids in the background. We went to the Cairo Museum to see centuries-old mummies and many other historical relics. Next we went to Amman, Jordan where we spent two nights. Dr. Porter and I were roommates on this leg of our tour. The first of the two nights his snoring was so vigorous and resonant that I could not sleep. In order to get some rest, I took my mattress into the bathroom and shut the door. When he woke up he wondered if I had been taken in the rapture or kidnapped by Arabian bandits. But he knew if I had been raptured he would not even *be* there wondering what had happened to me.

While staying in Amman we took a bus out into the Jordanian wilderness. Finally the bus came to a halt, and after disembarking, we mounted horses and rode down narrow trails between high rock walls. By and by we exited the narrow passageway for our first glimpse of the ancient city of Petra. Intricately carved out of the reddish-brown, sheer cliffs, this mysterious and foreboding looking place is surrounded by mountains and has only one narrow passageway into the city. Because of this some Bible scholars believe Petra is the place being described in Revelation 12:6 and 14 where God will protect a remnant of Jews from the Antichrist during the Tribulation (after the Rapture of the Church and before Christ's Second Coming to the earth to establish the Millennial Kingdom).

The second night in Jordan Dr. Porter's snoring was just as energetic as before. Because the bathroom was too small for my mattress to lie flat I took it outside on the balcony to sleep. During the night Wymal woke up and saw that my mattress and I were not in the room again. When he checked the bathroom I was not there. Could it be that someone had actually taken me? But why take the mattress also? Soon he saw me on the balcony. As dawn broke the bleating of the sheep, goats and calves in the pasture behind our hotel proved to be as effective as Wymal's snoring at encouraging wakefulness. Sleep in Amman proved in short supply.

The following day, after a very careful security check of all our luggage, we crossed the Jordan River into Israel. It was exciting to walk on some of the same sites where our Lord Jesus had walked 1900 years before. To look over Jerusalem from the Mount of Olives and to stroll through the olive garden where Jesus had often prayed was a unique thrill.

It was a most awesome feeling to walk into, and out of, the empty tomb from which our victorious Lord arose from the dead, just as He said He would. We also visited the well where it is believed that Jesus met the woman of Samaria and gave her the living water of eternal life. It was this account from John 4 that had caused Dr. Weigle to write his famous chorus many years earlier:

Jesus gave her water that was not in the well.
Jesus gave her water and sent her forth to tell.
She went away singing and came back bringing
Others for the water that was not in the well.

On August 17, 1974, we crossed the Sea of Galilee near where Jesus walked on the water in the midst of a storm, according to Matthew 14 and Mark 6. North of Galilee we saw some of the ruins of the city of Capernaum where Jesus delivered Peter's mother-in-law from her fever, cast out demons, and healed many others.

Ladies Whose Hearts the Lord Opened

We rode a bus to Beirut, Lebanon and flew from there to Athens, Greece. I sat beside a lady on the way to Athens who spoke English. She was a Roman Catholic who lived on the island of Malta ("Malita" in the King James Bible at Acts 28:1). The lady knew that we were a Christian group returning from the Holy Land and she was quick to tell me that the Apostle Paul in the Bible was once shipwrecked on her island. I told her that the Apostle Paul was one of my favorite Bible characters because he majored on telling people how to go to heaven. I asked, "Should our plane not make it to Athens are you sure that you would go to heaven." She responded, "I hope so, because I am faithful to mass, and I do believe in God."

"May I read for you what the Apostle Paul wrote in the Bible about this," I asked. She answered, "Yes, please do." I opened my New Testament and explained the key verses in Romans about how she could be sure of heaven if our plane were to crash. I showed her Romans 3:23 ("For all have sinned and come short of the glory of God,") and that sin is what's wrong with us, the reason that people can't just automatically go to heaven when they die. Then I read Romans 3:19 that states that all the world is "guilty before God." I explained that "guilty" means "obligated to pay a penalty." At Romans 6:23 we noted that this penalty is death.

We looked at Romans 5:8 which tells us that although we are sinners Jesus Christ died for us. It means that Jesus died in our place. Finally, I turned the lady's attention to Romans 6:23 and 10:9 where God promises that all who by faith accept Jesus' death as the payment for their sins will be saved and have eternal life instead of eternal death. I believe the Spirit of God enabled that lady to understand God's offer of salvation. She accepted Christ as her Savior and received assurance that if the plane should crash she would go to heaven. She gave me her address, and later I sent her one of Dr. Rice's Gospel booklets entitled *What Must I Do to Be Saved*. She responded to my letter by writing: "Your words to me on the plane to

Athens and the words in this little book make my heart glad because I have been taught that I must do good deeds and be faithful to my church to gain eternal life. But now I know my salvation depends on the truth that Jesus' death paid for all my sins." I expect to see that dear lady in heaven someday and renew our conversation begun on that plane to Athens, Greece, way back in August of 1974.

After we returned from that trip two of my students went to the Tennessee Temple administration and complained about me. They said, "Professor Winget is a Calvinist and he believes in election. He does not really believe 'whosoever will,' nor does he believe in soul-winning." When that accusation was aired one of my colleagues who had been on the trip to the Middle East with us, Dr. Bruce Lackey, stood up in my defense. He declared, "On our trip to the Holy Land the only person in our group to lead anyone to Christ was Brother Winget. On the plane from Lebanon to Greece he led a lady to the Lord." The whole issue was dropped for it was obvious to everyone that I *did* believe in sharing the Gospel with others. Years later at Dr. Lackey's funeral I remarked to his son, David, that I would always be so very grateful for his father's valiant rally to my defense.

Luke wrote in Acts chapter 16 about the Apostle Paul leading a lady to Christ in Philippi. Luke describes the lady as the one, "whose heart the Lord opened." This text reminds me of the two ladies to whom I had the privilege of sharing the Good News on airplane flights – first, the lady on the trip to Hawaii and also the lady on the trip to Greece. Seeing how gladly they accepted my witness about Christ it was clear that the Lord had opened their hearts.

Both Ends of the Line

The experience of those two ladies on the plane flights in '71 and '74, on opposite sides of the world, reminds me of a sermon I heard fifty years ago. It was a radio message by the late Sam Morris, the famous temperance crusader. The title of the sermon was "God Works at Both Ends of the Line." At one end of the line in Acts eight was the evangelist Phillip and on the other end of the line was the Ethiopian eunuch.

After a very successful evangelistic campaign in Samaria, where Phillip had witnessed the salvation of many people, God sent an angel to him to command him to go south to the desert road toward Gaza. Phillip may have thought this command foolish, but he obeyed. On the way he encountered an Ethiopian eunuch of great authority, according to Acts 8:27. This official was in his chariot and was reading Isaiah chapter 53. God, working on the eunuch's "end of the line," had used that Scripture to prepare him for Phillip's witness about Christ and the Gospel. God sovereignly arranged that one who needed the Gospel should encounter one who knew the Gospel. He arranged the circumstances to bring them together, and He gets all the glory for the eunuch's salvation.

A similar sovereign superintendence was demonstrated in Acts chapter ten. God sent an angel to a Gentile named Cornelius in Caesarea – the angel told Cornelius to send for Peter. While Cornelius' servants were en route to Joppa to the house where Peter was, God was teaching Peter, a Jew who had extremely prejudicial opinions toward non-Jews, that the Gospel was for the Gentiles as well as the Jews. When the men from Cornelius arrived the Holy Spirit told Peter to go with them. On one end of the line was Cornelius in Caesarea. On the other end of the line was Peter in Joppa. God arranged the circumstances to bring these two together and therefore He gets all the glory for Himself for the salvation of another sinner.

Just so, in 1974, God arranged for me to visit the Holy Land and to be assigned to a certain seat on the plane to Athens, Greece. God caused a lady of Malta who needed the Gospel to be assigned a seat on her flight to Athens beside this fellow who knew the Gospel. God moved her to tell me that her island of Malta was famous for the historical fact that the Apostle Paul was once shipwrecked on her island. Her mention of Paul presented a tailor-made opening for me to tell her what Paul said about how to go to heaven. Thus God arranged the circumstances and gets all the glory for her salvation. God likewise arranged the details of the flight to Hilo, Hawaii, and likewise deserves all the accolades for the conversion that occurred there.

I'm grateful to God that there were many other times in my life where He arranged the circumstances and used me as a part of His plan. In Ephesians 3:8 Paul wrote, "Unto me who am less than the least of all saints is this grace given, that I should preach among the Gentiles the unsearchable riches of Christ." Paul's words move me to say gratefully, "To me who am a good-for-nothing is this grace given that I should be granted even a smallest part in God's eternal program."

At 2 Timothy 1:8-9 Paul wrote to his young son in the faith, "Be not thou therefore ashamed of the testimony of our Lord, nor of me, his prisoner." He went on to say, "Timothy, God who saved us and called us with a holy calling, not according to our works, but according to His own purpose and grace which was given us in Christ Jesus before the world began."

I might paraphrase his thought: "Timothy, God did not just decide yesterday or last week to use you and me in His great plan. He did that before the foundation of the world. It was according to His own purpose and grace, which was given us in Christ before the world began." Paul emphasized that it was purely by God's grace, God's unmerited favor, that God would use him to proclaim the Good News of salvation to Gentiles. It is little wonder that Paul is called both "the apostle of grace" and "the apostle to the Gentiles." What's more, the Holy Spirit memorialized Paul's ministry to the Gentiles by also using him to pen a major portion of the New Testament – at least thirteen of the twenty-seven books of the New Testament were written by this God-called man.

The Gospel, of course, is totally of God's planning and provision. He sovereignly arranged the divine calculus of the Incarnation, according to Galatians 4:4-5: "But when the fullness of the time was come, God sent forth His Son made of a woman made under the law, to redeem those who were under the law." His calculations also engineered His Son's death for we read in Acts 2:23 that Christ was "delivered [to crucifixion] by the determinate counsel and foreknowledge of God." Peter's message in the next verse also speaks of the Father having "raised Him from the dead." In other words, Peter gives God the credit for planning the death and resurrection of his Son.

God also arranges the circumstances by which He brings sinners into contact with the Gospel. He gets all the glory when he gives individual sinners the wherewithal to accept salvation by faith. "For by grace are you saved through faith, and that not of yourselves. It's a gift of God, not of works, lest any man should boast," proclaimed Paul (Eph. 2:8-9).

Fishing for Fish, Too

In 1976, the congregation at Foust sent me to Alaska to visit missionary Don Stokes, one of the missionaries supported by the church. The August temperatures there were exactly the same as the August temperatures were when I visited missionaries in Iceland in 1970.

One of the most intriguing parts of my Alaskan visit was the fishing trip Brother Stokes, his son, and I took one day. So successful were our angling efforts that on several occasions all three of us were reeling in a big salmon *at the same time*.

We threw back most of the fish we caught because there was a state-mandated limit. I think our limit was seven, so we just kept the best ones. The fish were swimming upstream so thickly that you would throw in your hook and snag a fish in his back or side. Many times we caught big, beautiful salmon with a hook lodged in their fin on their back or in their tail. In fact, most of the fish we landed showed evidence of having been hooked before.

All This Travel Makes
a Fellow Want to... Move?

*B*y the mid-70s much had been done to improve the atmospheric pollution that had driven us out of Chattanooga to the suburbs a decade earlier. I had a busy Seminary schedule and we had three children enrolled in classes of various levels of the school, so we felt that it would be much more convenient to move back closer to the campus. In September of 1974, soon after my return from the Holy Land, I bought a building lot from Elgin Smith at 1806 Chamberlain Avenue within one block of the school.

Elgin, a Christian realtor we had known for many years, agreed to obtain a city building permit and to build a house for us for cost plus ten percent, but there was still the matter of selling our house in Georgia. The first couple to look at our Prigmore house offered to pay us for our equity and assume the monthly payments. Furthermore, they allowed us to continue to live there for three months, rent free, after which we were to pay $100 per week rent.

We thanked God many times for the good weather He sent so that it took only one week beyond the three-month period for us to complete the house on Chamberlain and move in. By doing much of the labor ourselves, including the digging of the foundation, painting, wall-papering, and so forth, we kept the cost down. Our brick layer allowed me to pay him in part by tutoring him in biblical Greek. Our new, two-story, five-bedroom house was completed before Christmas.

You might not be surprised to find out that I bui
ming pool for the house the next summer.

What Would We Do Without Our Government to Take Us?

The house had something very special and very rare in the Highland Park section of Chattanooga in those days, and that was central heat and air conditioning. Mr. Smith arranged for a low interest government loan because we were building in an older, deprived area of the city. Because the national economy was bad at that time and bank interest rates were very high, there was very little building being done. The government building inspectors had few building projects to inspect. Therefore they inspected and reported often on ours.

We were not cleared to move into the house until everything was finished, including the lawn and the shrubbery outside. Even after we moved in two leading government inspectors sat in our living room discussing whether anything had been overlooked in their final inspection. They did not recall if they had seen the government stamp on the timbers in the attic that supported the roof.

One of them climbed a stepladder into the attic and, with a flashlight, saw that the government stamp was neither on the ceiling joists nor the rafters. They phoned Mr. Smith because he was the building contractor and informed him that he must obtain an official letter from the lumber company that had furnished the lumber verifying that the lumber was all new and first grade lumber. It took only three days to have the letter from the lumber company sent to the inspectors.

The inspectors then told Mr. Smith that they could not accept the word of the lumber company because they knew that sometimes officials would lie about the quality of their lumber. Mr. Smith was informed that the only way for us to get an acceptable final inspection that would permit the Wingets to occupy the house would be to have a lumber expert to climb into the attic and to check the beams to see if they contained less than 10 percent knots. The inspector who checked the lumber in the attic said that he could not sign a less-than-10-percent guarantee for the timbers in the attic.

Then the inspectors said the only way to strengthen the supporting beams in the attic to make it safe for occupancy would be to add extra two-by-sixes and two-by-fours according to written instructions they would supply. Elgin wanted to know, whether the extra lumber was required to have the government stamp. The answer was "No"; for bracing it would be okay if it was just new lumber.

With great difficulty I carefully put the dozen or more beams into the attic through the opening in the ceiling of the hallway. I took great care to avoid causing any damage to the freshly-painted walls in the hall. Before the carpenter came the next day to nail up those new reinforcement beams, the inspectors phoned Elgin and said "Mr. Smith, we are sorry, but the new bracing beams must have the government stamp." Do I need to tell you that I was more than a little aggravated to tediously put that beautifully stamped lumber into the attic? Nonetheless, I was able to remove the unstamped timbers without scratching the finished walls in the hallway, and then replace them with the government-approved lumber.

During these days when it seems our government is making every effort to regulate more and more of our lives, I sometimes have an occasion to narrate this episode. I often make the sarcastic observation that I probably should have been *glad* to go to the extra trouble because that stamp on that lumber obviously made the lumber stronger and my family more safe.

Yeah… sure. I've got a hot lead on a bridge in Arizona that's for sale, too.

Burglar Proof but Not Prankster Proof

To make the house burglar proof I had iron bars cemented into the downstairs brick walls in all the windows. Steve's and Dave's bedrooms were on the ground floor and thus their bedroom windows were also a part of my attempts to protect from break-ins. I found out some years later that Dave was more afraid of fire than he was of burglars, so he secretly sawed through a couple of the iron bars in the window in his bedroom so that he could easily remove them in case of fire. David's measures at making his room "safe" from my safety precautions reminds me of a related incident.

You have to understand that I have always been a very light sleeper. Nearly any unusual noise around the house at night awakens me. Anytime one of our teenagers came in late from an "away game" with one of their athletic teams the opening and closing of the downstairs door would inevitably wake me up.

We found out, sometime after the fact, that David had his reasons for wanting to leave the house during the night, but my tendency to awaken at the slightest noise presented a challenge. David employed his secret "escape route" through his window so that he could leave the house and rendezvous with his cohorts on campus to pull off an April Fool's prank. That night they rappelled down from the tower roof of the Phillip's chapel and put a Mickey Mouse face and hands on the chapel clock! I have to admit that it was one of the more humorous pranks in Temple history.

The next year on April Fool's Day Dave and his cronies unlocked the back double doors to the administration building and rolled a compact car into the lobby right in front of Dr. Roberson and Dr. Faulkner's offices. They took the wheels off of the car so that vehicle could not be so easily removed. Unfortunately – or perhaps in hindsight, fortunately – David had a reputation as the campus trickster, and the administration of the school knew exactly who to call to begin their investigation as to who the culprits might be.

Integrity Inventory

Our payments on the house were about $200 per month, including the city property tax. At more than twice as much as we had paid a decade earlier on the State Line Road house, it was quite a stretch on our family budget. Amazingly, some eighteen months after we closed on the house the finance company notified me that our house payment had been reduced by $50 per month. That was a huge surprise and something which neither I nor any of my friends had ever encountered. Within a few days I figured out the explanation for the $50 reduction. A serious error had been made at the city tax office

– they were billing the finance company for my lot as if it were still vacant, but the city tax officials were unaware of their error. I could have kept quiet and pocketed the extra $50 per month. On second thought, I could have put the extra $50 in a savings account and earned interest until such time as the tax people discovered their error. I could then pay the back tax. I reasoned, however, that this would be earning interest on money that really didn't belong to me. What to do? My integrity was at stake, and so I called the tax office and they immediately saw their error. I was commended for my honesty, but I didn't keep the money – they still charged me the $50 per month. I am confident, however, that the Divine Appraiser of Rewards made due annotations on my record.

"Shug, I Love You" & "It Don't Depend on Good Deeds!"

Tennessee Temple held its annual Bible conference early each April. During the conference of 1977, I received word from Winter Haven that Dad had suffered a heart attack, and for the first time in his life found himself in the hospital. I flew to Tampa, Florida, and Buck and Bobbie picked me up there for the two-hour drive east back over to the hospital.

During the next couple of days I had several opportunities to talk with Dad. I took that time to review with him many Bible verses regarding salvation, its basis in Christ's cross work, and faith, the means by which God applies the benefits of Jesus' sacrifice to us. Dad made a clear statement to me that he was trusting Christ, and Christ alone, as his Savior. Within a few days he seemed to be much improved, and I flew back to Chattanooga. He was dismissed to go home after only a couple of weeks.

A couple of days after he was released I was eating breakfast at the college dining hall when I was summoned to the dining hall office for a phone call. I immediately recognized the caller as my mother. "David," she said calmly, "Your daddy died in bed just a few minutes ago." She went on to explain that he had suddenly rolled over in bed toward her, put his arm over her, and said, "Shug," – that was his pet name for Mom – "I love you," and then passed away just as suddenly. They had been married for 47 years, and I had never known him to be very demonstrative of his affections. His final gesture was a wonderful farewell gift for my mother.

Pastor Dale Simpson, who had been Dad's pastor at Rifle Range Church since my resignation to go to Dallas Seminary in 1956, allowed me to deliver the main message at Dad's funeral service on the third day of May in 1977.

During my sermon at the funeral I related an interchange that had occurred some 20 years earlier. It was one of the most comforting of memories I had of my father. The incident involved an episode in which I was seeking to explain the Gospel of grace to Uncle Dick. Uncle Dick was adamantly declaring a lengthy recitation of his good deeds, when Dad, who overheard his brother's self-justifying pretext, blurted out, "David, tell Dick it don't depend on his good deeds!" My dad's exclamation was most assuring that he understood this cardinal issue related to his own relationship to Christ. In the context in which it took place, it was a clear indication of my father's affirmation of the point that I was trying to clarify for Uncle Dick, that one's salvation is directly the result of simple faith in what Christ had done and had nothing to do with what any mere human had done. Dad's interjection was extremely reassuring that he understood and had affirmed the Gospel, and I have every confidence of seeing him again someday.

Let Me Show You My Grandchildren's Pictures...

*W*e've all encountered the proud grandparent who just happened to have "a few" recent photos of their adorable grandchildren that they must show you along with an exhaustive explanation of the provenance and complete narrative of each picture. For the next half hour you are held captive as you listen to excruciating details of their grandchildren's exploits. Well, we didn't have any grandchildren yet in our story, but we did have some children that I want to crow about just a little.

In 1975, Dave was captain of his high school soccer team and was named to the all-district team. He led his team to a perfect season, 11 wins and no losses, and they also won the district championship.

The same year Joy, as a freshman at the academy, was chosen as a varsity cheerleader and home-coming princess. She also received several music and speech awards. The next couple of years she had a job which curtailed a lot of her extra-curricular activities, but in her senior year she was elected as one of the class officers and again made the cheerleading squad.

While we lived on Chamberlain, Dave, won a leading role in an on-campus production of Gilbert and Sullivan's musical, "The Pirates of Penzance." The production was directed by Mrs. Joy Martin, conductor of the Concert Choir at Tennessee Temple. He practiced many nights until well after midnight, and I sometimes complained to him about his late hours. All that preparation paid off, and David gave a super performance as the *Pirate King*. After

I attended the performance and saw what an excellent job Dave did in singing and acting, I apologized to him for complaining about his many nights practicing so late.

Steve was a four-year starter on the Temple College soccer team and also the captain in 1976 when the Crusaders took the NCCAA District V championship. That same year Steve was a unanimous choice for the National Christian College Athletic Association First Team Soccer All-American Team – the first All-American in any sport that Tennessee Temple ever produced.

One game that year stands out in my mind. It was against their cross-town rival, Covenant College. The match was on Temple's field on a Saturday afternoon, but that morning Steve and the goalkeeper on his team had gone out witnessing to people and telling of their faith in Christ. Early in the game a foul was called against Temple, and Covenant was awarded a penalty kick. I thought to myself that if Temple falls behind this early in the match against a team as strong as Covenant it will be almost impossible to come back to win. The Temple goalie, John Meyer, guessed correctly which way the kick would probably go and saved the penalty kick, knocking the ball way out into the field of play. On a quick counter attack Steve received a beautiful pass just outside the opponents' penalty area and sent a hard left-footed shot into the upper left corner of the Covenant net. Temple fans let out what may well have been the loudest cheer in the history of Temple soccer. That goal proved to be the only tally of the game, and Temple earned a hard-fought 1-0 victory. I believe God honored the two Temple guys on that team who had honored Him in their ministry earlier that Saturday morning.

It reminds me of how God honored those Hebrew fellows who honored Him in the face of a furnace of fire in Daniel chapter three. Those fellows didn't bow, and they didn't budge, and God saw to it that they didn't burn.

In 1978, Steve finished his Master of Divinity seminary degree and was awarded the Lehman Strauss Expository Preaching Award. In the fall of '79 he was invited to join the college Bible faculty and became a favorite Bible teacher. One year a particularly large number of students were enrolled for a course on Bible Doctrines, so many in fact that four sections of the course were offered. Steve taught one of the sections. Sixty-seven students chose to be in his section. Less than 30 students signed up for any one of the other sections. I know because I saw the computer printout of all of the four rosters and I actually counted the numbers.

Someone once bragged on Steve's teaching to me and I commented, "Well, I taught him all of his theology in seminary." Their immediate rejoinder was, "I see, but I guess he got over it."

Steve met Cheryl McCowan at Temple in '78 and they were married in June of 1979, in her home church, Burge Terrace Baptist, up in Indianapolis, Indiana. They themselves planned their own wedding service – it was unique and quite beautiful. At a certain point in the ceremony Steve surprised Cheryl with a special song. I think it was entitled "My Love Is Like a Red, Red Rose." Some few years later when Cheryl earned her master's degree in education from Temple's graduate school, I had the privilege of teaching her in one of her courses. I might add that she did well.

Dave met his wife, Penny Brim, when she came to Tennessee Temple. Interestingly Penny was from Cheryl's home church, and consequently, a second son of ours said his wedding vows at Burge Terrace in June of 1983.

I'll save a recitation of the weddings and exploits of our other two children until a bit later in this account.

The Fly

*A*s was the case with all our children, our lastborn child was a real joy to Norma and me. He was always abuzz with activity of one kind or another, first here then there, hither and yon, and he was dubbed "The Fly" by his brothers. The name stuck for several years. I recall a number of anecdotes about him, some humorous and some not so humorous.

The Meaning of "Behave" & Other Words

One evening at supper in the Chamberlain house when Phillip was two or three years old he was misbehaving at the table. I looked at him and told him, "Son, *behave*," but he shortly was acting up again. With a still more stern tone I inquired, "Are you going to *behave*?" He shook his head and replied, "No." It seemed that he was being belligerent. I took him from his high chair and spanked him on his bottom a couple of times and warned him, "You must obey Daddy." When he was back in his high chair I asked again, "Now are you going to *behave*?" He began to weep and cry, saying, "No, no, Daddy." It suddenly dawned on us that he misunderstood my term "behave." He thought that when I asked if he was going to "behave" that I was asking if he was going to "disobey." He therefore was answering in the negative – he meant, "No, Daddy, I won't disobey." I scooped him up and hugged him and explained that to behave meant to "be good" or to "be obedient."

This little episode was very uncomfortable for Phil, but it was a no less painful reminder to me that father's must be very careful to communicate clearly to their children and take special precautions that their instructions are understood. I have also used that incident to illustrate for my students who were prospective preachers and teachers that they must carefully explain the meaning of words. We must not assume that listeners attach the same meaning to words as we do.

For instance, Romans 5:8 says, "Christ died for us." The final phrase, "for us" is often misunderstood by many people. They often understand it to mean "as an example to us" or "to teach us something" or "to show us something," as in the sentence the teacher acted out the meaning of the word for us." "The teacher acted out the meaning as an example to us, to teach us something, to show us something." Rather, Paul's language requires us to interpret his phrase "for us" to mean "in our place" or "in our stead" or "as our substitute." Paul was teaching that Jesus died "instead of us, as our substitute, in our place." While His death does demonstrate and teach and show us things, that's not what the Apostle's terminology in the last of the verse means, and if we are going to be faithful teachers we must explain what *his* words *mean*.

Jesus paid our debt of death, the penalty for our sins, in order that we may be delivered from the obligation to pay that penalty. Christ died in our stead in order that we may be justified; that is, that we may be declared righteous by a holy God.

I was once talking to a star athlete and regular church-attendee about this verse. I asked him, "Al, do you know what this verse means when it says, 'Christ died *for us*'?" He said, "Sure, it means He died for you, for me, for everybody." "OK, you're exactly right," I replied. "The word 'us' does mean 'everybody.'" But I pressed further, "What does the word '*for*' mean?" He said to me, "That He died *for* us means that Christ died *to teach us to stand up for what is right* even if we get killed in the process." In essence this young man was suggesting that "for us" meant that Christ died as our example, to teach us, to motivate us to live godly lives. That is definitely *not* what the Greek word that Paul used means.

Salvation

When Phillip was in the first or second grade his teacher had urged all the kids who had accepted Christ as their Savior to obey the Lord in baptism. The Lord used this to spark a spiritual recognition of his need.

One morning as I lay asleep in our bedroom at the Chamberlain house – I think it was about 2:00 a.m. – Phillip crept into our room and awakened me. It was evident that he was quite troubled. He said, "Daddy, I'm afraid I'm going to hell because I haven't been baptized."

I immediately took him in the living room and sat in an upholstered chair with him in my lap. I carefully explained the simple story of God's way of salvation. I emphasized that God's way of salvation doesn't require baptism or any other religious activity we might do. After about thirty or forty-five minutes he, in his pajamas, accepted Christ and came to the assurance of salvation based on the fact that Christ's death paid for all his sins. He was able to go back to bed and fall asleep, his anxieties fully relieved.

Perfect Memory

Later during the second grade there was a special elementary school chapel program on the subject of Christian character. A portion of the presentation involved six students, all of which had a one-word description of Christian character printed in large letters on a large sheet of poster board. The first student marched out on stage with the word "courteous." Then the second student came on stage carrying a sign with the word "kind." A third word, "honest," was displayed. The fourth word was "sincere," and the fifth word was "truthful." Finally the sixth student appeared highlighting the descriptor "trustworthy."

The six students marched off the stage one at a time and the principal then asked if anyone could repeat the six words they had just seen. Phillip raised his hand and repeated all six words. It was not the first, and certainly not the last, that Phillip's mental faculties have surprised us.

Flags, Fibs, & Fainting

One day when The Fly was in third grade we were notified that he had fainted at school. They suggested that we have a doctor to check him. They, and we, were concerned that his fainting spell could be evidence of an epileptic seizure. The doctor checked him over, kept him in the hospital for a day, and ran all kinds of tests but found nothing wrong.

As we questioned him more closely we came to understand the problem was probably not of a physiological nature. Phillip said that the class had been studying early American Presidents. When the discussion turned to James Madison, mention was made of Dolly Madison. Phil had raised his hand and asked to tell something he had read.

"I read a story about Dolly Madison," he began. He proceeded to relate that it seems that Dolly was more popular than her husband, the President. He explained that in the War of 1812, a U.S. ship had defeated a British ship and captured the British flag. In a special celebration ceremony the captured British flag was first presented to Dolly Madison and she then gave it to the President.

For some reason the story sounded implausible to his teacher. She told Phillip that she did not believe he was telling the truth, that he was just making up his story. He insisted that he had indeed read it in a book. (Sometime later we were able to verify Phil's story about Dolly Madison – we found a narrative that recounted the incident just as Phil had related it to the class.) Nonetheless, the teacher instructed him that he would stay after school, standing at her desk, until he declared that he had lied to the class. Under the anxiety and tension of the moment and not willing to acknowledge a lie that he felt he had not committed – and perhaps because he locked his knees – Phil fainted. Fortunately, he regained consciousness again after only a few moments, and the teacher relented.

My having misjudged Phil's responses to my instructions to "behave," and this teacher's misjudging the veracity of Phil's story are good illustrations of how adults can so easily misjudge children, either by assuming too much or too little.

Missionary Ridge

*A*fter we moved to Chamberlain Avenue, Norma quit her child care business, but she worked a few years for the Chattanooga school system as a teacher's assistant. For most of this period she was assigned to work at Brainerd High School with students with various physical challenges. Norma enjoyed this work very much.

For various reasons we decided in 1979, on yet another move, this time up on the slopes of Missionary Ridge about three miles from campus. I bought a steep lot with a beautiful view overlooking Chattanooga. With a chainsaw, pruning shears, and a sling blade I labored several weeks during that fall and winter clearing trees and brush preparing the lot for excavation in the spring of 1980.

We had come to enjoy having a private pool at our other houses very much. The steep slope of our new lot required that, if we were to have a pool on this property, it either had to be below our house in the front yard, or I would have to build it in the backyard above the house. If we built the house first, none of the heavy equipment necessary to build the pool could get up behind the house where the pool was to be built –there was some doubt as to whether the heavy equipment could in fact get to the site at all. Therefore, strange as it may sound, we built the new pool before we built the house.

Of all the pools I built – from 1968 through 1997 I constructed over 50 – this one was the most difficult of all. For this pool I was forced to hire four different men with heavy machinery: a bulldozer leveled the pool site and pushed the dirt down the slope, a backhoe excavated the hole, and a front-end loader put the dirt on a large dump truck that hauled it away.

The concrete blocks for the pool walls, as well as all the other tools and most of the supplies, were carried by hand well over 100 feet up the steep incline.

We ordered ready mixed concrete for the patio around the pool. The first truck driver to arrive – I remember that he was a rather large gentleman that surely must have weighed over 250 pounds – refused to try to back up the hill, saying it was too dangerous, and simply drove away.

A second driver was dispatched and, upon arrival – I recall that he seemed to be not much over half the previous man's size – surveyed the precipitous incline and said, "I'll give 'er a try." However, his first attempt to navigate that multi-ton beast of a truck backward up the hill was unsuccessful, and so was the second effort. On the third try, his engine revved wide open and his dual exhaust pipes furiously belching black smoke, he bounced, and spun, and slowly crept his way up to within reach of the worksite. From there we were finally able to offload the concrete and maneuver the heavy slush into the proper forms for the patio.

The pool, with diving board, slide, and ladder was completed in April of 1980. With considerable difficulty I put up a chain link fence with a gate around the pool so that we could secure the area. Many of our friends kidded us by saying that they had known of people to build a house without a pool, but had never before known of anyone to build a pool without a house. Over the course of the next several years it provided much enjoyment, not only to our immediate family, but to many of Phil & Joy's friends, and various others as well.

With the pool completed we set to work clearing the lower slope between the pool and the street and preparing the building site for the construction of a three-story house. Over the course of the next number of months we labored diligently and were able to move into our new yellow and red brick abode at 2934 Westside Drive.

Shortly after the house was completed I invited Dr. James Price, a fellow faculty member and Hebrew professor at Tennessee Temple, to be our special speaker at Foust Chapel. After the morning service we asked the Prices as well as all the congregation to join us for a celebration meal and special prayer of thanksgiving and dedication at our new house.

Until the new dwelling was completed, we continued to live in, and make monthly payments on, the Chamberlain house. But now it was time to divest ourselves of that financial obligation. My temperament had always favored a quick sale over a more lucrative, but more protracted, sale. (I had learned this lesson trying to sell a certain car. My newspaper advertisement for the car set the price at $1,500. A man showed me twelve one hundred dollar bills and offered them for the car. I refused his offer. I kept paying for newspaper ads for two more weeks. Finally, after the extra expense and frustration, I sold it for – you guessed it – $1,200!) In order to liquidate our liability in the Chamberlain house rapidly I advertised the house for $10,000 below appraised value. The first couple to look at it, bought it.

There were many good things about the house on the side of Missionary Ridge. It was easily the roomiest house we ever owned, it had gorgeous dogwood trees that bloomed beautifully, and we enjoyed cooler temperatures in the summer. However, being at a higher elevation and shielded from the afternoon sun made for colder temps on winter evenings.

A few times our long, steep driveway was covered with snow or ice. One evening when freezing weather was forecast I parked my car on the edge of the street at the bottom of the driveway. When I started for school the next morning I, with briefcase in hand, tried to creep slowly down the icy driveway to my car. Suddenly, my feet shot out from under me, and I skidded on my back about 100 feet all the way down to my car. It would have been just about impossible to make it back up to the house to change clothes, so I attended breakfast and taught my classes that morning in a soiled suit and with skinned knuckles.

A Wedding at Home

The most significant event that happened at the three-story house at West Side Drive was the marriage of our daughter, Joy

Lynn, to John Lee Smotherman on August 16, 1986. Her plan had been to have a garden wedding in our backyard between our house and the swimming pool. The plan was for the bride, groom, and the minister (me), to assemble for the ceremony under the flowering, vine-covered arbor near the foot of the walkway leading down from the pool. The steeply sloping hillside would form a beautiful green backdrop to the proceedings. We rented dozens of chairs which were arranged on the patio on each side of the arbor. John's dad, Tom, set up a camera on a tripod to film the proceedings. Special musicians and singers were to perform from the balcony overlooking the scene below.

The August weather had been dry; there had been no rain for at least a month, and we were quite concerned that the grass would be scorched and brown. We took great pains to water the shrubbery and lawn so that it would be pretty for the big event. The ceremony was to take place at 5:00 p.m., but you can guess what happened. Around 3:30 it began to rain, and didn't stop until well after the ceremony. Tom ran to cover the movie camera on the tripod in hopes that the rain would stop in time for the much anticipated event, but the rain continued.

To our surprise most of the invited guests came anyway. We moved the festivities into the foyer and front mirrored stairway of our house. The guests were pretty cramped, but it was a lovely ceremony nonetheless. More than 70 people looked on from the den through the double doors on my right and through the double doors from the living room on my left and also from the stairway landing above.

A couple sang a duet entitled "I Will Love You Till the End of Time," and Joy and John sang to each other. Though John's song came off well, he stumbled slightly when giving his vows. His defense was that although he had sung in public before, he had never had any experience at repeating marriage vows.

In spite of the rain and the missteps in the repetition of vows, they have enjoyed God's blessings together for almost 25 years, and we granted them permission to raise three of our most beautiful, healthy, intelligent grandchildren.

Foust Farewell &
the Union Gospel Mission

$\mathcal{I}$n 1985, Dr. J. Don Jennings became president of Tennessee Temple University and Seminary. At the time that he took on those responsibilities a goodly number of the faculty also served in various churches in the area as pastors and in other leadership roles. For decades the fact that so many of the faculty were personally involved in various practical ministries and not sequestered away in an academic "ivory tower" was viewed as a major strength. In spite of the fact that he himself was both pastor of Highland Park and president of the university, Jennings, however, was of the opinion that we teachers could be more effective in the classroom if we did not have the responsibility of leading a church at the same time. He instituted a ruling that teachers were no longer allowed to pastor churches. Therefore in mid-November of 1985, I ended twenty-one years of ministry at Foust Chapel by tendering my resignation to the church.

Among the blessings of that pastorate was the joy of observing my two oldest sons mature in Christian ministry. For several months prior to their marriage in '79, Steve and Cheryl did a wonderful job directing the music there at Foust. Steve taught the main auditorium Sunday School class, and it is my opinion that the main reason some people attended Foust was to hear Steve teach God's Word in the Sunday School hour. He supplied the pulpit a number of times when I was away. Through those opportunities at Foust he gained valuable experience in the exposition of Bible truth.

In the same way, David was afforded valuable experience in leading cooperate worship and the study of the Scriptures at Foust, especially in the summers of 1980-82, when his older brother and sister-in-law were away traveling across the country representing Tennessee Temple Schools. David also developed a great capacity to stand before people and give exposition of the Word.

Both Steve and David later employed that early training in local church ministry as foreign missionaries.

During the early years at Foust I scheduled a special four-day Bible conference once a year, Sunday through Wednesday. The conference speaker spoke twice in the morning and twice in the evening on Sunday and once each evening, Monday through Wednesday. Because of their work schedules and other obstacles, many of our people were forced to miss the Monday through Wednesday messages. That meant they missed three of the seven messages during the conference. In order for more people to profit from more messages delivered by our special expositors, I began to schedule quarterly, one-day conferences. Sixteen messages by four gifted men during the year proved to be much better than only seven messages a year by one gifted teacher. My good friend, Wymal Porter, spoke some 75 times during my 21 years there.

After my 21-year ministry at Foust came to a close in 1985, I began a nine-year ministry with Dr. Porter at the Union Gospel Mission in downtown Chattanooga. We took turns preaching or leading singing every Wednesday night. We would often have the opportunity to speak one-on-one with some of the men who were helped by the mission. At times such as this I simply opened my Bible or pocket New Testament and showed the gentleman to whom I was speaking the familiar "Romans Road." I would point out from Romans 3:23 that all have sinned. I would emphasize from Romans 6:23 that the penalty for sin is death. I would point to Romans 5:8 which tells us that Christ died in our place and paid our penalty of death for us. With great care and slow and emphatic tones, I would put my finger on the text of Romans 10:9, and I would read, "If thou shalt confess with thy mouth the Lord Jesus, and shall believe in thine heart that God has raised him from the dead, thou shalt be saved."

"Confess whom?" I would ask. "Confess *the Lord Jesus*," I would reiterate. I would clarify that "confess" is from two Greek words that mean literally to "say the same," or "agree with" God about the Lord Jesus as to who Jesus is and why he died, and that God raised him from the dead to prove that God accepted Christ's death as the full payment for our sins. When a sinner prays from his heart and sincerely agrees with God concerning his own sins and God's son, God promises that that sinner *shall* be saved.

I would then call them by name and ask them, "Now, Joe, if you really want to accept God's offer to save you, just bow your head and pray something like this: 'Dear God, I admit I'm a sinner and I believe that Jesus died in my place to pay for my sins. And right now, I accept Him as my Savior. I thank you for saving me. In Jesus' name, amen.'"

I would conclude by pointing again to the phrase "shall be saved," and I would say, "Now Joe, remember, this is not Dave Winget's promise, but it is God who cannot lie, who promises that when you trust Jesus and His death as your ticket to heaven, 'you shall be saved.' Joe, I just now heard you say to God that you are accepting his Son as your Savior. Tell me, Joe, on the basis of God's Word are you now saved?"

I have had those to whom God had granted the gift of faith in his Word to look me in the face and say, "Yes, I am." Often I would tell them, "If God really wants us to go to heaven He would provide a way, and He'd tell us how to apply that remedy of Christ's death personally to our lives by faith. This topic is too serious for Him to be joking about it. If He's not telling us the truth, there's nowhere else for us to turn. We are shut up to faith, to just believe and accept and bank on God's promises given in his Holy inspired Word."

Double Duplex & Double Departure

*I*n 1983, I bought a very steep lot at the highest point of Missionary Ridge just off Main Street. It was even steeper than the lot on Westside Drive and at least as heavily wooded, but the property was on sale for just a few hundred dollars. The lot had a beautiful view overlooking Chattanooga, and I had planned to develop it as rental property. As time went by it became clear that it would have been too expensive to build there, so I abandoned that plan.

In 1985, I purchased a level lot on which to build a duplex. The plot of ground was at the foot of the Ridge on 28th Avenue within a few blocks of our house. I traded the other (steep) lot to a private contractor as partial payment for his help in the more technical aspects of the construction of the new duplex on 28th Avenue; however, I still did a lot of the construction work myself. I dug the footing by hand, poured the concrete, and laid the foundation blocks and the white bricks on the front. Norma, our kids, and I did a lot of the finishing work, such as wall papering and painting.

In February of 1986, for the same amount of rent they had been paying for a much smaller apartment, Steve and Cheryl moved into one side of the new duplex. A few months later Joy and John moved into the other side of the double apartment after they were married. As a wedding gift we allowed them to live there rent free for ten months. (They wisely saved the money they would have paid on rent and later used it as part of a down payment on a house.)

Adjacent to the duplex where Steve and Cheryl and Joy and John lived, I purchased a second lot and erected another duplex with a much better floor plan. Because they liked the floor plan of the second duplex better, John and Joy moved into one side of it when it was finished. It was great to have our first and third offspring and their mates living only a few blocks away from us.

Left for Another Fellow

As to our second offspring and his wife, an interesting incident occurred not long after the first duplex had been built. Tommy Crider, one of my students and pastor of Maranatha Baptist (the church we had planted years earlier near Calhoun, Georgia) invited me to preach in some special services. When I arrived at the church that particular Sunday morning in July, several asked me, "Why isn't Norma with you." My answer was, "I'll tell you in a few minutes."

After the pastor welcomed me to the pulpit I said, "Some of you have wanted to know why my wife is not with me. Okay. I'll tell you. Two days ago she left me to go to see a fellow in Indiana." I paused for a moment while many who had known us for many years sat breathless with astonishment. I continued: "She called me last night and told me that guy was sitting on her lap at that very moment." I paused again and added, "I did not mind at all to hear this. In fact, I was glad that she was enjoying her time with our first grandchild, Nathaniel Winget, the firstborn of our son David Earl and his wife, Penny." My explanation, though having caused general shock at first, at last was met with smiles of relief and great rejoicing.

Three More Arrivals

Steve and Cheryl followed suit and thrilled us with the arrival of their firstborn in January, 1987. They named our first granddaughter, Karis. To make matters even better the following year, David and Penny added Andrew to the tribe in February, and Joel, our fourth grandchild in less than two years, was born to Steve and Cheryl in June.

In October of 1988, Steve's family was able to buy their first house – it was an older, ranch-style abode northeast of town on Paw Trail in Chattanooga.

Two Departures

Both Dave and Penny were graduates of TTU and had been teaching for a couple of years at a Christian high school in Anderson, Indiana. Since they were considering foreign missions aviation as a life ministry, David joined the Navy to learn aeronautical mechanics. In God's providence the Navy assigned him to a job of working on jet aircraft ejection seats, an area not easily applicable to missionary aviation. Therefore after his seven years in the Navy he and Penny joined the Association of Baptists for World Evangelism in 1994, and were commissioned to plant churches in Eastern Europe.

Before their departure for Europe it had been my joy to preach David's ordination sermon at the First Baptist Church in Pikeville, Tennessee, and to observe their commission to foreign mission service. After raising their financial support they transplanted their family to Kharkov, Ukraine, about 30 miles from the Russian border. Within a few years they had organized the Lighthouse ("Mayak" – pronounced "my-AHK") Baptist Church in that city of about 2 million people.

Back in 1991, Steve and Cheryl had publicly surrendered to God's call to missionary service at a missions conference at Grace Baptist Church. For the previous five years or so they had been very active in the ministry of that church. They attended the ABWE candidate school in 1992, and were accepted for service in Hungary. By late winter of 1993-94, they raised their financial support for missionary service, and were preparing to fly to central Europe.

Steve had requested ordination to the Gospel ministry by Grace Baptist earlier that spring. His detailed written doctrinal statement was submitted beforehand and his oral questioning began at 9:00 the Saturday morning before the formal laying on of hands service was scheduled to be held the following evening. The pastor, Dr. Steve Euler, called the ordaining counsel to order. He told the dozen or so invited pastors and Christian leaders that the questioning of a candidate's doctrinal qualifications could easily take several hours, but on this occasion the proceedings needed to be completed at 12:00 noon. That would allow three hours.

As it turned out, the questions and discussion continued until 12:30. Steve was sent out of the room for the council to vote on recommending him to the church for ordination. One of those present was Dr. Ron Bishop. He spoke up: "I have participated in many ordination councils and have never heard a candidate for the Gospel ministry set forth a more thorough defense of his Biblical convictions than this young man has done this morning." Of course I was glad to hear that recommendation, not only because I was his dad, but because I had been Steve's theology professor in seminary. The council voted to present him to the church for ordination the following Sunday, and at that service I was privileged to offer one of the dedicatory prayers.

Steve and Cheryl, along with Karis, age 7, and Joel age 5 and a half, left by plane for Budapest, Hungary to begin their missionary service in late April of '94. Some three years later David and Penny and their escorts, Nate and Andy, were winging their way to the wide rolling plains of eastern Ukraine.

It had been a bittersweet decade. It had begun back in the mid-80s with the births of the first of nine grandchildren and ended in the mid-90s with the departure of four of those beloved little ones along with their parents in tow to destinations of service to the Lord halfway around the world. Don't be mistaken though; our tears were tears of joy and gratitude for what God was doing in our family. We had already begun to experience some rather remarkable compensations in the form of grandchildren – physical as well as spiritual – that the Lord would grant us. I'll show you those snapshots a bit later, but first I need to back up in the story a bit.

Just When We Were Getting Settled...

By the close of the 1980's Norma and I were both approaching our 60's, the many stairs in our three-story house were beginning to become a bit toilsome, and the nest was almost empty – only Phil remained at home, and his high school graduation was on the horizon. We no longer needed as much room as our house provided.

In 1989, Mr. Horton retired from Tennessee Temple security and put his house up for sale. It was a one-level house about four blocks up the road from us at 3030 Westside Drive. The house was plenty large enough, and what remodeling was needed could be completed while we waited for a buyer for our house.

Mr. Horton agreed to wait for full payment on the house until we could sell ours if we would agree to make his monthly payments until our house sold. After several months the three-story house finally sold, and we made the move up the street.

As you might by now expect, the next year we set about building a pool at the "new" house. It would turn out to be the fifth and final pool we built for our kids and grandkids over the course of 25 years, but it was the first to have steps and a ladder as well as a waterfall. Water circulated continually from the pool to the top of a rocky waterfall about 18 feet up the bank and back into the pool. One of the most enjoyable aspects of this pool was that it had a constant depth of four feet – it was great for playing water volleyball!

May I Brag Just a Little?

Like his two older brothers, Phil had become an outstanding high school athlete. He excelled at soccer, but he shone brightest on the basketball court. In his sophomore year his team qualified to compete in the national Christian high school tournament in Watertown, Wisconsin. Norma and Joy and a vanload of ladies went to Wisconsin to support the team, and although I went to almost all home games and numerous away games, my heavy teaching load at the seminary kept me from going to the tournament with them. Temple lost in the quarter-finals to an Ohio team coached by a man named Kevin Templeton.

The following year that opposing coach came south to work at Temple Academy. We were pleased that he did; he was a good coach who motivated his players in high spiritual principles. [Note: Kevin happened to have been a former student of mine. He turned out not only to be an excellent coach and mentor of young men, but an exceptional preacher of the Word, as well. I like to think that I may have influenced his preaching to some degree, but I'm quite certain that his successes in coaching owe nothing to my input.]

During Phil's junior year his mother and I saw him play in a basketball tournament on Lookout Mountain. Just prior to one of the games he stumbled into a bench in the dressing room and broke his toe, but still led all scorers for the game. Norma later remarked to the coach that he might consider breaking one of Phillip's toes before every game.

Phil was chosen as team captain for his senior year. I purchased a video camera and recorded many of the games. Allow me to describe some of them.

One game I filmed was at South Pittsburgh. Phillip sank 35 points in a big victory for Temple Academy. That effort received an impressive write up in the *Chattanooga News-Free Press*. One of my prized keepsakes is a copy of that article.

In a losing effort at cross town rival Boyd-Buchanan's gymnasium Phil led the individual scoring for both teams with 27 points.

Phil was voted Most Valuable Player by the coaches at a tournament in Jasper, Tennessee, totaling 52 points in the two-game tournament.

On another occasion Phil's team was slated to play archrival Chattanooga Christian. The week before the game Phil came down with the flu and was unable to practice at all. In his weakened condition Phil was unable to start, but came off the bench and played well. The newspaper article stated: "With 45 seconds elapsed in the ultimate stanza, Temple guard, Phil Winget, who was virtually unstoppable in a 25 point performance, launched a 25-footer to finally knot the game at 42." Alas, the opponents had their own excellent shooters, one of which sank another 25 footer with only two seconds on the clock. Those three points ultimately provided the winning margin.

Regarding another game I have a clipping whose headline read, "Temple Shocks City Behind Phil Winget's 24." The article continued:

> For Tennessee Temple this was two years in the making. In just the second season of its TSSAA berth, Temple is fast becoming one of the teams to beat in District IV-A, a fact that was underscored in a big way Tuesday night as the Crusaders picked up their biggest win since rejoining the TSSAA, and perhaps the biggest win in the school's history, with an 81-77 upset of defending regular season district champions and currently number 10 in the state.

I recorded another game, a meeting between Temple and another rival, Lookout Valley, in a Christmas tournament. It remains one of Phil's favorite memories. With less than 10 seconds remaining in the game Phil intercepted a pass intended for the opponent's leading scorer and raced down court. Fouled in the act of shooting he calmly went to the free throw line and sank both tosses to win the game.

Phillip had little interest in attending college. Instead he garnered a full-time job as a rookie salesman at Wolf Camera Store. He learned the camera business so quickly that his boss told Norma that within one month Phil knew more about cameras than some of his other salespeople had learned in six months.

After working in one of the Wolf chain's Chattanooga stores for about three years the organization called him to join their sales staff in one of their largest outlets down in Birmingham, Alabama in the summer of '94. At the end of '95 he sent this note to his mom and me: "You should be proud to know that tonight I was named '1995 Wolf Sales Associate of the Year.' My district includes Atlanta, Birmingham, Huntsville, Memphis, Louisiana and Mississippi. There are 96 salespersons in our district...[The] district manager told me privately that he expected me to be the first salesman in his district to lead the entire company of 300 stores in the nation in gross profits next year." This was at a time, I might add, when Phil was barely 22 years old.

In 1996, Phil became the manager of that Wolf Camera store with oversight at that time of nine employees. Under his leadership the store grew within four years to 32 employees and was earning several millions of dollars each year for the company.

In 2000, Wolf sold the company to a competitor. Salaries were cut drastically, and so many new rules were brought to bear that Phillip left the business in 2001.

You may take exception to my bragging on my boy, my last born child, but after all, that's what fathers are supposed to do when there's something to tell.

Another Farewell

In 1990, my sister, Bobbie, and her husband, Buck, brought my mother from Florida to visit us at the "Horton House" at 3030 Westside Drive. At the time Mom had moved out of her small house where she was living alone and had taken up a new abode living with Buck and Bobbie in a nice little apartment they had added onto the back of their house.

Buck and Bobbie had a mobile home they kept on a scenic lot they owned up in the mountains of North Carolina. They left mom to stay with us while they went up to their vacation getaway in the hills. After several days Norma took mom to North Carolina, and after a few more days Mom and the Snipes returned to Florida. It proved to be Mom's last visit to our home.

The next summer Mom suffered a major stroke while taking her morning walk. I got "the call" from Bobbie shortly thereafter. Mom had fallen in the street in front of my sister's home in Eagle Lake and had hit her head on the pavement. The blow caused massive damage, and by the time she reached the hospital she was already in critical condition. Surgery to relieve the pressure on her cranium was performed, but shortly thereafter she slipped into a deep coma and never regained consciousness. In obedience to her instructions in her living will the doctors shut down all life support systems, but my mother's body was still strong enough to hold out until after we arrived at the hospital. Several of our family and her pastor stood by her bed for her last two or three hours. We sang hymns and quoted Scripture passages while we watched Mom breathe her last breath and leave her frail body to go to be with Jesus.

At that point someone quoted a Scripture that the Apostle Paul wrote in 2 Corinthians 5:6-8: "So we are always confident, knowing that while we are at home in the body we are absent from the Lord. For we walk by faith, not by sight. We are confident, yes, well pleased rather to be absent from the body and to be present with the Lord." Because of the grace of Calvary our sorrow was "not like the sorrow of others which have no hope," according to 1 Thessalonians 4:13. Actually, we sensed a subjective peace that was the result of the objective "cessation of hostilities" purchased by the Warrior-Savior's violent death spoken of at Colossians 1:20, the peace provided by Christ when He "made peace by the blood of His cross." We enjoyed the "peace of God" (Phil 4:7) because we had "peace with God," (Rom. 5:1).

A calm came over me at that moment as I recalled that mom had accepted Jesus as her personal Savior back in 1947. It was during the same week of Gospel preaching when God secured my own salvation. On August 17, we celebrated mom's home going in the chapel of Glen Abbey Memorial Gardens near Auburndale, Florida.

At the service my brother Darrel sang a song written by Dr. Charles Weigle about God's amazing grace entitled "O, What Glory."

It was an amazing display of that grace and a credit to His glory that God enabled "Potsy" to sing so well at his mother's funeral.

It was my privilege to deliver the funeral sermon. The Scripture I chose for my message was Psalm 116:15, "Precious in the sight of the Lord is the death of His saints." I explained that according to the Bible all who have a saving relationship with God by grace through faith is a saint. The idea that a saint is one who has been canonized by the church is not biblical. The Greek word for "saint" means "a set apart one;" that is, one that is set apart from the world and the rest of humanity to the service of God. Every saved person – that is, every truly born again person that has believed in Jesus Christ and has based his assurance of salvation and eternal life on the substitutionary death and resurrection of Jesus Christ – is a saint.

Mom's body was laid to rest beside my dad (in the gravesite I had sold to them back in 1956). This was only a few weeks shy of what would have been Mom's 78th birthday. We didn't have any way of knowing then that this detail would later appear to be a peculiar precursor to something that loomed almost two decades into the future.

Forty Years & Counting

$\mathcal{M}$ay 30, 1992, marked our 40th wedding anniversary. We had a special time of celebration in the backyard of the "Horton" house. This is how it all came about.

Mona Skidmore, our seminary office secretary, and her husband, Jim, helped me arrange a surprise party for Norma. I had planned a ruse to the effect that Norma and I were supposedly going to a nice restaurant downtown with the Skidmores. I arranged for us to arrive at the Skidmore's house – only a few blocks from our house – at 5:00 p.m., but Jim agreed to intentionally delay getting home from work so as to allow plenty of time for the decorations to be set up back at our house. It was actually almost 6:30 p.m. before we actually left the Skidmore's.

As we headed down the street I blurted out, "Guess what, Jim. I left my billfold with my driver's license at home. I need to go back and get it." It was true. I had intentionally left my billfold and license. (I suppose I had subconsciously reckoned the "minor sin" of driving that short distance without my license as less grievous than having actually carried my license with me and having "lied" about not having it in order to have an excuse to return to the house.)

As we drew near our house I said to him, "Jim, I want to show you how powerful the engine is in this new Saturn." At that moment I turned from the street and with a loud roar charged up the rather steep bank beside the house to the level plateau in the backyard. A crowd of 25 or 30 friends and family, including David and Penny and their boys who had come in from Texas, surrounded our car yelling, "Happy anniversary!"

Four of our five grandchildren, all under six, sang a special song for grandma and granddad. (Joy and John's first child, Zac, only 15 months old at the time didn't sing because he didn't know the words.)

You are my sunshine, my only sunshine.
You make me happy when skies are gray.
You'll never know, dear, how much I love you.
Please don't take my sunshine away.

Cars & Camping Trips

Two weeks after our 40th anniversary celebration we switched vehicles with Steve and Cheryl for several days. They drove our car to ABWE missionary candidate school in Cherry Hill, New Jersey, and we drove Steve's van to Dallas, Texas to visit Dave and Penny and their boys, Nate and Andy. The six of us took a camping trip to Colorado in the van.

On that camping trip we slept in tents one uncomfortably cold night; but the rest of the trip we rented cabins. Visiting the Royal Gorge was the highlight of our trip. From the highest bridge in the world we took pictures of rafters braving the rapids in the Arkansas River below.

Helping Grown Up Kids

In 1993, I purchased a lot in the Woodgate subdivision of Catoosa County of northern Georgia near I-75 as part of a plan to help John and Joy build a house. In order to avoid either John and Joy or me paying high interest on a conventional bank loan I arranged to use our tax sheltered annuities to finance the construction. Through a series of extraordinary financing procedures we were able to assist John and Joy to become home owners.

Sometime later we were able to assist Steve and Cheryl to purchase a home in Budapest, Hungary, as well as help David and Penny and Phil with similar gifts.

Georgia on My Mind

In the time that we had lived in the "Horton" house on the Ridge, Chattanooga property taxes had become quite burdensome. Just across the state line where John and Joy lived the property taxes were considerably less, so we decided to build and move to north Georgia as well. I had built at least four pools in the Ross Hills subdivision and I knew that area to be a quiet and commodious neighborhood. When a nice hilltop lot on Richard Drive, about two miles from the Woodgate community where Joy lived, came to our attention we purchased it. In the fall of 1993, with a chainsaw and a few other tools, I set about clearing the land for yet another new house. The plot of land on Richard Drive afforded a fantastic view northwestward overlooking the countryside toward Chattanooga.

Our plan was to live there the rest of our lives, and I took special care during construction to make everything permanent: extra deep water lines to prevent freezing in the winter, special insulation, an alarm system, and redundant heating and air conditioning systems were installed. That peach-colored house in Ross Hills was the most beautiful, and in my opinion, the most ideal, house we ever owned. It was my thinking that this would be our final move.

Oh, well. Do you remember the line from Robert Burns? "The best laid schemes o' mice an' men Gang aft agley..."

First Visit to Hungary

During TTU's spring break in 1995, Norma, Phil, and I traveled to Hungary to visit Steve and Cheryl and their kids. It was a most delightful trip. The Iron Curtain had been withdrawn less than six years, and that part of the world was still shrouded in mystery and intrigue in many Westerners' minds.

Seeing the regular tourist sites around the picturesque capital of Budapest was fine, but I was much more interested in seeing things that were off the beaten path. For instance, Cheryl introduced us to one of the Hungarian church planters with whom they and their teammates were working, Géza Kovács, and his family. At his home in the Budapest suburbs we were shown a small room behind a false wall where Bibles and Christian literature were concealed until they could be distributed. They also took us to a mushroom cellar near their house where, under the former Communist regime, believers had held secret worship meetings.

On the last day of March we all rode in Steve's van westward from Budapest for about six or seven hours into the Austrian Alps to a little village just outside Salzburg. There we stayed at a "bed and breakfast" inn which, during the Socialist era, had served as a stop-over for people involved in smuggling Christian materials into the Eastern Bloc. I was fascinated to chat with the landlady of the inn and hear her stories of their work in assisting the Church in Eastern Europe.

While we were driving to Salzburg the Lord was busy preparing a bit of an April Fool's surprise for us. When we awoke the next morning we were amazed at the breath-taking vista that greeted us from our 2nd floor window. A foot or more of fresh brilliant snow blanketed the ground. Not more than a mile or so from our cozy lodging there arose a sheer mountain face straight up into the sky. That panorama was one of the grandest I'd ever beheld. Norma, especially, could hardly get over the native beauty of the area.

Phil had talked us into allowing him to travel alone on a side trip by train through Austria, Switzerland, and Italy. He purchased a student "Eurorail" pass, and Steve and I took him to the train station in Salzburg. It was quite a "stretch" for Norma and me to let our "baby" go "gallivanting" around Europe all alone, but after all, he was 21 years old by that time. We were all relieved, especially his mother and I, when he arrived back in Budapest, safe and sound. To our amazement, he not only survived the trip, but apparently he thrived!

Another interesting portion of the trip involved riding with another of the ABWE team, Chris Johnson, headed for Timisoara, Romania. We were hoping to visit a Bible institute in that northern Romanian city where the uprising against the Communist dictator,

Nicolae Ceauşescu, had begun during the Christmas season of 1989. After about four hours of travel we approached the Romanian frontier and encountered some rather surly border guards. Chris had just days earlier bought the used van in which we were traveling, and unfortunately the guards would not let us pass into Romania. Due to some technicality they were unwilling to accept Chris' paperwork on the van, so we were forced to turn back only a couple of hours from our objective and make the long trek back to Budapest that evening. [Note: A year later we visited Hungary a second time, and Steve took us down to Timisoara. On this occasion we crossed the border without incident, and I had the privilege of preaching in one of the churches there.]

All in all, we were very glad that we had taken the chance to visit Steve and Cheryl and their little ones, and to see a bit of their new life on the mission field.

A New Sister & Daughter-in-Law

A most significant event that happened at the Ross Hills house involved Tanya Sliwinski, Phillip's girlfriend. Tanya had been taught since early childhood to trust in her church baptism and good works for salvation. When Phillip brought her to meet Norma and me, Tanya, allowed me to open the Bible to show her Bible proof that good works and baptism are not the bases of forgiveness and assurance of going to heaven when we die.

We looked at such verses as Ephesians 2:8-9 ("For by grace are you saved through faith, and that not of yourselves, it is the gift of God, not of works lest anyone should boast."), and Titus 3:5, ("Not by works of righteousness which we have done..."), and Galatians 2:16. In that one verse the inspired Apostle Paul stated three times over that salvation is not by good works.

I showed Tanya from the book of Romans the reason why all humans need God's forgiveness. "What is wrong with us," I asked rhetorically, "that causes us to need to be saved?"

"The answer," I suggested, "is given in Romans 3:23: the verse explains that our salvation is necessary due to our sin. 'All have sinned and fallen short of the glory of God.'" I put my finger under the word "all" and asked her to notice that the word "all" means "everyone, male, female, white, black, rich and poor, absolutely everyone, without exception – all have sinned."

I went on to point out that Romans 3:19 says that everyone is "guilty." I pointed out that in legal contexts the word "guilty" means "obligated to pay a penalty for some crime."

We then looked at Romans 6:23 which emphasizes that that penalty which our sin obligates us to pay is death. It says, "The wages of sin is death." I explained that the "death" in this verse includes both physical and spiritual death. Physical death involves the separation of a person's soul, or immaterial part, from his material part, his body. Spiritual death involves a sinner, because of his sin, being separated from God.

All are sinners and all are disqualified for heaven. Heaven is a perfect place and soiled sinners cannot be allowed inside. We can't just automatically go to heaven; something has to be done about our sin problem. Something has to be done to qualify us.

The great news is, as Romans 5:8 informs us, that the penalty we all owe has already been paid by Jesus Christ. It says, "While we were yet sinners Christ died for us." Jesus paid our debt of death for us, in our place.

I pointed to the last part of Romans 6:23 which says, "The gift of God is eternal life through Jesus Christ our Lord." Forgiveness of sin and the certainty of heaven is a gift that is free, but it was not cheap. It cost Jesus His life blood when He bore our sins on the cross (1 Pet. 2:24).

I explained to Tanya that we sinners must simply accept the gift by faith. Romans 5:1 says that sinners are justified by faith. We read Romans 10:9 where Paul taught that when one in his heart agrees with God about why Christ died and believes that God raised him from the dead, God promises such a one that he is saved.

Tanya permitted me to explain the meaning of two Scriptures about baptism that are often confusing. The first was Acts 2:38. Peter told his listeners, "Repent and be baptized for the remission of sins."

I tried to make clear to her that the word "for" can either anticipate the future or review the past. Among other things this preposition can mean "in order to bring about a future result" or "because

211

a past result has been achieved." The context usually makes it clear which meaning the word carries. For example: "The team practiced *for* the game." That is, "they practiced *in view of* the upcoming game, because the game was approaching, in order to achieve victory." There the word "for" is forward looking. They practiced – looking forward – because they wanted to make a good showing.

On the other hand we might say, "The team received a trophy *for* winning the game." "For" here reviews the past; it looks backward. They received the trophy because a victorious result had been achieved.

In Acts 2:38 Peter's "for" looks backward. He is instructing the believers to be baptized "because of a past result," namely, "the remission of sins."

The same Greek word Peter used in Acts 2:38 and translated "for" is used at Matthew 12:41, only there it is translated "at." That verse speaks about the people of Nineveh who repented "at" the preaching of Jonah. I asked, "Did the Ninevites repent in view of Jonah's upcoming preaching, or in order to get him to preach? Of course not. They repented because of a past event, because he had preached to them the warning of God." I drew the comparison: in a similar way Peter was instructing his audience to repent, and thereby receive forgiveness for their sins, and in view of this result, they should also be baptized.

There was a second Scripture that Tanya wanted me to explain, namely 1 Peter 3:20-21, where we are told "In Noah's day eight people were saved by water the figure whereunto even baptism doth also save us." Yes, baptism saves. But in what sense? How? In what way?

Tanya recalled the Old Testament story of the big boat that Noah built that spared him and his family from drowning. She agreed that certainly the water did not save Noah's soul. He was surely a saved man before it ever began raining. We know this from passages such as Genesis 6:8-9 and 7:1 where it says, "Noah found grace in the eyes of the Lord," and "Noah walked with God," and "The Lord said to Noah, 'I have seen thee righteous before me.'" If Noah had suffered a fatal heart attack before the flood started he would have enjoyed heaven for eternity.

Water saved Noah in the sense that it separated him from his evil generation. Water baptism separates us and distinguishes us from our former unsaved friends. Unbelievers who see us baptized know that we want to be identified with God's people. No longer do we want to be identified with the old crowd. Believing sinners in the Book of Acts were baptized because they had been saved by faith in the death and resurrection of their Substitute, Jesus Christ, and they wanted the world to know it.

By baptism they proclaimed their identification with the Christian message and with Christian people, God's people. They wanted to be counted on the side of all others who also accepted that same message.

I reminded Tanya that in Acts 10:47 Cornelius was baptized after he was already saved by faith. Peter wanted to baptize this man because he had "received the Spirit." Having "received the Spirit" proved to Peter that Cornelius was saved and thus he was qualified for baptism. Peter no doubt knew the truth of Jesus' words at John 14:17 that "no unsaved man could receive the Spirit." Paul wrote in Romans 8:9 that only saved persons have the spirit of Christ. Cornelius, therefore, is absolute proof that in the New Testament people were saved before, and apart from, water baptism.

Another key passage demonstrating this same truth is 1 Corinthians. Paul made a sharp distinction between baptism and the gospel in this epistle. He said, "Christ sent me not to baptize, but to preach the gospel," (1 Cor. 1:17). Later he remarked to the Corinthians that he was their spiritual father. He said, "I have begotten you through the gospel," (1 Cor. 4:15), and the instrument Paul used to birth them into the family of God was the gospel. Later, in 1 Corinthians 15:1-4 he explained to those Corinthians what he meant by gospel. He said, "The gospel that you have believed and received, by which you're saved" was the good news that "Christ Jesus died for our sins and that He was buried and that He rose again the third day according to the Scriptures." The only conclusion we can draw from these statements that the gospel and baptism, while related, are separate and distinct.

Because of Tanya's upbringing it was important to give a thorough rebuttal of the false doctrines she had been taught and a careful explanation of some of the pet passages used in that false portrayal of the gospel. It was necessary for her and for all others to understand what the Bible says about salvation. First, the need for salvation is caused by sin. Second, the remedy for sin was provided by the substitutionary death and resurrection of Christ. Third, the means, or the instrument for the appropriation, or the application, of salvation to individual sinners is faith, and faith alone.

It is a joy for me to report that that night Tanya professed faith in Christ as her Savior. Some months later, after she and Phillip were married, both our son and our new daughter-in-law were baptized on the same evening at Dawson Baptist Church in Birmingham. Although Phillip had been saved in early childhood, Tanya's courage to publicly obey Christ's command spoke volumes to him. It influenced him to obey his Lord in a matter that had weighed heavily on his mind for many years.

I want to regress a moment to say a word about Phil and Tanya's wedding. The ceremony took place in 1998 at Shades Mountain Bible Church in Birmingham. They asked me to help officiate, but because of the emotions of watching our youngest take such a momentous step I fumbled the words a bit. I inadvertently got some of the words of the vows out of order. I paused and sheepishly addressed the audience, "Ladies and gentlemen, please understand: this is our baby."

All four of our children, including Phillip, were married during their 24th year, but we still thought of him as "our baby." He never indicated that that bothered him.

Icecapades

While living on the hill high up on Richard Drive we experienced a number of snow and ice days. One icy day the road crews had salted and sanded the roads, but our driveway down to the street was still iced over. Norma and I needed to go to the store, so I decided that I could maneuver the car down to the cleared street by sliding slowly down the steep driveway with the brake on, but Norma didn't think that plan was to her liking. It seemed far too dangerous to her. She said, "I'll walk on the grass beside the driveway down to the street." As I sat in the driveway contemplating my route down the incline I watched my wife take one step onto the grassy slope and immediately thereafter a very sudden tumble straight onto her back followed by a very rapid skidding decent down to the street three or so car lengths below. I crept over the edge of the flat upper driveway and slowly slid down to the level area, so glad to discover that Norma's most significant injury was her slightly bruised dignity.

Creek View & Coughing Spells

A number of times through the years we had difficulties with snow and ice on the hill on Richard Drive, and although we had intended to spend the rest of our earthly lives in that beautiful location, we decided to move again. Just after the Y2K scare at the turn of the century, we moved four miles to Creek View Drive just inside the city limits of Ringgold, Georgia. Our good friends, the Porters, had just recently bought a house on Creek View Drive, and this detail made the move all the more inviting.

Another Trip East

In August of '01 Phil and Tanya joined Norma and me on a third trip to Europe to visit our missionary sons and their families. One key difference from earlier trips was that this time we were able to travel also to eastern Ukraine where David and Penny and their boys ministered. We had spent a few days in Budapest and then taken the four hour flight to Kiev where David picked us up in their vehicle to take us another seven or so hours east. We finally arrived in their city of Kharkov very near to the Russian border.

After spending a few days in Kharkov we began our return leg back to Budapest. It proved to be a bit more tricky than the trip in to Kharkov had been. Instead of taking his van back to Kiev, all eight of us – David, Penny, Nate, Andy, Phil, Tanya, Norma, and I – boarded an overnight train bound for Kiev. Upon arrival, and having several hours until we needed to check in at the airport, David hired a Russian-speaking van driver to take us around to see some of the sites of the city. At one point we arranged to have the van to take our luggage and meet us at the bottom of a certain hill near a certain big church while we went on foot through an open air bazaar. We were assured that our luggage and travel documents would be safe with the driver.

After a couple of hours we arrived at the place that David had indicated we were to meet the van, but – you guessed it – no van! At that point my legendary propensity for always taking extra pre-cautions was looking pretty good, because I had decided to keep Norma's and my passports and plane tickets in my pocket. Phil and Tanya's tickets and passports, as well as all our luggage, was, so far as we knew, in the back of some black marketeer's van on its way to be sold. Finally, though, David realized that while we were at the church he had in mind when conversing with the driver, there was another large church still further down the hill. You can only imagine how we felt when, after walking a bit further, we spied our driver waiting patiently in the van in front of *that* church. Can you spell "relief"?

We said goodbye to Dave, Penny, Nate, and Andy and boarded our flight back to Budapest to spend a few more days with Steve and his family before heading back to the States. It was the last time my wife would visit Europe.

Diagnosis

For quite some time Norma had been plagued by a periodic cough that became progressively worse. Finally, after a biopsy in November of 2001, the lung specialist in Chattanooga diagnosed Norma with pulmonary fibrosis. He privately told me that the prog-nosis suggested a survival time of two to five years.

Within a matter of weeks the doctor wanted to start Norma on a very expensive experimental regimen of interferon – the cost would be $5,000 per month. I immediately made plans to sell our two-year-old brick house on Creek View to pay for the medicine.

Tanya, however, suggested that we get an appointment with a certain Dr. Sutton, a recently retired pulmonologist, who attended her mother's church in Birmingham, Alabama. He was, she informed us, known to be one of the best pulmonologists in the country, but more importantly, a longtime, personal acquaintance. With Tanya's help we were able to set up a rendezvous with Dr. Sutton – we met around the dining room table at Phil and Tanya's with this specialist.

We sat there in silence for quite a while as Dr. Sutton studied Norma's x-rays and reviewed her doctor's reports. At last he spoke. He expressed a belief that a different medicine could slow the progression of her lung disease and would help with her breathing difficulty. He recommended Dr. Vines, a pulmonologist who had been a colleague of his before his retirement, and try a different, much less expensive, medicine (that, unlike the interferon, our insurance would cover). Dr. Sutton looked at us with a bit of a sly grin and said, "You know how hard it is to get an appointment to see a specialist of Dr. Vines' quality, but I think I can help. My daughter is his appointment secretary." Even while walking through the darkest valley of our half century together, we knew that our Shepherd had not abandoned us.

Within short order we were able to begin regular appointments with Dr. Vines. We came to appreciate this man, not only because he proved to be a brother in Christ, but because he seemed to have a genuine interest in Norma's condition. Those visits started in 2002 and continued for five years. We drove the 160 miles down to Birmingham once every four months. His treatment and prescriptions seemed to be helpful, and we were grateful for the Lord's provision through this kind Christian physician.

Simply Golden

During our third year on Creek View Drive our four children with the help of some of the grandchildren favored Norma and me with an exciting 50th anniversary celebration. Although our true anniversary date fell on the 30th of the month, because of various scheduling necessities the festivities were held on May 18, 2002.

Friends and relatives travelled from far and wide to join in the big event. It was staged in the fellowship hall at John and Joy's church, Woodland Park Baptist, in Chattanooga. We were thrilled to have all four of our adult children along with their spouses present as well as our seven grandchildren. (Phil and Tanya were by this time expecting our eighth!) From the Lafayette area and from around Cummin in north Georgia several of Norma's side of the family drove in: Bill and Elizabeth Garner, George ("Buddy") and Betty Hicks, and Harry and Barbara Hicks. My side of the family was represented by Raymond ("Buck") and Bobbie Snipes, their son-in-law and daughter, Grady and Barbara Walker, Bobbie and Buck's son and daughter-in-law, Charles ("Lucky") and Carol Snipes, and Darrel and Millie Winget who traveled up from central Florida, and by Earl Winget who drove all the way from El Paso, Texas. In addition to these were numerous close friends, some from as far away as Indiana.

For the celebration a picture of Norma and me with a script title which read, "Celebrating God's Faithfulness for 50 Years" had been prepared. On the back of the photograph was inscribed the following words: "Many of you know that last fall our mother was diagnosed with pulmonary fibrosis. This ailment normally causes a progressive decrease in lung capacity... Please join us in asking the Lord to provide the grace, patience and wisdom our family needs in the coming days."

After a banquet-style meal with those who had gathered, our children presented an hour-long program of pictures, memories, music, and laughter. One of the highlights was a duet performed by David and Penny. In costume they sang a nostalgic number from *Fiddler on the Roof*. Taking on the persona of Tevye and his wife, Golde, David and Penny sang, "Do You Love Me?"

Tevye:	Golde...Do you love me?
Golde:	Do I what?
Tevye:	Do you love me?
Golde:	Do I love you?
	With our daughters getting married
	And this trouble in the town
	You're upset, you're worn out
	Go inside, go lie down!
	Maybe it's indigestion

Tevye: Golde I'm asking you a question...
           Do you love me?

Golde: You're a fool

Tevye: I know...
           But do you love me?

Golde: Do I love you?
           For twenty-five years I've washed your clothes
           Cooked your meals, cleaned your house
           Given you children, milked the cow
           After twenty-five years, why talk about love right now?

Tevye: Golde, The first time I met you
           Was on our wedding day
           I was scared

Golde: I was shy

Tevye: I was nervous

Golde: So was I

Tevye: But my father and my mother
           Said we'd learn to love each other
           And now I'm asking, Golde...
           Do you love me?

Golde: I'm your wife

Tevye: I know...
           But do you love me?

Golde: Do I love him?
           For twenty-five years I've lived with him
           Fought him, starved with him
           Twenty-five years my bed is his
           If that's not love, what is?

Tevye: Then you love me?

Golde: I suppose I do

Tevye: And I suppose I love you too

Both: It doesn't change a thing
           But even so
           After twenty-five years
           It's nice to know

At one point in the festivities I stood to sing my own song to Norma. While the musicality of the rendition was surely questionable the sentiment of the song was real.

God gave the wise men their wisdom,
And to the poets their dreams.
To father and mother their love for each other,
But he left me out, so it seemed
I went around broken hearted,
Thinking life was an empty affair
But when God gave me you it was then that I knew
He had given me more than my share.

Norma and I were so thrilled we sent them the following note written in Norma's own beautiful, flowing script:

To our dear children and your spouses, Daddy and I want to tell you how proud we are of all of you and thank you for all your effort put forth to make our special occasion such a great success. All of you did a great job in planning, decorating and producing a sweet program and the wonderful food. We appreciate your hard work and sacrifices financially. Many have told us it was the very best celebration program they had ever witnessed.

We pray for, and thank the Lord for, each of you every day. He has been so good to us over these 50 years together for which we don't deserve, but give Him praise. We love each of you deeply and all the grandchildren you gave us are a special joy. We pray the Lord will use each of them in years to come. We joyfully anticipate the arrival of another beautiful granddaughter in another few months. Your ever-loving mom and dad.

PS: Mrs. Bartlett cried and thanked us over and over for asking Kent and her to sing that beautiful song, "Love Till the End of Time." It was the last song they sang together.

Moving On Up to the Basement

During late 2001 and well into 2002 John and Joy were formulating plans to build a beautiful new brick home a mile or so from our place on Creek View in a subdivision called Calloway Farms. Shortly after we turned the calendar over to 2003 they were able to occupy the new residence. At about the same time that his sister and brother-in-law were constructing their new house, Phil and Tanya were discussing with us the possibilities of buying our dwelling on Creek View. (They had expressed interest in moving to the Chattanooga area several months earlier.)

When the severity of Norma's illness became known I approached John and Joy with a request: I asked if they would consider allowing me to fund the construction of a simple apartment for Norma and me attached to their new house. We all knew that someday I would likely need help caring for her. John and Joy eagerly agreed.

And so we found ourselves moving one more time – this time into a spacious, two-bedroom basement apartment beneath their new home. God's provision for us was exactly what our situation demanded.

Norma and I thanked God many times for friends who helped us build that apartment, especially a former colleague at Temple, Doug Griffin. This dear brother did carpentry, plumbing, and tile work over a period of many months. Mrs. Griffin and John Hain, another teaching colleague, also did many hours of painting. These precious servants would not accept any pay for their labors, but they saved us many hundreds, if not thousands, of dollars.

As another example of the Lord's abundant provisions to us, I want to mention a gracious kindness extended by our friends, Mike and April Rittichier. Mike was a former student of mine and a pastor of a church in southern Indiana. On their own initiative Mike, April, a church deacon, his wife, and a daughter took their vacation time and came down before we moved to the Calloway Farms apartment, and worked diligently doing renovations and repairs on our Creek View house in preparation for it being sold.

Thus, within a twelve month period several important events took place in our family for which we thanked God. I can list a few of them: first, Phil and Tanya presented us with a new grandbaby, Mia Mae, born in October of '02; second, Joy and John completed and moved into their new house the following winter; third, Norma and I completed the apartment in Joy's basement and moved there from Creek View; fourth, Phil sold his Birmingham house, bought our Creek View house, and moved closer to us; and finally, in the summer of '03, I had successful heart surgery during which a stent was inserted to remedy a blockage. Praise God. Thank God. He was proving yet again for the unnumbered time that "all things work together for good to them who love God, to them who are the called according to His purpose."

A Lifetime of Teaching

9 t is very difficult to summarize a lifetime of teaching at Tennessee
Temple. So many thoughts come to mind. Here are a few of
them.

A Crucial Omission?

During my 46 years at Tennessee Temple, I taught mostly in the
seminary. However, I did teach some in the undergraduate division
of the university. The first course I taught in the lower division was
a study on premillennialism. This came about because in January of
'61 Dr. Roberson wanted the faculty to offer new courses to spark
interest for the summer school. For financial reasons we needed a
good enrollment that summer in the college especially.

From its beginning in 1946 Temple had always emphasized its
premillennial position; however, no detailed course explaining the
biblical basis of the premillennial perspective had been taught. I saw
this as a crucial omission in the curriculum and suggested that such
an offering be added to the college summer school schedule. I proposed to develop the course and teach it. Dr. Roberson liked the
idea, and so beginning that summer, though most of my teaching
load remained in the seminary division, I taught *Premillennialism*
every semester for many years to the undergrads. Later I was told by
Dr. Roberson that students had written notes to him expressing their
appreciation for the course.

Unfortunately, years later the head of the Bible department in the college, Dr. Don Davis, abruptly discontinued the course with no discussion from the rest of the Bible faculty. His dismissive explanation was that all the Bible courses at the institution were taught from a premillennial point of view and a single course on the topic was superfluous. One could have responded that all the Bible department courses were taught from a Trinitarian perspective therefore there was no need to discuss the Trinity as a particular doctrinal category in Doctrines class, or since all the Bible courses were taught from a Christological perspective there was no need for a course on the Life of Christ.

It was my opinion that unless the school offered a thorough defense of dispensational premillennialism in short order that distinctive issue in hermeneutics would be disparaged and jettisoned under the adverse weight of opposing opinions. Such, in fact, seems to be the case in churches and schools today. Fewer and fewer preachers and teachers hold to dispensational premillennialism, not necessarily because it has been weighed and found wanting, but because it has not been fairly weighed. Further, it is my opinion that if a school makes premillennialism a key component of its doctrinal creed, as TTU still does, it is obligated to prepare its students, at least its Bible majors, to intelligently defend that tenet.

What Does "Master's Level" Mean?

In North America "master's degree" is an educational term that speaks of training in a particular field to a high level of professional proficiency. Also, in North America the word "seminary" usually refers to a graduate level or postgraduate level school seeking to train students for religious vocational leadership roles. A seminary normally offers master's or doctoral degrees in various disciplines of study. Thus, at Temple Baptist Theological Seminary the basic degree offerings were the Master of Religious Education degree and the Master of Divinity degree. It was my view that any who are called masters in theological studies should have a mastery of certain strategic Bible verses. That is, they would be able to cite accurately from memory certain key Scripture passages. One should expect a "master" to be able to give Bible proof of what he believed and taught and explain how those texts were germane.

In most of the courses I taught I emphasized by example as well as by course requirement the memorization of a number of verses that were significant to the course at hand. Never were my students required to memorize verses that I had not memorized myself. In one course I required students to memorize seven verses per week for seven weeks and then to review all 49 for seven weeks. They were expected to be able to quote all of them perfectly and demonstrate a clear understanding of the meaning of the verses.

For example, a question on an exam might read something like, "Give a reference to show the *purpose* of the death of Christ, and show how this verse would be used to teach one of the purposes of Jesus' death," or "Give a reference that might be used to prove that His death was *substitutionary*, and explain how the verse supports this doctrine."

Some students felt that this was an unfair way to word the questions because none of the verses assigned used the word "substitution." (Indeed, the word does not occur at all in the King James Version.) However, the concept is taught numerous times in Scripture, and we specifically discussed several of the assigned memory verses showing how they supported this cardinal tenet. There was no intention to trip up or trick the student. The objective was to allow the student an opportunity to show how the verses they had memorized could be used in teaching key doctrines.

I showed them how to use these in their preaching to prove certain Bible truths, and this memorization of Scripture proved to be more profitable than the writing of research papers. Students were urged to review the verses throughout their lives, and many have written or phoned me over the years to say that the memorization of those key verses proved more helpful in their ministries than any other seminary experience.

I recall a particular incident involving one of our seminary students. The course was Systematic Theology and the student was currently also laboring as a pastor. He had failed the course once, partly because he found the discipline of memorizing the required Scripture passages very difficult. He came to resent that portion

226

of the curriculum. In private he approached me about it. "That's what kids do in Sunday School," he reasoned. "I can be a successful pastor without knowing all those memory verses by heart."

He took the course a second time and failed again for the same reasons. He contended that I should not fail him simply because he could not memorize all those verses. I replied, "I never have failed any of my students." He insisted, "Well, you *did* fail me." My rejoinder was, "I did not fail you, nor any other. Some of you failed *yourselves*. I only recorded the grades."

That student phoned me later and threatened to take his case before the administration for being unfair to students. I politely responded that I would be glad for him to present his case to the school leadership. I told him, "It may be that they would agree with you. They may believe that graduate school students preparing for the ministry of the Word of God should not be required to memorize key Bible verses. I sincerely hoped to find out the opinion of our school leaders concerning my requirements."

To his credit that student never went to the authorities, and to his credit, he enrolled for the course yet a third time. This time he "buckled down" and did the hard work necessary to memorize those key verses and passed the course.

Another staff member who thought this approach was unrealistic and overbearing did go before the administration to challenge my methods. Before Dr. Roberson he demanded an explanation of the memory work that I required. After viewing a copy of one of the exams Dr. Roberson remarked, "I do not think this is asking too much of master's degree students in graduate school." I silently rejoiced that I had been vindicated.

Dr. Lee Roberson

Lee Roberson was an impressive man, physically as well as otherwise: tall, having a steady gaze and an imposing voice, always attired in his famous blue double-breasted suit, in later years possessing snow white hair. He was a commanding presence in every sense of the word, a man of iron will, courageous, decisive, but sometimes given to spur of the moment reactions and somewhat impulsive.

I remember distinctly hearing him repeat several of his trademark slogans: "Don't be a quitter, Young People. Quitters are a dime a dozen!" or "Where God guides, He provides," or "Everything rises or falls on leadership."

It was an encouragement that Dr. Roberson called on different members of the faculty at least once a year to preach in chapel. A few times just before chapel began he would ask one of us to be ready to give a personal testimony of our salvation experience. On one such occasion I told how my sovereign Lord rescued me from the making of booze and brought me to salvation and a ministry of the Bible. Several faculty members and students were astonished at my testimony and asked, "Did you really make moonshine whiskey? How do you make that stuff?"

After lunch one Friday Dr. Roberson invited me to give a short talk on Bible prophecy to his training union class which met for an hour before the Sunday night service. His plan, he shared, was for me to give a 15 minute introductory talk on the topic, and then he would ask for questions from the audience. He said that he felt this would be an interesting time of Bible teaching. When I inquired as to when he planned to do this he replied, "This Sunday night."

Of course, I showed up on time that Sunday night – Dr. Roberson was not the kind of man one wanted to disappoint, and his legendary punctuality was remarkable. (Before a speaker would go to the pulpit to speak in chapel Dr. Roberson would often hand him a terse, handwritten note on a 3X5 card: "Stop at 10:50," or "You may go until 10:55." Woe be to the speaker who did not heed the time limit!) After my 15 minute talk someone asked whether or not I felt that Old Testament saints and New Testament saints would be resurrected and raptured together. I responded that I felt that New Testament, or "Church Age saints," would be resurrected and raptured preceding the time of the Great Tribulation. Paul taught in 1 Thessalonians 4 that the "dead in Christ" would be raised, and that terminology was common New Testament nomenclature for those who had put their faith in Christ during our era of redemptive history. On the other hand, Daniel 12 speaks of a time following the period we call the

Tribulation in which "many will rise from the dust of the earth." It seems likely that this is a reference to the rising of Old Testament saints after the time of Jacob's Trouble (the Tribulation) and preceding the inauguration of the Millennial Kingdom.

Dr. Roberson could sense that my answer was not convincing to some in the audience and commented, "David, it seems like there might be a difference of opinion on that, but let's go on to the next question."

Following the service one of the Bible professors from the college, a dear brother with whom I had very good times of fellowship, engaged me regarding that first question and his disagreement with my position. I reminded him of the passages I used to support my opinion and asked what Scripture he would use to sustain his view. He replied, "I don't actually have a Scripture verse, but your view makes Israel second rate citizens and I cannot agree with that."

The next morning we saw each other at breakfast in the school dining hall. I said to that brother, "Did you find a Scripture that supports your view?" Again, he said, "No...but I still don't like to make Israel second rate citizens."

This encounter reminds me of a particular seminary student – I remember his first name was Alan – who once had a problem with a certain essay question I asked on an exam. I had asked whether or not the students felt a particular statement was true or false and then to give an explanation along with Bible passages that buttressed that response. Alan came up to the front and whispered to me, "Brother Winget, I do not know any Scripture that supports my view. I only know Scriptures that support your view."

Dr. Roberson sometimes asked for particular subjects to be dealt with in chapel messages. He once asked me to speak on the subject of prayer. On another occasion we had a special chapel service emphasizing the library so he instructed me, "Speak on the value of books."

I suspect that one of the reasons he decided to ask me to deal with that topic was because for years I sought to assist the students in acquiring good books. I was able to buy bulk orders of certain titles and resale them to the students at drastically reduced prices.

Some of the students who had no idea of my real name knew me simply as the "Book Man."

Dr. Roberson was always very much in control and rarely at a loss for a decisive response. Before one Monday morning chapel session – I recall that it was in October of 1962 – one excellent Bible professor told him that he had accepted a pastorate and would be resigning at the end of the semester. Dr. Roberson responded to that professor by saying, "If you plan to leave at the end of the semester you might as well leave now."

At the end of the chapel service that day Dr. Roberson announced that he wanted all Bible faculty to meet him in his office immediately following the service. The resigning teacher's schedule was in Dr. Roberson's hand and the meeting went something like this:

Dr. Roberson: Who does not have a class first period Monday, Wednesday and Friday?

Someone raises his hand.

Dr. Roberson: Okay. You will teach the Epistles of Paul in Room H-11 beginning Wednesday. Now who doesn't have a first period class on Tuesday and Thursday?

Another teacher raises his hand.

Dr. Roberson: Okay. Beginning tomorrow you will teach the Book of Romans in Room H-11. Which of you does not have a class third period, Tuesday and Thursday?

I raise my hand.

Dr. Roberson: Okay, David. You will teach Methods of Bible Study beginning tomorrow in room H-14.

And so it went. Within five minutes all the classes of that resigning professor were summarily reassigned. And such decisiveness was typical of Lee Roberson. In keeping with such brevity I will simply recount that...

In April of 2007, the old warrior went to glory.

Dr. J.R. Faulkner

Moses had his Aaron and Lee Roberson had his J.R. Faulkner. To say that Dr. Faulkner was "vigorous" or "energetic" would be far short of the truth. He was a dynamo – a very efficient and organized dynamo, I should add – who was in many respects the genius behind the scenes who made things happen around TTU. Ever the gracious personification of a gentleman, this North Carolina native had an incalculable impact on thousands of students and church members as he ably functioned as both Dr. Roberson's vice president in the schools and his associate pastor at Highland Park Baptist. In my estimation he was the world's foremost church song leader. His noble wife, Magdalene, was a fantastic pianist in her own right, and my daughter-in-law, Cheryl's, piano teacher during her undergraduate studies. The Faulkners had five sons, four of whom are in vocational ministries. The fifth inherited his father's gifting in visual arts and makes his living as an industrial artist. Dr. Faulkner went to be with his Lord in June of 2009.

Dr. Elmer Delancy

The best single phrase that I can think of to describe one of my all-time favorite colleagues, Dr. Elmer Delancy, is "a prince of a fellow." He taught education for many years in a state school, and then took on a second career teaching in the same field but at Tennessee Temple. It was my considerable privilege to eat at least one meal a day for well over a decade with him at the school dining hall, and as one simple signal of his sterling character I can tell you that I never heard him say a single word of complaint about the food. I came to consider him an excellent theologian, and on one occasion I heard him give a synopsis of the book of Philippians that I still consider the best I ever heard. I can still remember Dr. Roberson coming to the end of faculty meeting on a certain occasion, and turning to Dr. Delancy, asking for a brief word of advice to the faculty regarding the art of teaching. His masterful response is etched in my mind for even today I can see that short giant of a man – he may not have weighed more than a hundred pounds – stride to the front of the room, pick up a piece of chalk, and mark on the board in large bold letters: K-I-S-S. He turned to the assembled faculty and said, "Keep it simple, Stupid," and immediately sat down. He knew how to practice what he preached!

Dr. Aubrey Martin

Another colleague who held the highest esteem in my thinking was the blind Bible prof, Dr. Aubrey Martin. As a young boy Aubrey fell out of tree one day and the injury resulted in the permanent loss of his sight. His testimony was that it was one of the best things that ever happened to him because he learned to pass the tedious hours of darkness by the study and memorization of the Word of God. He later earned a Th.D. from Southern Seminary in Louisville. Though he and I had our different views of a few secondary doctrinal matters, I never tired of interacting with this godly brother. I can remember how he would sometimes flash his winsome grin and say, "Well, I don't see anything wrong with that." Yes, our many discussions were definitely an occasion for his iron sharpening my bronze.

Dr. Howard Vos

Howard Vos came to Tennessee Temple in the late 40's after having earned his doctorate from Dallas Seminary. To show you how inaccurate first impressions can be, especially impressions of young college students a little too big for their britches, I didn't have a great opinion of him at first. I took Dr. Vos for Old, and New Testament Intro, Greek and Roman History, and Methods of Bible Study. As I matured I began to appreciate his well-organized, focused teaching methods, and in one of the biggest turn-arounds in my life, he became my very favorite teacher during my college days. It was he who impressed me to go to Dallas Seminary after college.

Some years later he wrote a textbook entitled *Effective Bible Study* in which he used as an example of a certain type of Bible study an outline that I had written for one of his course assignments in college.

Dr. Charles Mashburn

My Old and New Testament Survey, Shakespeare, and Homiletics teacher in college was Dr. Charles Mashburn. He had earned his doctorate at Golden Gate Baptist Seminary in California. He was a very gifted orator – once, while speaking in chapel, he so vividly described an auto accident in which he sustained a bloody injury that at least two girls fainted. You'll perhaps recall that it was in a collision with Dr. Mashburn during an informal football game that I sustained a broken arm, but that was not the only "impact" he left on me. I regard him as one of my best teachers in college.

Dr. John Economidis

John and Sophie Economidis came to be two of our very closest friends. For years Norma and I enjoyed their warm camaraderie and fellowship, and after Norma's passing they proved their love for me in numerous ways. At only about five feet, three inches tall John is not a big man in stature, but I have absolutely the highest regard for this friend. Of Greek descent – what was your first clue? – and a graduate of the University of Texas, John took every single course I taught in the seminary, and scored well in all of them – I believe he scored straight A's in seminary. So far as I know he is the only student I ever had who took all my courses and never missed a single class. John was a member of Temple's business faculty, but in my view, he was one of the best Bible expositors and theologians on campus.

Dr. J. Don Jennings

Dr. J. Don Jennings became the president of TTU in 1985 after Dr. Roberson had resigned. Much like his predecessor he was a serious minded man of resolution and command, tall and impeccably dressed. He was a gifted orator and expositional preacher.

In May of 1988, Dr. Jennings wanted to bestow honorary doctoral degrees on five Christian leaders. He chose a pastor, a lawyer, a songwriter, a missionary and an educator. I well remember the missionary was Margaret Stringer who spent 30 years among a cannibalistic tribe in the remote jungles of Irian Jaya, reduced their language to writing, and translated the New Testament for them.

The pastor was Gene Payne, a Temple classmate of mine from the early 50's. The songwriter was B.C. Jennings, Dr. Jennings' father. The lawyer was John Stoffel, who had practiced law in Chattanooga for nearly 50 years. The educator was a former moonshiner. After 28 years on the faculty Dr. Jennings needed to do something, I suppose, to help raise the final recipient's status or else get rid of him.

Hard Times & Hard Decisions

The old adage says, "When the going gets tough, the tough get going." Well, the going got tough at Tennessee Temple in the early 90's. Falling enrollment required the university to take some drastic measures to try to remain solvent. Several faculty and staff positions were eliminated, and the faculty took a ten percent pay cut. I even took home a couple of paychecks made out in the amount of $0:00!

Hard decisions continued to be required. In 1997, three of my older colleagues were asked to retire. To take up some of the slack in the teaching schedule left by their departures I was given a larger teaching load than I had had the previous several semesters. My salary had previously been so low that the $16,000 I received that year was a considerable raise.

In November of 2004, I was informed by Dr. Roger Stiles that starting the following term, the undergrad division of the school, due to financial restrictions, would have to drop my courses from the class schedule. There was no money in the college budget to pay me even the $8,000 per semester. Paul's words to Timothy came to mind: "The things that thou hast heard from me among many witnesses, the same commit thou to faithful men who shall be able to teach others also," (2 Tim. 2:2). I replied, "Well, Dr. Stiles, I appreciate the 45 years of opportunity God has given me to equip young people to proclaim His truth." Immediately he added, "We want to hold a retirement reception for you in the spring at a time that is convenient for you and your family."

Later that day the seminary vice president, Dr. Trachian, called to inform me that he wanted me to teach one seminary theology course the next term, the spring semester of 2005. I then phoned Dr. Stiles to tell him to hold off on any plans for a retirement reception, because I would be teaching theology in the seminary in the spring.

The next day I informed Dr. Kemp, the head of the Bible department in the university, that should there be a need for my services in the Bible department I would be willing to teach one two-hour course for no pay if it could be arranged to have the course scheduled for one two-hour period on Tuesday afternoons. This would save me having to drive into school an extra day per week. He was glad for my offer and told me that he would inform Dr. Stiles.

The next week I received the following letter from the office of the vice president:

Dear Mr. Winget,

I am writing as a follow-up to our meeting on Tuesday, November 23, 2004. It is impossible to describe how difficult it was to meet with you and present this matter to you. As one of your former students and a great admirer of your teaching gift, it was harder than I would have thought it to be to meet with you and deliver the message that I had to deliver.

Dr. Kemp called me on Wednesday and he told me that you wanted to teach one of the theology classes as a gift to Tennessee Temple University. We are pleased to accept this offer and count it a privilege to have you continue with us in this capacity during the spring semester of 2005.

There is one question I have for you. In light of the circumstances surrounding the completion of your career at Tennessee Temple Schools I am asking your permission to hold a reception in your honor at an agreed upon date in the spring of 2005.

I so appreciate the gracious way you accepted the decision reported to you on Tuesday, November the 23rd. I appreciate your kind response and it overwhelmed me. You exhibit extraordinary Christian grace and love. If you will permit us to do so, Tennessee Temple will plan a reception for you in honor of your many years of dedicated ministry and outstanding teaching at Tennessee Temple.

We will schedule this reception at a time most convenient for you and your family. I again want to express my admiration and appreciation and look to receive a positive response from you regarding the reception.

Sincerely,
Roger Styles, Executive Vice President

No reception ever took place, because I did not really care for a reception.

As it turned out Dr. Kemp wanted me to continue to teach a two hour class for three more semesters if I wanted to do so. This I did. In the spring and fall semesters of '05 and the spring semester of '06 it was understood that I was not expecting any pay; however, Dr. Lovett, the new president of the university, decided to pay me an adjunct fee of a total of $2,800 for those last three courses anyway.

Course Evaluations & Concluding Commendations

As do most educational institutions, TTU requested that students submit course evaluations at the close of each semester. Of course, a given student's opinion taken alone is not nearly as valuable as are the collective judgment of a number of students, especially if a general trend is present. These responses provided one tool for helping the school assess its teachers and assisted the instructors in calculating the effectiveness of their methods and presentations. The following comments were submitted anonymously by four separate students:

- Dr. Winget is an awesome and inspirational man of God. I am honored and privileged to sit under his teaching. He is also the most structured and organized professor I have had.
- Just a thought, please pay Dr. Winget and buy his lunch. He volunteers his time to us. Show that you appreciate it.
- Dr. Winget is one of the best professors I've ever had, a godly example and passionate teacher. He deserves greater pay than most... It is a shame to treat such a loving man of God with anything except double honor.
- Dr. Winget is an example to his students not only intellectually, but spiritually. He displays a deep devotion to Christ, a love for God's Word and a humble life of servanthood. He is deserving of much recognition, yet receives and expects very little. God's hand is upon this man.

Actually, I'm a little bit embarrassed and hesitate to mention those comments about me and my teaching, but they're a part of the written record for the final semester in '05 in my file at TTU in the Office of the Administration. It is both humbling and a great encouragement that these students responded to my ministry so positively.

During Class Day exercises preceding Graduation in May of '05, Dr. Trachian presented me with the *Seminary Professor of the Year Award*. At the year's end seminary banquet that night, with Dr. Roberson, Dr. Faulkner, Dr. Bouler, Dr. Lovett, and many teachers and students in attendance, the seminary Student Body President honored me with a beautiful plaque which read: "In appreciation for 45 years of faithful Bible teaching."

In addition to the plaque the seminary students gave me another wonderful surprise, a check in the amount of $1,000 made out to me, that had been contributed in a special offering of gratitude from the seminary students themselves. I was quite taken aback by this magnanimous bequest, and for the want of something more profound to say, I remarked somewhat sheepishly, "This may be the only time in history that a student body has given $1,000 to get rid of a teacher." I will always be deeply grateful and profoundly humbled by that gesture of generosity and appreciation. It was my God-given opportunity to spend more years preparing young people for Christian ministry than any other teacher in the history of the school, and I consider that an amazing honor to be bestowed on me by a gracious Savior who rescued me from a low life of sin and wastedness.

It is not unusual for someone who labors faithfully for 20 or 30 years for an organization to be granted an annuity of several thousands of dollars. However, Tennessee Temple is not financially endowed by wealthy benefactors or rich corporations, and therefore is not able to give pensions to teachers even after many years of service. No financial pension at all has come to me for 46 years of teaching the truth of God, but I do not consider my lot negatively or count myself impoverished.

While no monetary pension has ever come to me, I consider of much greater currency the eternally valuable fruit I've seen in the lives of almost a half century of students. When I visit or hear from former students who are successful pastors, that's my pension. When, by phone call or letter, I learn of the fruitful ministry of a missionary or teacher who sat under my instruction, when I learn of their achievements and victories, that's my pension.

One of the many expressions of gratitude that have come through the years arrived in the form of a letter from Kerry Payne, the pastor of Emmanuel Baptist Church in Tuscaloosa, Alabama. It was dated April 6, 2005. He wrote:

Dear Dr. Winget,

I was one of the many, many seminary students who was changed forever because you said "Yes" to God's call to equip young men for the ministry. I attended your theology classes from 1978 to 1981. Because of you, Dr. Winget, I changed my major over to theology. I couldn't get enough of God's Word through you. I sat on the edge of my seat each time you took one verse and opened it up for our devotional thought at the start of each class. I have wrapped sermons around some of those gold nuggets you gave us.

Dr. Winget, for the first time in my life you taught me how to think and how to reason. You took deep truths and explained them in a way that I could not only grasp, but use as food for my soul. I have been serving as a missionary and now as a pastor ever since graduation in 1981. I would not have traded my experience learning at your feet for anything in the world. As you prepare for retirement, please understand that your ministry carries on through men like myself who had the privilege to hear God each day we took a seat in your classroom.

May God's richest blessings be yours forever.

Gratefully yours,
Kerry.

P.S. Thank you for changing and redirecting my life and ministry.

There's another letter I might mention. One former student whom I helped to train for the ministry of Christ became a successful and popular Bible teacher at Tennessee Temple University. He then obeyed God's call to foreign missionary service in central Europe. In this letter he recounted how God won the victory in the life of a young Hungarian atheist. After a number years of prayer and witness this young man named "Jozsi" – it's pronounced YO-zhi – came to believe in the existence of God and the reality of sin through reading 1 Corinthians. He began to refer to himself as a believer and a Christian.

The missionary letter reported:

Last Monday night I had a chance to have about a three and a half hour private conversation with him after our weekly small group evangelistic meeting with several university students. I asked him, "Jozsi, do you understand the difference between a theist and a believer in the Bible sense of the term?"

He was perplexed. "Aren't they the same thing?"

"'No," I gently responded. "The difference is the difference between life and death." I went on to explain that a theist is one who believes there is a God, but a believer the way the Bible uses the term is someone who calls that Person "my God." A believer, according to the Bible, is a person who has a personal relationship with that God. In fact he calls that God "my Father."

"Jozsi, you believe that you have a deathly cancer called sin and that there isn't anything you can do about it. You believe that there is a Doctor out there that can cure your cancer. But just knowing that there is a Doctor won't remedy your problem. You have to receive the cure. You have to take the medicine He prescribes."

I asked Jozsi, "Wouldn't you like to receive the remedy tonight, the finished payment for your sins that Jesus paid on the cross? Just take it. Just receive the truth. That's all you have to do. Just ask God for his remedy. He promises to give it to you if you just ask."

"Yes, I would." After a short pause Jozsi wanted to know, "May I ask him in Hungarian?"

"'Jozsi, the Lord speaks better Hungarian than you do," I assured him.

What followed, my friends, was a classic sinner's prayer that brought light and life to Jozsi. It brought a fatherly response from God who had been there patiently waiting all this time. It brought joy to the hosts of angelic creatures surrounding the throne, and it brought such a surge to my heart that the CPR unit would like to bottle it.

I have an appointment to see our new brother tonight. Please pray that he'll grow and be strong in the Lord. Please pray that the grace and patience of God will grow in my heart. Please pray for Jozsi's family. God desires that they come to know him too.

You might guess that this letter was from my oldest son, Steve. More recent word has come that Jozsi is growing in his faith and in his understanding of the Bible and in his witness for Christ. You will also be glad to know that Jozsi's mother has now accepted the Gospel, as well. [Note: I understand that Jozsi and his wife, Zsuzsa, continue to serve the Lord in northern Budapest, and that recently they brought home their first child, a daughter they named "Lili."]

Another whose life God allowed me to influence was Dr. Ray Prichard, author, speaker, president of *Keep Believing Ministries* whose web log on Wednesday, December 14, 2005 read:

> The current issue of *Dallas Seminary Connection* mentions that David Winget has retired after 45 years as a professor at Temple Baptist Theological Seminary in Chattanooga. Though I haven't seen him in over 30 years and I doubt that he would remember me, I sat under his ministry at Foust Baptist Church during my college days at Tennessee Temple University. I got to know him a little bit because I ran a *Word of Life* club at the church.
>
> I never took a course from David Winget, but I listened to him preach many times. He was one of the first Bible expositors I ever heard. I am happy to say that he played a key role in my life during my formative years. He graduated from Dallas [Seminary] in 1960 and came straight to Temple Seminary and stayed there until his recent retirement. That's a record of faithfulness that is hard to match these days.
>
> Congratulations, Professor Winget, on a distinguished career from one of your former youth workers.

The assurance that my sovereign Lord is using pastors like Kerry Payne is my pension. That I had the God-given privilege to help train missionaries God is using to point still others to Christ and salvation is my pension. Kind assertions of my small part in other lives, like Ray Pritchard's, are my pension.

I would be woefully shortsighted, however, not to emphasize that this pension of which I speak is a pension that I must share with many others. I must by all means share this pension with scores of people who invested in my life through the years. People like Millard Branson (who influenced me to attend Tennessee Temple), and Jane Currie (who financed a good portion of my studies there), and Dr. Howard Vos (who encouraged me to go to Dallas Seminary), Dr. Howard Hendricks (one of my most influential professors in grad school), Dr. Charles Ryrie (the author who had perhaps the greatest impact on me), Dr. Wymal Porter (one of my closest friends), Lester Roloff (who made such an impression on me regarding the memorization of Scripture), and so many others that only time and space inhibit their mention (and I humbly beg their forgiveness for this omission). Their investments in my life have been immeasurable and life-changing, and I am confident that the same God who took notice of Solomon's grand sacrifices and the widow's mite will surely have noted their sacrifices on my behalf and will reward them openly!

Students I Have Studied

*I*n heaven I will rejoice with scores and perhaps hundreds from all over the world who were led to Christ and motivated and taught to serve God by my former students. That will be a million times greater pension than any pension of money. To God be the glory for any contribution that He has enabled me to make towards the preparing of young people for the carrying out of the Great Commission. There are at least a few hundreds of these serving in different ways. Perhaps I should mention some of them by name.

I am especially glad of the achievements of four of my choice students who became presidents of major, God-honoring organizations. I had the thrill of teaching former president of Cedarville University, Dr. Paul Dixon, as well as chairing his ordination counsel at Duncan Park Baptist Church in East Ridge, Tennessee in July of 1964. Dr. Dixon is a powerful evangelist and gifted leader. Under his direction Cedarville grew by leaps and bounds. He was one of only two former students whom I invited to lecture to my systematic theology classes. Norma and I appreciated the beautiful Bible that Dr. Dixon and his wife sent to us as a 50th anniversary gift.

Dr. Michael Loftis, formerly the president of the Association of Baptists for World Evangelism, Inc. and presently the Executive Director of DNA Global Network, took all of the theology and Greek classes I taught in seminary. After completing his dissertation he received his doctor's degree at Temple Seminary in 1978 (at the same graduation ceremony in which I was presented with an honorary doctor's degree). Michael was a highly motivated and effective teacher at Temple seminary until 1989. He then served as regional director over ABWE's central and eastern European ministries until he was named the new president of the mission in 2000. I appreciated the gift Dr. Loftis sent in recognition of my *Teacher of the Year Award* at the graduation exercises in 2005. Our family was thankful that Dr. Loftis took time from his busy schedule to come to Tennessee to perform the wedding ceremony of Steve and Cheryl's daughter, our grand-daughter, Karis, in December, 2007.

Yet another of my former students who rose to significant leadership roles is Marvin Brubaker, former president of Heritage College and Seminary in Ontario, Canada. Marvin was an excellent student who later served with great distinction on the faculty at TTU for several years before returning to his native Canada. Marvin also serves on the board of directors of ABWE, Canada.

I am proud to list Dr. Ron Bishop as a former student. Ron is the founder and president of SCORE (Sharing Christ Our Redeemer Enterprises) International. His outstanding abilities in exhortation, vision-casting, and administration showed early on as Ron led the Tennessee Temple Crusader basketball program to several national honors before focusing his energies in evangelism and missionary endeavors. SCORE facilitates youth missions ministries primarily through sports evangelism, and Ron maintains a busy speaking schedule all over the western hemisphere.

There are other vivid memories of my teaching career – memorable because they were not so pleasant at the time – that I might relate.

We were on the second floor of the old red-brick Herrman Building just down the hallway and around the corner from my office. We were reviewing the results of a Biblical Greek Grammar exam. One rather stocky, fine-looking fellow whose name I will not mention, was exceedingly confident that his answer to a certain question was correct and energetically contended with me that it was I who had been mistaken when I marked his answer as incorrect. While I was attempting to explain the correct answer he interrupted me, blurting out, "Awh! That's asinine!" The word means "like an ass; obstinately stupid."

To a man his classmates froze, astonished at his audacity and curious as to how I might react to his impudence. I immediately pointed at him, and snapped my finger to give emphasis to my words. I exclaimed, "One more word out of you and you will be out of this class on your ear." You could hear the proverbial pin drop.

To his great credit that young man came to me afterward and apologized for his disrespect. He and I became good friends. He made his living as a private contractor installing home burglar alarm systems, and sometime later, perhaps as a gesture of contrition, offered to install a complete system in my house free of charge. After seminary he wrote me from New York about the ministry in which he was engaged – he was ministering to the city's drug addicts. I trust that the Lord granted him much fruit in his labors there.

But that's enough consideration of unpleasant memories for the moment. I'd rather turn back to more enjoyable recollections.

I fondly recollect an episode which transpired as a result of a detailed classroom discussion of soteriology, the doctrine of salvation. One particular student, a rather retiring young man as I recall, came to my office and in a solemn voice, confided, "Professor Winget, after our discussion in class about the relationship between sin, Christ's death, faith and so forth, I don't believe I've ever been saved."

Together we reviewed the Bible verses that made God's plan of salvation very clear, and he gladly accepted God's offer of salvation, as promised in Romans 10:9-10: "If you will confess with your mouth the Lord Jesus and believe in your heart that God raised Him from the dead thou shall be saved." I later had the joy of baptizing that fellow – it was the only time that I recall baptizing one of my seminary students.

Only once in all those years of teaching did a class member during a lecture ask if we could pause right then and praise God for his amazing grace in planning and providing the way of salvation for guilty, hell deserving sinners. That student, James Owolabi, was the son of a native African pastor named Solomon whom I had taught 40 years earlier. The father had been led to Christ by missionaries when he was a young man, and years later attended my class still bearing the tribal markings he had been given as a boy during pagan rites in his home village.

James' display of his deep gratitude impressed the rest of us with the realization that we all should be more grateful. We did indeed pause in the middle of that lesson for a time of prayer, praise and thanksgiving to our heavenly Father for His amazing grace.

Through the years most of my theology teaching was done from a seminary classroom or from a church pulpit. But a different type of teaching opportunity proved helpful to Pastor Ronald Campbell. In 1990, he became the pastor of the Rifle Range Baptist Church, the church we had helped plant back in the mid-50's outside of Winter Haven, Florida.

Pastor Campbell was an airplane mechanic and pilot who had helped train airplane mechanics at Bob Jones University. Though Ron was an eager student of the Scriptures, he had not had the privilege of formal training in theology. In 1991, he invited me to preach in the church, and during one conversation with him I learned of his desire to study more biblical theology. I proposed a method by which he could do so without any tuition. That pastor's passion to learn the Word of God is reflected in a letter he later wrote. It is dated as having been written on July 24, 1991. It read in part:

Dear Dr. Winget,

I enjoyed learning via tape. I am anxious to continue. My wife explained the situation as you told it to her. My question is if you don't expect the tapes back soon could I get started on another subject? I want to finish your course in eschatology, but I feel like I could be studying another subject while we wait. I'm not trying to be pushy. I just want to learn. I know there's a lot to learn.
In Christ,

Pastor Campbell, Ephesians 1:7

Most any teacher would be thrilled to have such a student, and though the method of instruction was a bit unconventional, I thoroughly enjoyed my interaction with Brother Campbell. Would to God that all teachers of the Word be blessed with such students.

Controversy

he year was 1950. They were seated in a semi-circle, probably 18 or 20 folks in total. Everybody in the audience was either in a wheelchair or rocking chair. We were at the retirement home in Polk County, Florida, and I was preaching my first sermon. Every time I lowered my voice a bit my listeners would all begin to lean forward and cup their hands around their ears as a sign that I needed to dial up the volume. I'd respond by raising my voice and they would lower their hands and relax back in their seats.

It has been a tremendous dispensation of the grace of God that I have been able to teach and preach the Word of God almost six decades since then. I have been both honored and humbled to serve as pastor or interim pastor of eight different Baptist churches in Alabama, Georgia, Florida, and Tennessee.

I would like to relate a portion of a story from one of those pastoral situations. In the mid-90s, while I was teaching seminary I also pastored Faith Baptist Church in Sparta, Tennessee. During my time there a bit of controversy arose. It was about Gail Riplinger's book entitled *New Age Bible Versions*. The primary thesis of her book is that the only authoritative English Bible is the 1611 King James Version and that all other English Bibles, including the New King James Version, promote false doctrine.

I prepared a series of messages giving documented proof that her book had a number of serious difficulties. Riplinger's book was full of misleading insinuations and outright errors and mistakes.

I'll discuss here one major error contained in her book as an example of many. Her assertion that the New King James Bible is supported by only 1 percent of Greek manuscripts has at least two major problems.

The committee that produced the 1982 New King James Bible employed exactly the same Greek text, the *Textus Receptus*, as was used by the men who produced both the original 1611 KJV and the revision of 1769. If the NKJV is suspect because of the Greek text upon which it was based, then so is the original 1611.

While it is historically accurate that Desiderius Erasmus had at his disposal only a handful of Greek manuscripts from which he collated his Greek New Testament back in the early 1500's, later called the *Textus Receptus*, and while it is now true that scholars today have in the neighborhood of 7,000 manuscripts of the New Testament, and while it might be said that the *Textus Receptus* was constructed from less than one percent of all Greek manuscripts that we have at our disposal today, it is exceedingly misleading to suggest that any King James Bible (1611, 1769, or 1982) is supported by less than one percent of the Greek manuscripts now available because the *Textus Receptus* has subsequently been supported by the vast majority of those thousands of manuscripts that we now have at our disposal. Thus, in actual fact, the Greek New Testament that underlies the New King James, as well as its predecessors from 1611 and 1769, reflects the overwhelming majority of Greek manuscripts.

In my presentations I also sought to show that, not only is the original 1611 King James Version published quite rarely – one *can* obtain copies by special order – but the overwhelming number of present-day copies of the King James published today are the 1769 revision or the 1982 revision called the New King James Version (even though some are misleadingly printed with the words "1611" on the cover). Many, if not most, who believe that the King James Bible that they use each day is an exact reproduction of the 1611 are totally unaware that the Bible they possess is different from the original 1611 in a number of important respects. Further, they are unaware that those differences can be easily ascertained.

For example, the 1611 King James Bible contained 80 books – 39 books in the Old Testament and 27 in the New Testament, plus an additional 14 books, called the Apocrypha and viewed as authoritative by the Roman Catholic Church, placed between the Old and New Testaments. The 1769 revision of the KJV contains only 66 books. Anyone who carries a Bible in which Matthew follows immediately after Malachi is not carrying the 1611 King James Bible. This is one of the most glaring differences between the original and later revisions, but certainly not a trivial one.

Some King James Only advocates counter this point by comparing the 1611 KJV's inclusion of the Apocrypha to some Bibles today including a concordance or maps in the back. However, it is a fact that the 1611 KJV listed the books of the Apocrypha as a part of the table of contents using the same format and typeface employed to list the other 66 books. In the body of the Bible, the Apocryphal books were printed exactly like Malachi and Matthew using precisely the same layout, font, formatting, etc. I must hasten to make clear that the translators of the KJV 1611 did not view the Apocrypha as authoritative or on a par with the 66 books of the canon, but the inclusion of this section in the early printings of the KJV and its exclusion in more recent revisions is a striking example of changes that have been made over the years.

Another easy way to show the numerous differences between the 1611 original and later revisions is by comparing just a few of dozens of verses where significant changes have been made.

The original wording of the 1611 edition of Genesis 39:16 read, "...until *her* lord came home." The 1769 revision, and all subsequent publications of the King James Bible read, "...until *his* lord came home." Anyone with a King James Version that reads "...until *his* lord came home," does not have the original 1611 KJV, and only one change is enough to prove that the King James Bible has indeed changed through the years. But the changes don't stop there.

The 1611 translation contained the following wording at Numbers 6:14 "...and one *he lamb* without blemish." When the revisions were made the wording became, "...and one *ram* without blemish." It is clear that a "he lamb" and a "ram" are arguable synonyms in some contexts, but they are decidedly not the same words. To anyone who holds to the inerrancy of the King James 1611, this presents a not insignificant difficulty.

The original translators produced the following reading for Job 39:30: "...where the slain are, there is *he*," but the 1769 revision of the same verse reads, "...where the slain are, there is *she*." Anybody who says, "It's just one letter..." hasn't tried to give little Johnny a dress to wear or asked him to be on the girls team in the Sunday School contest. "Just one letter" makes an even greater difference when the discussion has to do with inerrancy!

The 1611 of Jeremiah 49:1 has, "...why then doth their king inherit God..." The 1769 revision reads, "...why then doth their king inherit Gad..." Again, one letter makes a huge difference.

In the New Testament the original King James of Matthew 12:23 reads, "Is this the son of David?" Yet the revision has the reading, "Is *not* this the son of David?"

At 2 Timothy 4:13 the 1611 translation has, "The cloak that I left at Troas with Carpus, when thou comest, bring with thee, but especially the parchments." When this verse was revised an entire phrase was added: "The cloak that I left at Troas with Carpus, when thou comest, bring with thee, *and the books*, but especially the parchments." Any Bible, whether it has "King James Version" on the cover or not, which has the phrase, "and the books," is *not* a 1611 King James Version Bible.

Often those who hold to a King James only perspective accuse more recent translations of seeking to "water down" or diminish the doctrine of the deity of Christ when, for textual reasons, phrases like "the Son of God" are rendered simple "the Son." However, it is clear that the original 1611 King James rendering of 1 John 5:12 can potentially bring the same accusation against the 1611 translators because it reads, "he that hath not the Son, hath not life," while the later revisions have, "he that hath not the Son *of God* hath not life." Any Bible, whether it has "King James Version" on the cover or not, which has the phrase, "of God," in this passage is *not* a 1611 King James Version Bible.

After I had concluded the series of studies on the King James controversy at Faith Baptist some of the folks at the church wanted me to prepare a video of the material I had presented in order that they could share it with others. This I did.

When Pastor David Bouler of Highland Park Baptist Church in Chattanooga viewed the video he asked me to present those lectures to his church during a series of 45 minute sessions preceding the main service on Sunday nights.

Dr. Robert L. Sumner watched the video and gave a very favorable review of it in his bimonthly periodical called *The Biblical Evangelist* (Mar-Apr, 2006) which read as follows:

How We Got Our Bible and Why I Prefer the KJV is a one hour and 43 minute video by Dr. David Winget, a seminary professor of Bible and theology for 45 years at Tennessee Temple University. Pastors and laymen in 18 states have ordered copies of this video.

With the use of several charts and diagrams Dr. Winget traces the history of the inspired Scriptures from the Greek manuscripts to today's English Bible, including a discussion of the many English translations before 1611, and a comparison of the different revisions of the King James Version since 1611. Winget "prefers the KJV and the *Textus Receptus*" on which the KJV is based because the vast majority of Greek manuscripts support this perspective.

Dr. Winget contends that those who argue that the King James Version is the only authoritative English Bible are mistaken. Really, most people nowadays could not even read the 1611 King James, and most people nowadays use the 1769 version of the KJV. One thing we appreciate about Winget's lecture is the fact that he repudiated the nonsense that goes with KJV-onlyism. We urge folks everywhere to get a copy of this video. We urge you to get it, and share it. This is a timely study.

In-Laws & the Gospel

7 or over half a century my life has been based squarely upon the proposition that the Word of God and the message of salvation have been endowed with divine power. The sovereign Holy Spirit graciously saw fit to exert His compelling conviction upon my stubborn heart, and He wooed me to Christ, but for reasons not revealed to us, He sees fit not to do this for others. God is God and we are not, and to Him alone belongs all praise and thanksgiving for the way He sees fit to work in the affairs of man.

My personal encounter with the dynamic of the Good News and subsequent conversion has been reflected in the lives of many others. I'd like to share a few memories from Norma's family as examples of the power of the Gospel to save repentant sinners, and the refusal of others who fail to respond to the love of Christ.

Norma's mother, Eva, was a faithful wife to her husband and caring mother to her seven surviving children. (One daughter, Helen, had died in childhood.) Grandma Eva had been exposed to the Gospel early on, but in later adulthood had some difficulty with certainty about her soul's status. I recall back in the early 60's sitting with her in the kitchen at our home in Chattanooga and asking, "Wouldn't you like to be certain of the difference between believing *about* Christ and believing *in* Christ?" When she nodded her assent I took her down the old familiar "Romans Road," and she volunteered, "Yes, I would like to make sure I believe *on* Him." There, in that simple white frame house on Union Avenue, a simple call for mercy based upon the promises of God in His Son, Jesus Christ, affected the transference of a simple mother from the dominion of darkness to the kingdom of light. Simply marvelous!

George Hicks, my wife's father, was a man's man. A master brick mason, he possessed a strong work ethic and a vice-like grip. On several occasions I attempted to tender an explanation of the Gospel, but his was always a cold response. I remember once confronting Granddaddy Hicks about his need of the Savior while we were in front of his country house in the gravel driveway. He was in the cab of his pickup truck and I was standing with my left foot up on the running board and my left arm propped in the opened window of the open driver's side door.

As I was speaking to him, he cranked the engine and started to drive away. I looked him in the eye and said somewhat sternly, "Listen to me Old Man. After all the help that Norma and I have given you in taking care of your sick wife you owe it to me to hear me out." I'm sure that he was surprised by my boldness – so was I, if the truth be known. Nonetheless George allowed me to continue to share the Gospel with him, but he finally said, "Awh... I know all that!" I countered, "Do you really understand that Jesus Christ took your place and died in your stead so that you would not have to pay the penalty for your sins?" to which he replied, "No... I guess I didn't understand that." He insisted that he had to leave, and thus ended the final opportunity I ever had to witness to him privately. As far as we know he never surrendered to the claims of the Gospel.

I never got a chance to witness to Lawrence, the oldest of the brothers, but with George, Jr. ("Buddy") I did have an occasion to speak. Buddy dismissed the question with the excuse that he just didn't understand.

Joe Hicks was another of Norma's brothers. He was also a brick and block layer, like his dad, but he also was a weight lifter who had developed a truly remarkable physique. With his shaved head and massive arms he cut a memorable profile. I went to visit him after he had suffered a heart attack, and shared the old story of the Cross with him. He listened patiently and when I was finished he politely said, "David, I appreciate you telling me all that, but it's just not for me." With that he closed the discussion. Just a few weeks later, after being discharged from the hospital, Joe had another massive heart attack at home and died instantaneously.

There were also several instances to chat with brother Harry, but I'll save his story until a bit later in the narrative.

Charles Hicks was the youngest of Norma's five brothers and baby of the family. Like his dad and other brothers he had obstinately refused the appeal of the Gospel for decades. Something about the death of one of Norma's aunts awoke a glint of interest in eternal matters in Charles' heart, though, and he let me share a word with him at the funeral home. I gave him an article that I had previously written entitled "The Centrality of the Cross," and he read it.

Some weeks later Charles found himself in the hospital and he asked the nurse to contact me with a request to come visit. I suspected that he might want to have me explain the Gospel again to him; however, when I arrived at his bedside he told me, "David, I got right with God last night, and I wanted you to be the first to know." After further conversation I became convinced that he had indeed, come to face his need. In the privacy of his thoughts on that bed of affliction he had called upon the Lord for mercy and had placed his faith in Christ.

A few moments later Charles' son called. Charles related to him, "Son, you don't have to worry about your 'ole dad anymore. Last night I got right with God." I interrupted, "Charles, tell him that you accepted the Lord Jesus Christ as your Savior," I coached. I wanted his first attempt at sharing his testimony to be unambiguously Christocentric and theologically accurate. It was important that his son at least hear the essence of what the phrase "getting right with God" was intended to portray and how it took place. Charles immediately added, "That's right. I accepted the Lord Jesus Christ as my personal Savior."

The next day Norma and I returned to visit Charles and another son of his was there. In the course of the conversation Charles turned to this son and, motioning in my direction, said, "Son, you ought to listen to this man – he'll tell you the truth."

Approximately a year later Charles went to be with the Lord. At least one other Hicks brother was to join him later.

Farewell to the Queen

*A*fter her biopsy surgery in November of '01 and the prognosis of "two to five years" she survived another six and a half years. For something more than the last three years she employed the assistance of a portable oxygen tank to help her breathe more easily.

Norma loved to go shopping, sometimes not so much to buy, but to look. When it became difficult for her to withstand the exertion of the walking involved she used a little blue, battery-powered, three-wheeled scooter to maneuver around the mall. In the last year or so, even the effort to mount the scooter and drive it around became too great, and we resorted to transporting her by wheelchair at church or at other rare occasions when she felt strong enough to get out.

The Only True Source of Strength

While it is true that she occasionally would go out, especially for Sunday morning church services, Norma spent the last couple of years of life primarily in her bedroom. You might wonder how she spent those hours. One pastime she enjoyed was working at crossword puzzles. Another amusement she liked was watching reruns of old comedy TV shows like "I Love Lucy," "Andy Griffith," or "Leave It to Beaver," or game shows, especially those that had to do with guessing secret words or spelling out secret phrases, such as "Wheel of Fortune" or "Password."

However, she loved to sit quietly and meditate on favorite Scripture passages or simply read portions from her Bible. For hours Norma would sit in her easy chair by the table lamp and follow along in her Bible as she listened to New Testament books being read verse by verse on a tape player. She would quote certain favorite verses over and over again: "There is therefore now no condemnation to them which are in Christ Jesus," (Rom. 8:1) or "For I reckon that the sufferings of the present time are not worthy to be compared with the glory which should be revealed in us," (Rom. 8:18) or "We wait for the redemption of the body," (Rom. 8:23) With that verse in mind she often prayed, "Dear Lord, give me patience to wait for your time to bless me with that new body."

Norma also gained much strength from Paul's words to the Corinthians: "We know that if our earthly house were dissolved, we have a building of God, eternal in the heavens. Therefore we are always confident knowing that whilst we are at home in the body we are absent from Lord. For we walk by faith, not by sight. We are confident, I say, and willing rather to be absent from the body and to be present with the Lord," (2 Cor. 5:1, 6-8).

One night during her last few months I could tell that my wife was growing very weary of the waiting for the inevitable. Her body was very frail, but her emotional strength seemed to be waning as well. She weakly asked, "David, please quote the verse that says that our citizenship is in heaven where Jesus is." I said, "Sweetheart, you're probably thinking about Philippians 3:20-21, which literally says 'Our conversation is in heaven from whence we look for the Savior, the Lord Jesus Christ, who shall change our vile body that it may be fashioned like unto his glorious body." She said "That's it."

Then I added "The Greek word translated 'conversation' means 'citizenship.' Once a student of mine said that the phrase 'our conversation is in heaven' means that people in heaven hear what we're saying when we're speaking to each other down here on earth. Actually, 'citizenship in heaven' speaks of the fact that the names of Christians are written down in the book of life in heaven and that's where we really belong. We're just legal aliens here. People in heaven may know what we are talking about on earth, but that is not what this verse teaches. You see, Darling, the Christians in Philippi knew that the names of the citizens in their city were recorded in a roll in Rome, the capital of the Empire. But Paul was encouraging them with the awesome truth that their names are written down in a far more important place than Rome."

Norma at that point responded, "Honey, I thank you for quoting the verse, but I didn't expect a sermon about it. But I appreciate that too." She added, "I think I heard a man on 'Back to the Bible' use that term 'citizenship' when discussing that verse. Paul's words there in Philippians remind me of what he wrote in another place telling us to 'seek those things which are above where Christ sits on the right hand of God' and he urges us to 'set our affections on things above, not on things on the earth, because our life is hid with Christ in God and when Christ comes again we shall also appear with him in glory.'"

Then I told her, "Darling, you just quoted almost word for word verses 1 through 4 of Colossians chapter 3 which Paul wrote about the same time that he wrote Philippians and from the same Roman prison where he had been held for his loyalty to Christ. At that point I quit talking to let her get some rest.

May of 2007 marked our 55th wedding anniversary. Such a remarkable occasion called for a most remarkable gift, so I surprised Norma with an automobile. We had owned two separate red Mercuries over the years and she sometimes commented, "I still think that a red Marquis is the prettiest car of all." I don't think those comments were intended as a hint, but her observation got me to thinking.

Earlier in the year I asked our son, Phillip, to do a computer search for a clean, late model, low mileage, red Mercury Grand Marquis at the right price. He found a red one in Miami, Florida, but it was a nearly new 2007 model with only 2800 miles on it and the price was too high. For two weeks Phil searched on his computer and I phoned car dealers and looked at newspaper ads but nothing fit the bill.

Because our anniversary was fast approaching and no other cars matched my criteria, I told Phil that if that red 2007 was still available to put a deposit on it and I would take it. He placed the order, and I wired the money for the full price. I asked that it be delivered to Phil's store a few miles away in East Ridge, and I made arrangements with our next door neighbors to park it in their yard until May the 1ˢᵗ. Phil and Tanya and I were the only ones in our family who knew the secret.

My youngest brother, Potsy, and his wife, Millie, happened to be visiting until May 1ˢᵗ, and I didn't want to bother the neighbors by leaving the car in their driveway for several weeks so I decided to go ahead with the presentation before Potsy and Millie left. They were staying upstairs with John and Joy, our son-in-law and daughter. On the evening before I was going to spring the big surprise I asked everyone upstairs to help me "make a memory" for Norma the next morning at exactly 9:30 a.m. I asked them to wait quietly at the top of the stairs with cameras in hand until they heard my phone ring, then come down to our apartment for a big surprise.

Before daybreak I quietly drove the sparkling Mercury into our garage, and at 9:00 a.m. I served Norma her a bowl of her favorite breakfast cereal, Cheerios. I had arranged for our son, Steve, to phone us from his home in Budapest, Hungary at precisely 9:30 a.m. Eastern Time (the time in Budapest would have been 3:30 p.m.). Because Norma would hear me answer the phone I had told Steve I would say to him, "What year were you my student?" and then, "I am busy now. Call me back in ten minutes." In this way Norma wouldn't know that I was talking to our son and ask to speak to him. I would leave the phone off the receiver, but Steve would stay on the line so he could hear what was happening.

At exactly 9:30 Steve phoned from Budapest as planned. That was the signal that summoned everybody from upstairs. As they began to troop in the door Norma looked up in amazement wondering what was going on. I announced, "Listen now. We are about to make an anniversary memory. Let's pray first." After a prayer of thanksgiving for the many years of marriage God had granted us I read a freshly penned poem to my Queen.

"A Grand Marquis is a great gift," someone said,
    But for a queen it must be red.
To find a red Marquis I did strive,
    A gift for my Queen on her anniversary fifty-five

I know that May the 30th is the right date,
But I love you so much, I just can't wait!

With that I pressed the alarm button on the key ring in my pocket and the Marquis' alarm went off in the garage. Everyone was stunned and rushed for the garage door, but I called out, "Wait, wait. The honoree must be the first to see."

I quickly brought her three-wheeled scooter to her recliner chair, and she rode it through the door to the garage to see her anniversary gift.

I gave the phone to her and said, "Sweetheart, someone in Budapest wants to talk to you." She talked to Steve about her surprise anniversary gift for a few minutes. It would be the last wedding anniversary gift she would receive from me.

Epitaph

On November 16, 2007, I was on my way out the door to make a final payment on our burial property at Lakewood Memorial Gardens in Rossville, Georgia. In fact, my hand was actually on the doorknob when Norma spoke.

It may seem somewhat morbid, but for some days previous we had been chatting about what sort of epitaph she might like on her grave marker. We had considered several options that fit within the 19 letter maximum that the marker we had settled upon would allow: "Because of Calvary" or "Saved by Grace" had come to mind.

Just as I was about to leave the house that morning I heard my dear wife's weakened voice: "Breathing Heaven's Air." I turned to her and asked, "Darling, is that what you want on the marker?" She said, "Yes. I've been thinking that in my glorified body I'll no longer have to battle to breathe. I'll be breathing heaven's air." And so it was decided.

Since David's family lived in Ukraine and Steve's in Hungary it was quite rare that we were all able to gather for special family holidays. David and Penny were still in Ukraine at Thanksgiving '07, but Steve and his family were in the States preparing for Karis' upcoming wedding. Therefore they were able to join the family festivities. The Thanksgiving feast with all the trimmings was set at Joy's house. Shortly before everything was ready for the meal Steve, Phil, and John went downstairs and carried Norma up to the dining room in her easy chair. Though by this point in her illness she didn't have much of an appetite, she was happy to be able to meet with the family.

A month later, on Christmas Day, we arranged the same sort of thing. The weather was quite cold, blustery, and "spitting" a light rain, but Norma was able to be carried upstairs for a short time during the Christmas meal. After only a short while she began to feel unwell and requested to be taken back downstairs. I remember that awhile later the family all followed her downstairs where we opened some of her gifts. The mood was lighthearted and gay, but there was also an tinge of bittersweet that hung in the air. All the adults understood that this was almost surely Norma's final Christmas, but one of the things that made it all joy was the fact that the event we were celebrating – the Incarnation of the Son Who had willingly left the Father's side – gave us real hope of a future reunion with her.

A First & a Last

Four days later marked the first time any of our grandchildren had gotten married – Karis Grace, Steve and Cheryl's first child and our first granddaughter, was set to "tie the knot" with Joe Ervin. The wedding was set for 5:00 p.m. on Saturday the 29th in Cleveland, Tennessee. There had been considerable concern that Norma would not be strong enough to attend, and I was hesitant to leave her for the several hours it would take for me to be present. Almost at the last minute we decided to go, and I think Norma was really glad she did. It was the last time she left the house.

At the appointed moment for the entrance of the bride's paternal grandmother Norma was wheeled down the aisle by the bride's brother, Joel. She looked gorgeous to me in her striking blue suit – it really set off her beautiful blue eyes. So as not to have her wheelchair obstruct the bride's procession down the aisle, Joel later escorted Norma to her prearranged vantage point.

I took my seat near the front to fulfill my assignment a bit later in the ceremony – I had been asked to offer a prayer of blessing for the new couple later in the service. At my cue I rose to pray. I asked the Lord's blessing on this occasion and upon the new home that was being established. I must admit that the gravity of the situation bore upon me somewhat and my prayer was especially fervent. I later heard from one of my former students that his teenage daughter asked regarding my prayer, "Mom, was that man who prayed a charismatic?" Knowing my views regarding charismata and my normally subdued temperament the thought tickled her parents and they replied in the negative and asked, "What would make you ask that?" She explained, "Well, he was just so passionate in his prayer!"

So weak was Norma, that we had to leave before the reception that followed, but just before we departed she wanted to be wheeled into the reception hall to see the decorations. I suppose that there are much less pleasant errands to run or reasons to leave the house for the final time than to attend the first wedding of any of your grandchildren.

Twice a Brother

Hospice had entered the equation sometime late in November or early in December. For the most part this consisted of periodic visits to our apartment by a nurse to check on us. Gradually the details and extent of their care increased as Norma's condition declined. In mid-March of 2008, hospice brought Norma a hospital bed that could be mechanically adjusted to help her rest better. Later that month her only living brother, Harry, entered the hospital in Fort Oglethorpe, Georgia. His 84 year old heart was showing its age. Norma and I and others had prayed for Harry's salvation for more than 50 years, but this only caused us to intensify our pleadings before the Throne on his behalf.

Born in the "Roaring Twenties," and raised during the Great Depression, Harry Hicks was a member of what journalist Tom Brokaw described as "the Great Generation." My sons grew up with intense pride in the fact that several of their uncles, Harry among them, had fought in WWII. Harry had taken part in storming Omaha Beach in the third wave during the famous D-Day invasion.

Harry was just a young infantryman, like thousands of others, with no great distinction to make him stand out from the rest, but he was a hero nonetheless. He was an honest and upstanding man, humorous and kind to children. However, the brother-in-law I knew had a hard, rough aspect, too, with no place for God in his life. I repeatedly sought to share the Gospel with him for over 50 years, but Harry seemed to grow harder and more belligerent each time.

When Norma's brother, Charles, went to be with the Lord, only Harry was left of the five brothers. Harry was 82 years old at the time and in declining health himself, so I once again attempted to share the Good News with him.

I went to his home down in Rock Springs, Georgia. He was at home alone, and I thought that perhaps this solitude was providentially prepared so that we would have an uninterrupted opportunity to do eternal business with God. Harry and I sat at his kitchen table as I took my little Gideon New Testament from my pocket. Immediately he said, "Now, David, I know what you believe. You don't need to say a word." I opened my mouth to speak, and again he ordered me not to say a word. When I persisted a third time he slapped the table and yelled, "I said, 'Shut up!'" I tried to calm the situation by saying, "Okay. May I pray for you?" He answered "I don't care."

I bowed my head and began to pray aloud, but the substance of my prayer was a brief rehearsal of the gospel message. "I thank You, my heavenly Father, for sending Your own Son, Jesus, to die in my place to pay the penalty for my sins, and for sending the Holy Spirit to convince me of my need for a Savior, and for the assurance that I will now not have to go to hell but will go to heaven because of what Jesus did for me." As I closed the prayer it seemed as if Harry Hicks had turned away from the Savior and the gift He offered for the last time.

Some two years later, Harry's failing health landed him in a hospital bed. What the enemy failed to do over 60 years ago on that beach in northern France was about to be accomplished by the ravages of time as his aging body began to shut down. Our family, especially my wife prepared for the grief of losing Harry forever.

God, however, had a different plan, as He often does. Late in March Harry's only daughter, Tammy, took a couple of friends, a lady who attends the same church as Tammy and the friend's young son, to visit her father. Tammy knows the Lord and, of course, she and her friends were concerned about his spiritual condition even more than his physical. The little boy wanted to see the patient because several months earlier Harry had given him a little puppy. Indeed, the bond between the lad and my brother-in-law had become so strong that the little boy referred to his aging benefactor as "Uncle Harry."

Almost as soon as the trio entered the hospital room the little child said, "Uncle Harry, I want to sing you a song. Sitting on the edge of the hospital bed, and in a clear, bold voice, the little boy sang:

Jesus loves me, this I know,
For the Bible tells me so.
Little ones to Him belong.
They are weak, but He is strong.

Yes, Jesus loves me.
Yes, Jesus loves me.
Yes, Jesus loves me.
The Bible tells me so.

It was clear from the look on his face that Harry's hardened heart had been softened by the child's simple musical affirmation of the love of Christ. The little boy's mother prompted her son, "Now, say your Bible verse for Uncle Harry – the one you learned in AWANAs." Without hesitation the little preacher unashamedly quoted John 3:16, "For God so loved the world that He gave His only begotten Son that whosoever believeth in Him shall not parish but have everlasting life. John 3:16."

Tammy related to me in considerable detail how her stubborn 84 year old dad began to sob and cry aloud. She moved to his bedside and gently implored, "Daddy, don't you now want to receive Christ as your Savior?" The Holy Spirit conquered and Harry meekly responded, "Yes, I do." Tammy led her daddy in the sinner's prayer to accept God's offer of salvation.

Later that day the hospital chaplain came by and asked, "Mr. Hicks, is it true that you accepted Christ this morning?" Harry answered emphatically, "Yes, I did." It would be an understatement to say that Norma rejoiced when she was told that good news. She had been even more deeply concerned about Harry's critical condition because he was lost. Now that he was born again she knew that they both were bound for heaven soon. She only wondered which one would be the first to take that trip.

I Want to Go Home

Evelyn, her hospice nurse, came on Wednesday May 7th for her weekly visit. She checked Norma over and sat down with her laptop computer to make a report. Norma called to me to help her up. I did so, but immediately she fainted and her hands turned blue. "Evelyn help! Quick!" I called out. Norma was as limp as a dish rag, and although she had lost a lot of weight, it was difficult for both of us to put her back on her hospital bed. I was so very thankful that the Lord's providence planned it so that Evelyn was there to assist.

Norma just as quickly regained consciousness, and overheard Evelyn tell me "She's got to stay in bed. She doesn't have energy enough to get up any more." In a faint voice Norma said, "I want to go home." I was about to say, "Sweetheart, you are at home," but it suddenly occurred to me the full import of her poignant plea. I asked her, "Do you mean 'go home to heaven?'" She replied "Yes."

As she was about to leave Evelyn took me aside and said gently, "Mr. Winget, you need to now be thinking in terms of *days* not *weeks*." The hospice doctor came the next day, May 8th, and confirmed Evelyn's opinion. She told me to stop all medicine except the pill that helped her breathe.

I Wanted to Beat

Four days later my darling wife slipped into a coma. That was Monday morning, May 12. That evening around 10:00 p.m. several of the family were gathered in her bedroom and were quietly chatting when our daughter-in-law, Cheryl, said, "I wonder if she can hear us." Cheryl slipped to Norma's side, bent over her, and quietly said, "Ms. Winget? Are you awake? Can you hear me?" Norma weakly opened her eyes and looked up at Cheryl, who then turned to the rest of us and excitedly whispered, "She's awake!"

We quickly all crowded around. Norma indicated that she was thirsty so one of us used a straw to drop a little water and a few small chips of ice on her tongue,. At that exact moment the phone rang in my study, and I hurried to answer it. Harry's sister-in-law, Nell, was on the other end of the line. "David, we wanted to let you all know that Harry passed away at six o'clock this evening."

I later wondered to myself why Nell had waited four hours to call. Why call then? Why not wait twenty minutes longer? I believe God wanted Norma to be awake and lucid when the call came. This was yet another evidence of the tender and gracious providence of God.

I returned to Norma's bedside, took her hand, and said tenderly, "Sweetheart, I have good news for you. Harry went to heaven a little while ago. Isn't that good news?" She smiled wanly and nodded her head. I stepped back to allow others to talk with her, but in the momentary lull during which we were all wondering how this news might affect her, Norma spoke in a small, frail voice. We were unsure what she had said, but somebody suggested, "I think she said, 'I wanted to beat...'" We were at a loss as to what exactly what it was she was trying to communicate. One of the kids said, "Dad, I think she meant, 'I wanted to beat [Harry to heaven].'" I stooped closer and asked, "Darling, is that what you said? Did you want to beat Harry to heaven?" Again, she lamely nodded in the affirmative. My wife's competitive spirit and sense of humor was still strong.

I suggested that we have a prayer of thanksgiving for Harry's recent acceptance of the gift of Life and for his departure to heaven. For the last several days Norma slept for long stretches and only awoke for a few seconds or, at the most, a few minutes at a time. We didn't know how long she might stay awake this time, and in her weakened state it was a bit unclear exactly how lucid she really was. As I began to pray everyone bowed and closed their eyes – all except my son, Steve. Norma closed her eyes as I began to pray too, but Steve wanted to see if this indicated her reverence or simply her falling back to sleep. When I said, "Amen," Norma's eyes immediately opened wide giving strong indication that for several moments the Lord had granted her – and us – a blessed memory of sharing that time with her.

Among those in the room were Joy's three children. They each somewhat shyly embraced their grandmother or clasped her hand and told her of their love. She smiled and put out her hand to touch them, and told each, "I love you, too." At that point one of us asked her if she wanted us to stop talking so that she could go back to sleep. She nodded in the affirmative and closed her eyes... for the last time.

The Valley of the Shadow

Steve offered to stay by Norma's bedside the rest of the night so that I could get some sleep. "Dad," Steve urged, "we're all going to need you to be on your best game over the next few days – that means that you've got to get some rest." I *had* been staying up several nights running, and so I gladly consented.

I set my alarm for 3:00 a.m. to check on her, but Steve awoke me about 2:35 and said, "Dad, I believe Mom's gone." I got up and went to her bedside. She was completely still with no sign of breath, labored or otherwise. We stood there watching for some sign of life, some sigh, some rising and falling of her chest, but there was none. My wife of almost 56 years was with the Lord.

Steve and I took a few moments to bow in prayers of praise and thanksgiving that our Great Shepherd had guided her safely through this long, dark vale into perfect day and our Great Physician had healed his patient with eternal health. She was now, indeed, breathing heaven's air.

As I had been instructed I phoned one of the hospice nurses – she needed to come out and legally verify Norma's death and begin the process of having her body cared for. The same two funeral home staff people who had taken Harry's body to their facility only nine hours earlier arrived at about 5:00 a.m. Both Harry's and Norma's earthly remains would be held in state at the same funeral home. It would provide a wonderful opportunity for us to rejoice together over the recent events, and Harry's funeral was held on Thursday of that week, while Norma's took place on Saturday.

She Being Dead Yet Speaketh

*N*orma went to be with the Lord sometime early on Tuesday morning around 2:15 or 2:30. As Tuesday dawn turned to morning and then noon arrived one of the hospice employees named Demetrius Edwards came by. Demetrius, a black man of average height, jovial by nature, and a punctual worker, had helped us on a number of occasions. Norma always greeted him warmly, and he seemed genuinely impressed with her attitude in view of her sickness. On one visit I had been able to share briefly with him about the Gospel; at other times I urged him to read a tract I had given him.

I cannot help but mention the obvious fact that God's timing once again arranged for intersections to occur that resulted in His glory and man's good. Just as Demetrius entered the room that day to disassemble the hospital bed and to gather the oxygen equipment that Norma had used, my phone rang. It was a call from our friends in Indiana, John and Norma Greene. I spoke rather louder than necessary so that Demetrius might overhear my narrative of how Norma had indicated her desire to "go home," and about her response to the news about Harry's home-going, and her desire to have beat him there. God had arranged for that phone call at that exact time to set the stage for Demetrius to be influenced by the testimony of a faithful lady's final days and hours.

One of Norma's prayers had been that God would be honored by her passing, and God was answering that request. It is quite likely that had that call not come, and had I endeavored to confront Demetrius about the Gospel, he may have been defensive. Likewise,

Norma's brother, Harry, was always on the defensive when I or others, even his daughter, challenged him to turn to Christ. But he was caught off guard by the singing and quotation of Scripture by a dear six year old child. Regardless of the human messenger or tactic, however, it always takes the convicting ministry of the Holy Spirit for a sinner to really see his desperate need for God's salvation and a sovereign impartation of grace to supply the faith for that sinner to turn to Christ. God provided the Savior's atoning death, arranges the circumstances that sinners might be confronted with their plight, and supplies the grace that the guilty might call upon His mercy. Therefore, He alone deserves all the glory.

As he was leaving the house that day I said, "Demetrius, Norma prayed for you, and now that she is in heaven I am sure she still wants you to be saved. Here's another tract like I gave to you before. Please read it and think on the truth it teaches, and when you realize your need, won't you admit to God that you are a sinner, turn to Christ in faith, and ask God to save you?"

I noticed tears in his eyes, and I said, "I'm not going to pressure you, but would you like to receive Jesus as your Savior right now?" He said, "Will you tell me what to say?" I led him in the sinner's prayer and told him that he now was qualified for heaven because Jesus paid the penalty for all his sins. We hugged each other, and I thanked God in prayer for my new brother in Christ. I wanted him to know that he, a black man, was appreciated and accepted by me just as well as any brother in Christ.

God used Norma's perseverance in sickness, and even the circumstances of her passing, to draw Demetrius to Himself. In her death my wife won at least one that may not have been brought to Christ had she lived.

Hebrews 11:4 says, concerning Abel, "By faith, Abel, being dead, yet speaketh." And Norma's testimony to Demetrius was not the final message she left. Many months in advance of her homegoing, Norma had planned almost her entire memorial service. She notified the persons she wanted to participate and assigned them their roles, but I'll save those details for later – I want to share a few lines about what happened before the memorial service.

Is This Heaven?

It seems that one of the reasons that God allows us the privilege of raising children is so that we get a chance to enjoy their simplicity and the straightforwardness with which they face life's challenges and to learn what it should mean to trust the kind hand of our heavenly Father. They may not possess an adult vocabulary, but it is amazing how well even small children can reduce the complex to simple terms and yet grasp the essence of reality.

Tuesday afternoon, the day Norma left her earthly dwelling to go to her home in glory, Phillip's wife, Tanya, picked up their six year old daughter, Mia, from school. They were planning to go to the funeral parlor that evening, and her mother wanted to gently prepare her. She explained, "Mia, Grandma died last night and went to heaven. We are going to the funeral home to see her body. Grandma's not in her body. She's in heaven." As they were walking out of school, Mia shouted to her teacher. "Bye, Ms. Lee. My grandma died, and she's in heaven. We are going to see her skeleton tonight."

Later Tanya told Wilson, her three year old son that "Grandma has died and gone to heaven. We are going to where we are keeping her body. She's not in her body. She's in heaven." When Wilson arrived at the funeral home and saw his grandma's body in the casket he gazed around at the people and all the flowers and asked, "Is this heaven?" He was informed that they were not in heaven, but that Grandma's body which reposed before him in the casket was all that was left of her. She had already gone to another place – she had gone to heaven.

That night he told his Nana, his other grandmother, that "Grandma died. Grandma is in a box. She is going to heaven in a box." As older sisters are sometimes want to do, Mia corrected him by saying, "Remember, Buddy, we saw her skeleton."

The outpouring of consolation and encouragement from friends and loved ones was a wonderful salve to my soul and to the hearts of all our children. Many family members and dear friends came from far and wide to share condolences. Their many kindnesses were a part of God's means of providing the indescribable peace we enjoyed during those days.

I can truly say that our family's demeanor was an amazing mixture of gratitude, joy, appreciation, relief, happiness, and thanksgiving to God for His grace, and we wished to honor Him above all. We also desired to give due honor to my wife and the mother of our children for her life's legacy. Finally, we so very much wanted to be an encouraging testimony to our extended family and the acquaintances of Harry Hicks – whose body was being kept in the same building down the hall from Norma's – as well as our own extended natural family and our church family.

I'm not sure that little Wilson was that far off – we were indeed experiencing a foreshadowing of the peace we will someday know to the fullest in heaven where we will fellowship forever in our dear Savior's presence.

I Find No Fault

As I mentioned earlier, Norma had given much careful thought about how she wished her memorial service to be presented. She had asked Cheryl, an excellent musician and songwriter, to play the piano for the memorial service. In the days between Norma's passing and the memorial Cheryl began contemplating the words that my wife had chosen for her grave marker, "Breathing Heaven's Air," and authored a song which, after an opening Scripture reading by Pastor Steve Euler from John 14, she sang while accompanying herself at the piano.

Just a few days ago
She stepped upon the shore.
The glories she experienced
Were like none she'd ever known before
Complete relief, no pain, nor fear,
With loved ones gathered round,
At home at last forever
On heaven's hallowed ground.

Breathing heaven's air,
Breathing like she never has before,

More alive than ever,
Eternal joy forever
In her lovely heavenly home,
Breathing heaven's air

She heard a voice; she turned around
To see him face to face.
She recognized him straightaway;
She'd been purchased by his grace.
He took her hand, she bowed her knee,
She worshiped at his feet.
In the beauty of Christ's presence,
Now she is complete.

Breathing heaven's air,
Breathing like she never has before,
More alive than ever,
Eternal joy forever
In her lovely heavenly home,
Breathing heaven's air

Following Cheryl's song Phil rose to give some personal memories of Norma's life. His words, offered in a poignant yet light-hearted way, gave the service an immediate lift. After Cheryl's touching words, Phil's very tasteful humor, allowed us all a much needed chance to relax and smile. As he closed, Phil introduced me with the words, "Now Dad is going to share some of Mom's favorite Scripture portions."

I strode to the front of the auditorium and took up a position next to the casket. I then quoted several passages: portions from Romans 8, 2 Corinthians 5, Philippians 3, and Colossians 3.

Norma had planned for David to sing the song "I Find No Fault." The words of this song by an unknown author had been a special comfort to her in the final years and became somewhat of a theme for the entire program.

Crowds moved into Jerusalem
    On Lamb Selection Day,
As every family sought a lamb
    The price of sin to pay,
The priest inspected closely
    And looked for a flaw,
And when he was sure the lamb was pure,
    He declared to all:
I find no fault, I find no fault,
    Not one spot, not one wrinkle, not one blemish.
This lamb of white will pay sins price,
    I declare to you: I find no fault.
The crowd moved on to Pilate's Hall
    On Lamb Selection Day.
As Jesus stood before the mob
    Accusations hurled His way,
Pilate listened closely
    Looking for a flaw,
But he was sure my Lamb was pure,
    He declared to all:
I find no fault, I find no fault,
    Not one spot, not one wrinkle, not one blemish.
This lamb of white will pay sins price,
    I declare to you: I find no fault.
Soon I'll walk that golden morn
    And stand before God's throne.
Oh, I don't fear the words I'll hear
    'Cause I won't stand alone.
Jesus' blood has covered
    My every sin and flaw,
And God will look me up and down –
    He'll declare to all:
I find no fault, I find no fault,
    Not one spot, not one wrinkle, not one blemish.
This lamb of white will pay sins price,
    I declare to you: I find no fault.

Norma had asked Steve to preach the sermon, and she requested that he speak on the theme of the song David had sung. Most of the text of his sermon follows.

The Lamb With No Blemish

How do you live with a perfectionist? Some of you know just what that question insinuates. Living with a perfectionist is tough. One of the keys to living with a perfectionist is praying that the Lord will show that perfectionist that he himself isn't so perfect or that she isn't exactly faultless herself.

May I ask you another, even harder, question? How do you live with a perfect perfectionist? Do you realize that that is exactly the situation we face whenever we seek to have a relationship with God? God is perfectly holy and requires precisely that from us. He says to us: "Be perfect as I am."

The passage we read just before David sang speaks about this issue. In the first official month of Jewish history God wanted to teach His people this crucial lesson that a relationship with Him required perfection. The way He chose to teach this is through the Passover Lamb.

Each family was to choose a lamb that was, by all appearances, perfect and then put it in a stall for 4 days. The idea was to spend those 4 days keeping a close watch on that lamb to see if it really was perfect. It couldn't have any blemish: no weak limb, no blindness, no malformed ear, not even sneezing or wheezing with a cold. No, that little animal had to be perfect.

You see, it was obvious that none of the people was morally perfect – each person's sinfulness was clear – and sin, i.e., anything short of perfection, was punishable by death. Many years later a famous Jewish rabbi known as Saul of Tarsus – or more commonly called Paul the Apostle, today – put it this way: "For all have sinned and fallen short of God's perfection...and the wages of sin is death."

Back in Moses' day God's solution for the death sentence hanging over their heads because of their sin was to prescribe that an animal sacrifice be made. This sacrificial animal was chosen to die – in a figure, the animal substituted for the sinners. The perfect took the place of the imperfect. The faultless died instead of the one at fault. The unblemished lamb stood in for the blemished and died vicariously for the other.

After four days and proof of perfection the lamb was taken out of its pen. Just before this innocent lamb was put under the knife, the father, as representative for his family, would place his hands on the little sheep's head and figuratively the sins of the family would be transferred to the unblemished animal. The key requirements for this sacrificial lamb were that it had to be without blemish and it had to die! The key requirement on the part of the sinner was to believe God's promise of grace to the extent that the blood of the sacrificial animal would be applied to the family's doorway. This act of trust in God's promise sufficed to figuratively answer the death penalty imposed upon every sinner in that family.

And the Jewish people did this year after year, decade after decade, for almost a millennium and a half. The lesson of the unblemished lamb and faith in God's promise was deeply impressed upon their national consciousness.

The Perfect Man

Fast forward 1400 years from Moses' day to the time of Christ. Jesus came to the earth that He had created and became a baby born to a Virgin Mother – you see, for Him to fulfill His task He had to avoid even the inherited taint of Adam's sin passed down from father to son.

He walked and talked among His people, ever in the public eye. He ate. He slept. He worked. He celebrated weddings, and He mourned at burial scenes. He worshipped in their synagogues and taught at their festivals. Yet no one, not even His fiercest critics ever witnessed Him commit a single sin. One highly respected prophet of the time caught an inkling of what the man from Nazareth was going to accomplish and called Jesus the "Lamb of God who takes away the sin of the world." It was He, said John the Baptist, who had come to be God's final sacrifice for the people.

Jesus told the people that if they would simply believe His message they could enjoy an eternal relationship with God His Father. If they refused they would bear eternal isolation from God and His wrath for eternity.

For 3½ years, under the most intense scrutiny anyone had ever faced, Jesus Christ demonstrated perfection. No Supreme Court nominee ever underwent such inspection by a Senate committee than did this Man. No would-be suitor ever faced such interrogation by a skeptical, over-protective father. Yet Jesus challenged His accusers: "Which of you can prove me guilty of any sin?" You can be quite sure that *if* He had been guilty of *anything* they would have jumped all over it!

Finally, when He appeared before Pilate Jesus found Himself being judged by anything but an impartial adjudicator. Pilate was under all kinds of pressure to keep the pesky Jews off his case and render the verdict they wanted. In spite of the pressure he repeatedly declared that Jesus was guiltless.

Yet Jesus voluntarily suffered an unspeakably cruel death for you and me.

The Faultless Sinner

Here was the ultimate Perfect Sacrifice that our holy God required. In His death Jesus fully met all the demands of God's perfection. Now an imperfect sinner could still enjoy a free and open relationship with the Perfect God. A Perfect Sacrifice, God's own Son, had died in the sinner's place and provided a basis by which God could offer the sinner a free pardon for his sin. This was no figurative and short-term bandage for the problem, like the animal dying for the human being. No, this was a Perfect Man dying for all mankind.

All that is necessary is that the guilty sinner admit that he can't do anything about his problem, that God has done everything necessary to solve the problem, and believe God's promise of forgiveness.

When the sinner accepts that free gift, God grants His forgiveness and declares the believing sinner as being legally acquitted and faultless before His law.

It's like a NASCAR driver trying to enter the big race with a engineless, rusted chassis he finds at the flea market – but he trades in his smashed and useless auto for a pristine, new racecar. It's as if a quadriplegic on life support is given an entirely new body in some sci-fi body transplant. It's as if a shabby beggar trades in his Goodwill rags for a brand new tuxedo.

Paul talked about this in one of his letters to the church at Corinth. Speaking of Jesus, Paul said: "He who knew no sin, took our sins, so that we could be made as perfect as He is." He takes off our filth-encrusted, sin-sogged rags and offers us His gleaming robes of righteousness. Anyone who accepts His offer is legally blameless, faultless, without blemish before a Perfect God.

That's how to live with a perfect perfectionist. It's the only way. And because God is perfect His promise will always prove trustworthy.

That's why my mom could look forward to meeting a Perfect God. She'd accepted His promise of being declared faultless because of Jesus' perfect sacrifice in her place. Just a few days before she left us Mom told Dad that she wanted to go home. She had no fear of that encounter – she knew God's promise would prove true....

...[O]ur perfect God has designed a plan by which guilty and filthy sinners can be clean and faultless. Only He would do this – only He *could* do this. You or I, had we been God, surely would not have! But God, while we were sinful, sick, helpless enemies, demonstrated His unspeakable love and mercy toward us, to the extent that He planned the cruel death of His only Son on our behalf so that we could be made as perfectly righteous as He is.

In the Lamb we are faultless. Moses and the people of Israel learned this lesson. My mom knew this truth... And Walter Wangerin knew it, too.

Walter Wangerin is a pastor and extremely gifted author. He has expressed these sentiments so ably that I would like to conclude with a reading from his pen. In his graphic allegory entitled "The Ragman" Wangerin vividly portrays this cleansing that Jesus offers.

The Ragman (by Walter Wangerin, Jr.)

I saw a strange sight. I stumbled upon a story most strange, like nothing in my life, my street sense, my sly tongue had ever prepared me for. Hush, child. Hush now, and I will tell it to you.

Even before the dawn one Friday morning I noticed a young man, handsome and strong, walking the alleys of our City. He was pulling an old cart filled with clothes both bright and new, and he was calling in a clear tenor voice: "Rags!" Ah, the air was foul and the first light filthy to be crossed by such sweet music.

"Rags! New rags for old! I take your tired rags! Rags!"

"Now this is a wonder," I thought to myself, for the man stood six-feet-four, and his arms were like tree limbs, hard and muscular, and his eyes flashed intelligence. Could he find no better job than this, to be a ragman in the inner city? I followed him. My curiosity drove me. And I wasn't disappointed.

Soon the Ragman saw a woman sitting on her back porch. She was sobbing into a handkerchief, sighing, and shedding a thousand tears. Her knees and elbows made a sad X. Her shoulders shook. Her heart was breaking. The Ragman stopped his cart. Quietly, he walked to the woman, stepping round tin cans, dead toys, and used Pampers. "Give me your rag," he said gently. "and I'll give you another."

He slipped the handkerchief from her eyes. She looked up, and he laid across her palm a linen cloth so clean and new that it shined. She blinked from the gift to the giver. Then, as he began to pull his cart again, the Ragman did a strange thing: he put her stained handkerchief to his own face; and then he began to weep, to sob as grievously as she had done, his shoulders shaking. Yet she was left without a tear.

"This is a wonder," I breathed to myself, and I followed the sobbing Ragman like a child who cannot turn away from mystery.

"Rags! Rags! New rags for old!"

In a little while, when the sky showed gray behind the rooftops and I could see the shredded curtains hanging out black windows, the Ragman came upon a girl whose head was wrapped in a bandage, whose eyes were empty. Blood soaked her bandage.

279

A single line of blood ran down her cheek. Now the tall Ragman looked upon this child with pity, and he drew a lovely yellow bonnet from his cart. "Give me your rag," he said, tracing his own line on her cheek, "and I'll give you mine."

The child could only gaze at him while he loosened the bandage, removed it, and tied it to his own head. The bonnet he set on hers. And I gasped at what I saw: for with the bandage went the wound! Against his brow it ran a darker, more substantial blood – his own!

"Rags! Rags! I take old rags!" cried the sobbing, bleeding, strong, intelligent Ragman.

The sun hurt both the sky, now, and my eyes, too; the Ragman seemed more and more to hurry.

"Are you going to work?" he asked a man who leaned against a telephone pole. The man shook his head. The Ragman pressed him: "Do you have a job?"

"Are you crazy?" sneered the other. He pulled away from the pole, revealing the right sleeve of his jacket – flat, the cuff stuffed into his pocket. He had no arm.

"So," said the Ragman. "Give me your jacket, and I'll give you mine."

So much quiet authority in his voice, the one-armed man took off his jacket. So did the Ragman – and I trembled at what I saw: for the Ragman's arm stayed in its sleeve, and when the other put it on, he had two good arms, thick as tree limbs; but the Ragman had only one. "Now, go to work," the Ragman said.

After that the Ragman found a drunk, lying unconscious beneath an old army blanket, an old man, hunched, wizened, and sick.

He took that blanket and wrapped it round himself, but for the drunk he left new clothes.

And now I had to run to keep up with the Ragman. Though he was weeping uncontrollably, and bleeding freely at the forehead, pulling his cart with one arm, stumbling for drunkenness, falling again and again, exhausted, old, old and sick, yet he went with terrible speed. On spider's legs he skittered through the alleys of the City, this mile and the next, until he came to its limits, and then he rushed beyond.

I wept to see the change in this man. I hurt to see his sorrow. And yet I needed to see where he was going in such haste, perhaps to know what drove him so.

The little old Ragman – he came to a landfill, to the garbage pits outside the City. And I waited to help him in what he did – but I hung back, hiding. He climbed a hill. With tormented labor he cleared a little space on that hill. Then he sighed. He lay down. He pillowed his head on a handkerchief and a jacket. He covered his bones with an army blanket. And he died.

Oh, how I cried to witness that death! I slumped in a junked car and wailed and mourned as one who has no hope – because I had come to love the Ragman. Every other face had faded in the wonder of this man, and I cherished him so; but he had died. I sobbed myself to sleep.

I did not know – how could I know? – but I slept through Friday and Saturday and its night too. But then, on Sunday morning, I was wakened by a violence. Light – pure, hard, demanding light – slammed against my sour face, and I blinked, and I looked, and I saw the first wonder of all. There was the Ragman, folding the blanket most carefully, a scar on his forehead, but alive! And, besides that, totally, completely healthy! There was no sign of sorrow or age, and all the rags that he had gathered shined for cleanliness.

Well, then I lowered my head and, trembling for all that I had
seen, I myself walked up to the Ragman. With shame I told him
my name, for I was a sorry figure next to him. Then I took off all
my clothes in that place, and I said to him with dear yearning in
my voice: "Dress me, too."

And He did dress me. My Lord, He put new rags on me, and I
am an unblemished, sinless, faultless wonder beside Him. The
Ragman, the Ragman, the Christ!

No More Night

As a climax Norma chose to ask Fred Holcombe, Grace Baptist's
music director, to sing "No More Night" by Mark Harrah. Several
months previous to her passing Norma had heard Fred's stunning
baritone rendition of the song, accompanied by his wife, Tina, and
on that occasion had emphatically requested that Fred and Tina offer
this song to close the service. It was an altogether fitting finale to
a wonderful memorial in which the Bible had been prominent and
Christ had been honored.

The timeless theme,
    Earth and heaven will pass away.
It's not a dream,
    God will make all things new that day.
Gone is the curse
    From which I stumbled and fell.
Evil is banished
      To eternal hell.

No more night. No more pain.
No more tears. Never crying again.
And praises to the great "I AM."
We will live in the light of the risen Lamb.

See all around
    Now the nations bow down to sing.

The only sound
    Is the praises to Christ, our King.
Slowly the names
    From the book are read.
I know the King,
    So there's no need to dread.

No more night. No more pain.
No more tears. Never crying again.
And praises to the great "I AM."
We will live in the light of the risen Lamb.

See over there, there's a mansion,
That's prepared just for me,
Where I will live with my Savior eternally.

No more night. No more pain.
No more tears. Never crying again.
And praises to the great "I AM."
We will live in the light of the risen Lamb.

All praises to the great "I AM."
We will live in the light of the risen Lamb.

Temporary Resting Place

That afternoon under a clear, blue sky my darling wife's body was escorted by a troop of pallbearers consisting of her nephews and grandsons to the grave site in Lakewood Memorial Gardens near Rossville, Georgia. There, after a short recitation from 1 Thessalonians 4 and a brief prayer, her remains were laid to rest – at least for a while.

The Bible promises a wakeup call, and someday Norma's body will be revived and renewed, glorified and perfected. We patiently await the time when...

The Lord Himself shall descend from heaven with a shout, with the voice of the archangel and with the trump of God, and the dead in Christ shall rise first, then we which are alive and remain shall be caught up together with them in the clouds to meet the Lord in the air, and so shall we ever be with the Lord.

Memory Lane

*C*ertainly one of the unintended blessings of funerals involves
the opportunity to renew fellowship with friends and family
members who live far away. Such was the opportunity afforded by
Norma's home-going. Since Earl had driven all the way from west
Texas, someone suggested a day trip down to our old home place
in south Georgia. Therefore, the Monday following the memorial
services my brother Earl, my sons Steve and Phil, and I drove about
300 miles to Blakely, Georgia, the county seat of Early County
where, you might recall, Earl and I had grown up.

In many ways the small southern town seemed not to have
changed much. In other ways it was unrecognizable. One of the first
landmarks I did recall was the old county court house that sat astride
the central roundabout in the middle of Blakely. (I had once visited
there back in 1945 when I was 14. I witnessed a man who had earlier
been convicted of murder being sentenced to death in the electric
chair. You might imagine what a vivid recollection I have of that
event.) During our visit we were allowed to look in on a few minutes of a court session in that very courtroom. I must admit that the
dimensions of that courtroom had seemed to shrink a lot since 1945!
Funny how that happens.

We also visited the area we called Boozey Bushes. It was mostly
overgrown with wild bushes, vines, and trees draped with beards
of moss. The house in which my mom had demanded that my dad
must quit the moonshine business had burned long years ago, but
we were able to find among the underbrush the decayed ruins of

Mr. Madison Freeman's old house. It had not been inhabited for decades. So thick, in fact, was the undergrowth that even from just a few feet away the remains could have been easily missed. The other fellows went inside the dilapidated wooden shell and took several pictures, but I didn't care to scramble through the rotting ruins that seemed to me to be teetering on the verge of collapse.

We visited some of Mr. Madison's relatives, including his granddaughter Helen whom I had not seen in 62 years. Helen was the girl with whom I had argued when we were both teenagers. She said she did not remember our argument, and I am glad for that. Our visit with her and her husband was very friendly.

We wanted to find the school house in Hilton where Earl and I had studied. All that remained were some overgrown foundations and steps. Nonetheless, it was fun for Earl and me to be there and relate old stories of bygone exploits to my sons.

We drove west about five miles to Columbia, Alabama. I discovered that the movie theatre that I had attended many times during the 1940s had been renovated and turned into a combination grocery-hardware store-gas station-pharmacy. One big difference was that in the 40s I could attend the "picture show" for a dime – in 2008 there was virtually nothing on sale for 10 cents. We did, however, find something of much greater value: we met some of the children and grandchildren of our former landlord, Mr. Madison, and discussed events that happened over the six decades since I had last been there.

It was a wonderful stroll down memory lane.

Unshackled

$\mathcal{B}$y the beginning of 2008 Norma had no longer been able to accompany me to church services. Though I had known of, and enjoyed for many years, the radio drama entitled "Unshackle" produced by the famous Pacific Garden Mission in Chicago it so happened that the program was aired over our local station at precisely the time I was making those lone trips to church on Sunday evenings. It became my habit to listen attentively each week. After hearing several dramas it occurred to me that perhaps my life's story may be relevant and of some encouragement to someone. Just maybe…just maybe the "Unshackled" people would be interested in producing my story. I decided to write out a sketch of my life and send it to Chicago.

Some weeks after submitting my draft to the program I received a request for a list of references and a number of detailed questions regarding my submission. Apparently the folks at Pacific Garden Mission were intent on making certain of the veracity of stories they aired, and they were in the process of "checking me out."

A few days after my wife's funeral, Mrs. McNeil, the executive producer of "Unshackled," phoned me from Chicago with news that they had decided to produce a radio drama of my story. During that conversation she patiently allowed me to recount the events of the last several days dealing with my wife's home-going and the many manifestations of God's sovereignty surrounding it. She seemed to be truly blessed by what I shared, and several times exclaimed, "Praise the Lord," and "Amen!" Mrs. McNeil insisted that I send a written account of how God had used my wife's life and death – she felt it had great potential for another dramatization.

I immediately set to work and over the course of the next few days was able to complete a rough, hand-written draft. As soon as I had finished I faxed it to Chicago. That very afternoon Mrs. McNeil called to say that she had already sent the story to one of the drama writers.

In mid-June it was confirmed that Norma's narrative was also in production. Both dramas were to be recorded in July in Chicago in front of live audiences. Our stories were due to be aired on consecutive weeks in the late autumn over the program's network of over 1,800 stations.

I began to pray that it would be possible for me to go to Chicago to view the taping of Norma's drama. I was a bit intimidated at the thought of flying into Chicago, but the idea of taking a cab all the way downtown to the production site was even more imposing to me. It wasn't long, however, until the Lord's gracious provision showed itself, because on July 1 the pastor of Grace Bible Church in Lansing, Michigan called. He was a former seminary student of mine named Dr. William Barber, and he was inviting me to preach at his church on July 13th, the day after Norma's production was to be recorded!

During his seminary days he and his lovely wife, Lalanne, had attended Foust, and Norma and I had enjoyed sweet fellowship with both of them. I told him about the production in Chicago on Saturday the 12th, and he said that if I would preach for him on the 13th he'd drive the 200-plus miles from Lansing to Chicago, pick me up at Midway Airport, drive me to the production, and then drive back to Lansing by bedtime. He assured me that we could get a good night's rest that night so that I could preach twice on Sunday. I was more than happy to agree to his proposal, and I thanked the Lord for His answer to my prayers.

I very much enjoyed the taping of Norma's story. Sitting among an audience of approximately 100 I watched with rapt attention as five or six actors, several technicians, and the drama director put together in about an hour's span the entire half-hour production. I was told that it was rare to have the subject of the drama in attendance when the production was being taped. As soon as the taping was finished Mrs. McNeil asked me to tell the audience if the story they had dramatized was true. I said, "Yes, indeed, it was the truth." It was a thrilling conclusion to a most enjoyable adventure to have my picture taken with the actor and actress who portrayed Norma and me.

On November 24, 2008, my story was broadcast on the "Unshackled" network of over 1,800 stations. It was drama #3015 and Norma's dramatized story was #3016. They can be heard through the website at www.unshackled.org.

You might expect that the opportunity to preach at the Barber's church the next day might have seemed to me to be anticlimactic. Far from it! Even after almost 60 years of proclaiming God's Word, I still find it a special honor whenever the opportunity arises. I must say, though, that the Barber's and the flock at Grace Bible Church went a long way out of their way to make me feel special. Lalanne and a number of the musicians at the church presented an excellent musical program centered on the theme of heaven that day as an encouragement to me in light of my wife's recent departure. It had been exactly two months since Norma's passing.

After the morning service I met a man with a most interesting story. This gentleman had been listening to Brother Barber's teaching for quite some time, but only the preceding morning, while I was en route to Chicago, did the man come to realize his need of the Savior and accept His free offer of forgiveness. This man had been born again barely 24 hours! That man's testimony, as well as many other successes of Brother Bill's 20 years of effective exposition of the Bible in that church, made me glad that I had had even a small part in his theological preparation.

The knowledge of that pastor's spiritual accomplishments was a tremendous encouragement to me. Only a few weeks later Dr. Barber resigned his pastoral responsibilities in Lansing to take a new role as the Professor of Mentoring and Development at Shepherd's Seminary in Cary, North Carolina.

Through the years I've learned of the fruitfulness and spiritual productivity of scores, yes even hundreds, of my former students like him. It moves me to borrow the words of Paul from 2 Timothy 2 and shout them aloud:

> To me who am less than the least of all heralds of the Word of God is this grace given that I should be granted the God-given opportunity for well over half a century to teach the manifold grace of God to faithful men who would be able to teach other faithful men who would be able to teach still others also.

This is the way our sovereign Lord planned to perpetuate His truth through succeeding generations.

Epilogue

7here have been several key events that have occurred over the last few years as I've trod past the eight decade marker. Some of them have been cause for great rejoicing; some have been very painful. Grandchildren have taken first steps in public Christian ministry, excelled in academics and athletics, and chosen life partners. Close friends have been called home, and I've undergone two serious surgeries. And one of my son's marriage dissolved in divorce.

It began shortly after Norma's home-going, and it was one of the saddest episodes of my life. Tanya began to exhibit very strange behavior. She was not the delightful and charming Tanya that we had all come to love over the past 10 years. I am convinced that an acute chemical imbalance that she refused to deal with properly was at least partly to blame. Though Phil openly admitted his faults to church leaders and steadfastly sought reconciliation by every possible means, Tanya adamantly refused. The situation became so desperate that they agreed to a divorce in June of 2010. With great sorrow I must admit that this heartrending turn of events has created serious doubts in my mind regarding the authenticity of her earlier profession of faith. Only the Lord knows the full truth, but God graciously brought into our family a wonderful new daughter-in-law in the spring of 2011 when Phil married Amy Herring. Through all of these events, and others I've not mentioned, our good and loving God has proven Himself faithful over and over again.

I wish I could have known more about my grandparents, their happy times as well as their times of sorrow. On my daddy's side, I'm not even sure of their names, and I feel a great loss for having not known them and learned from them. For this reason these auto-biographical sketches have been written for my grandchildren Nate, Andy, Karis, Joel, Zac, Josh, Brianna, Mia and Wilson, but also for my future great grandchildren and perhaps my great great grandchildren.

It would be my greatest delight if my offspring were to someday blend their own soul song of the grace of God with mine. To them I say: the first crucial step in learning this music is to accept Christ as your personal Savior; the steps that follow can be summed up in the words of Colossians 1:10: to "walk worthy of the Lord unto all pleasing being fruitful in every good work." Such a chorus of my earthly progeny would be most wonderful "for I have no greater joy than to hear that my children walk in truth," 3 John 4.

All praise and thanksgiving are due only to God's wonderfully sovereign providence. His grace transformed a good-for-nothing booze maker into a Bible minister. He moved my mom to issue an ultimatum that took me from Georgia to Florida, to the Gospel and salvation, to Temple to Dallas Seminary, and back to Temple again for a life of ministry. His magnificent grace gave me a royal wife whose love and companionship was second only to the One who gave her to me. I can only shout the words of the Apostle:

O, the depth of the riches, both the wisdom and knowledge of God. How unsearchable are his judgments and his ways past finding out. For who hath known the mind of the Lord or who hath been his counselor, or who hath first given to him that it shall be recompensed unto him again. For of him and through him and to him are all things to whom be glory forever and ever, amen," Romans 11:33-36.

There's an endless song
Echoes in my soul
I hear the music ring

292

And though the storms may come
I am holding on
To the rock I cling
How can I keep from singing Your praise
How can I ever say enough
How amazing is Your love
How can I keep from shouting Your name
I know I am loved by the King
And it makes my heart want to sing

– Chris Tomlin

CPSIA information can be obtained at www.ICGtesting.com
Printed in the USA
LVOW040948231112

308307LV00002B/3/P

9 781622 308910